25/8/15

2 FEB 2016

D&A
3/12

Books should be returned or renewed by the last date above. Renew by phone **08458 247 200** or online *www.kent.gov.uk/libs*

Libraries & Archives

THE COMPLETE

Jewellery Maker

THE COMPLETE
Jewellery Maker

PACKED WITH ESSENTIAL PROJECTS
AND TECHNIQUES

Bloomsbury Publishing plc
50 Bedford Square
London
WC1B 3DP

A CIP catalogue record for this book is available from the British Library.

ISBN 978-1-408-1-3399-6
10 9 8 7 6 5 4 3 2 1

A Quantum Book
This book is produced by
Quantum Publishing Ltd.,
6 Blundell Street,
London N7 9BH

QUMJMYE

Publisher: Sarah Bloxham
Consultant Editor: Jinks McGrath
Editor: Diana Craig and Anna Southgate
Designer: Kate Harris and Tim Scrivens
Managing Editor: Julie Brooke
Project Editor: Samantha Warrington
Assistant Editor: Jo Morley
Production Manager: Rohana Yusof
Printed in Singapore by Star Standard Industries Pte Ltd

Publisher's note:
The Publisher and author can accept no liability for the use or misuse of any materials mentioned in
this book. Always read the product labels, and take all necessary precautions.

This compilation is comprised of material previously published in BASIC JEWELLERY MAKING TECHNIQUES, copyright ©
1993 by Quintet Publishing Limited, JEWELLERY MAKING MANUAL, copyright © 1985 by Quill Publishing, THE CREATIVE
JEWELLER, copyright © 2000 by Quarto Publishing plc, TWO IN ONE JEWELLERY, copyright © 1999 by Quarto Publishing
plc, JEWELRY MAKING TECHNIQUES BOOK, copyright © 2001 by Quarto Publishing plc and THE ART OF JEWELLERY
DESIGN, copyright © 2002 by Quarto Publishing plc. All published by arrangement with Quantum Publishing Ltd.

Contents

Introduction

FOR CENTURIES JEWELLERY AND THE MEANS OF SELF-ADORNMENT HAVE FASCINATED BOTH MEN AND WOMEN – FROM THE TRADITIONAL CREATIONS OF TRIBAL PEOPLES TO TODAY'S SOPHISTICATED PRODUCTS OF THE WELL-KNOWN JEWELLERY HOUSES OF NEW YORK, LONDON AND ROME.

AN AGE-OLD TRADITION

Jewellery has long been used as a public display of wealth and culture as well as, more intimately, an expression of self and of perceived taste. Yet the creation of jewellery goes far deeper than the desire simply to reveal wealth and to set or follow fashion. In most cities of the world, in basements and hidden away in back streets, are the workshops that produce the glittering displays that appear in the windows of fashionable stores. Throughout the world there are hundreds of skilled men and women producing work in conditions and by methods that have changed little over the centuries. For some of these people, their workshop is little more than a block of wood held in sand and a few simple well-chosen tools, and the skills they use have been unchanged for many generations.

Technology has made its influence felt. Machines produce intricate chains; heavy mills and presses extrude sheets of fine metal; complicated electroplating and photo-etching systems produce in minutes what once took hours; CAD/CAM software enables amazingly intricate designs; and sophisticated casting techniques create high-quality finishes. But these processes do not eliminate the role of the hand-worker; they have merely made the world of jewellery a more competitive place. Traditional methods of producing jewellery continue to thrive, but a more contemporary school has found its niche in the market. Specialist jewellers, who design and make everything themselves, play an important part in the art and craft movement.

Jewellery design in itself requires an understanding of likes and dislikes when it comes to the visual, tactile, sensual and functional elements of a piece. This understanding is essential to the design process, and is an exciting learning experience. It provides a designer with a personal perspective necessary to give character to a design. Personality is what distinguishes design and saves it from being just another eternal, anonymous, eclectic repeat; it makes a design noteworthy, exciting, provocative, distinctive and individual.

Left A suite of jewellery, featuring a number of recurring themes and motifs, including the alternating bands of colour, intricate chasing and smooth sculptural forms.

Above A set of deep rings with an enamelled finish. The enamel does not cover the entire surface, but leaves a thin silver border. Gold elements add to the decorative finish.

INTRODUCTION

USING THIS BOOK

Anyone new to the art of jewellery-making will find this book a useful resource on many levels. At the core of the book there is a wide range of techniques that are used across all disciplines of the craft – from manipulating metal wire to doming and forging sheet metal and from setting stones to etching and enamelling. Arranged in two separate chapters, Basic Techniques and Advanced Techniques, they demonstrate the processes required for making infinite pieces from start to finish. Following each section are a selection of, first, Basic Projects and, subsequently, Advanced Projects that will allow you to practise the techniques demonstrated with confidence. Each project is described in detail, with step instruction and can, of course, be modified to suit your own interpretation of the design.

The majority of the projects in this book use silver – either in sheet or wire form – although in many cases, copper or brass could be used instead. Annealing and soldering temperatures do vary a little and details of this are given. Using gold for jewellery-making is also wonderful but can be very expensive, so it is advisable to familiarise yourself with how to work with silver before embarking on an ambitious gold project. Again, the working properties of gold differ from those of silver and special care must be taken when annealing, soldering and polishing different carat and coloured golds.

DEVELOPING YOUR SKILLS

Many of those who use this book will find that they want to go on to make jewellery professionally; others will find that they enjoy the challenge jewellery-making offers as a hobby; and still others will want to pursue it on a part-time basis only, so that they can enjoy the creative aspects without having to rely on it as a means of earning a living. Those who are fortunate enough to have jewellery-making as a hobby can allow themselves to be wholly creative in their approach, following some silver-smithing or jewellery ideas through to the end and abandoning those that do not seem to 'work', without the pressures of the marketplace putting constraints on their inventiveness.

Whichever group you fall within, as you become more familiar with the required techniques and processes presented in this book, you will start to develop a unique style of own, which may involve your using some techniques more frequently than others. A section on designing your own jewellery follows the project sections, and breaks down each aspect of designing and making pieces for yourself. First comes the theory – where to seek inspiration, coming up with a concept, brainstorming and researching to fine-tune the idea. Then come the practical considerations, such as shape, function, colour and so on. All in all, this section offers a comprehensive overview of how to take your jewellery-making skills very much further.

Left Oval labradorite and aquamarine engagement ring and interlocking wedding ring set with a ruby.

Right Pages from a sketchbook show how various ideas and designs for the engagement ring were developed.

THE RIGHT SET-UP

Jewellery-making can be time-consuming and, depending on which areas you decide to specialise in, may require a wide range of specialist tools and equipment. It is important, therefore, to have a clean, comfortable workspace, with plenty of light and good storage. In order to help you get started along the right lines, the first section of this book focuses on how to set up a small workshop – how best to lay out your space, and the kind of equipment to buy. For some of the more advanced techniques, quite a lot of specialist equipment is needed, so it is worthwhile experimenting at an evening class before deciding whether or not you want to invest in your own tools. If you get the work-

shop right, you will enjoy making jewellery there, finding it a place in which ideas can flourish and your skills develop, and where you can enjoy the satisfaction of creating something personal and beautiful every time.

It will not take you long to discover that jewellery design and making requires a healthy curiosity and an appetite for understanding and enjoying the fundamental ingredients of design. Learning how to design jewellery can be easy; it can be incredibly enjoyable and exhilarating. It can be a challenge and it can be a frustration; but there is no doubt that it can also be a wonderful journey that has the potential to enrich your life!

Tools and Materials

There is a considerable range of specialist equipment involved when it comes to making jewellery, and selecting tools can be a daunting exercise, initially. This section of the book outlines the various items used by jewellery makers, presenting them in three major categories: essential tools for everyday use; useful additional and specialist tools; and large-scale equipment. There is also information on the chemicals used in a number of jewellery-making processes and on the metals used for many of the projects that follow.

Planning a workshop

THE GREAT ADVANTAGES OF MAKING JEWELLERY ARE THAT YOU NEED ONLY A RELATIVELY SMALL SPACE IN WHICH TO WORK, IT IS A TREMENDOUSLY CHALLENGING AND EXCITING CRAFT TO LEARN AND YOU NEED NEVER AGAIN WORRY ABOUT BUYING GIFTS FOR LOVED ONES.

LAYING OUT YOUR WORKSHOP

Making jewellery can be an expensive pastime, especially at first when there seems to be an endless list of tools to buy. Don't be discouraged, however, as you can produce a wonderful variety of items with just a few basic tools.

Firstly, it is surprising how little space you need, and, if you plan your workshop carefully, it will serve you for many years.

There are a few basic Do's and Don'ts, which are listed opposite, but in general you should work in an area where you feel comfortable, adding equipment as and when you find you need and can afford individual items. If you are fortunate enough to have a special workroom, you should make sure that there is a stainless-steel sink and draining board, and a north-facing light.

WORKSHOP LAYOUT UNDER THE STAIRS

Even the smallest space can be used as a workshop, as long as it has good light and ventilation and adequate storage.

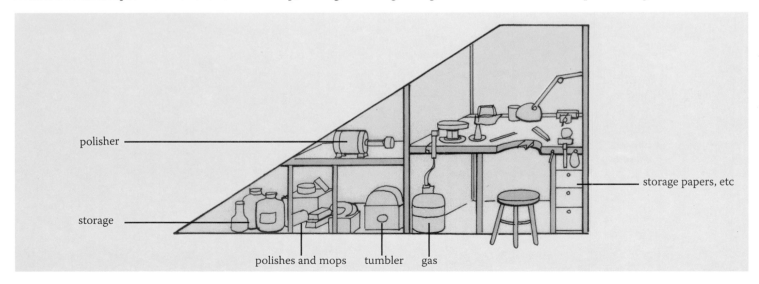

polisher

storage

polishes and mops   tumbler   gas

storage papers, etc

Do's and Don'ts

- DO make sure that the space you are using is well ventilated when dealing with acids and other chemicals. There must be a good flow of air.

- DON'T site your workshop in an area where bright sunlight will fall directly on your work, especially the soldering area. It is difficult to see colours change as you heat up silver if the light is very bright.

- DO have access to several electrical outlets so that there are no extension cords trailing across the floor or benches.

- DO keep the area in which you polish your work separate, because the dust created by polishing is dirty and will get onto your other work.

- DO keep a lighter next to your soldering torch for ease of use.

- DON'T leave the flame on when your torch is not in use, unless it has a pilot light.

- DON'T keep tools and equipment made of ferrous metal above or near acid because the fumes will quickly cause them to rust.

- DO use an electric heater rather than a portable gas one if your workshop is cold in winter, as the condensation caused by gas heaters will quickly make your ferrous tools rust.

TIP

Have a bulletin board in your workshop with a sheet of paper pinned to it. When you think you need a particular tool, make a note of it. Before you go to the craft-supply shop, list only those items and tools that you really do need, omitting those that you can manage without. You will, over time, build up a stock of carefully selected and versatile tools.

WORKSHOP LAYOUT IN A ROOM

Being able to dedicate a larger space to your workshop – a spare room, loft conversion or garden shed, for example – needs to fulfil all of the criteria listed to the left.

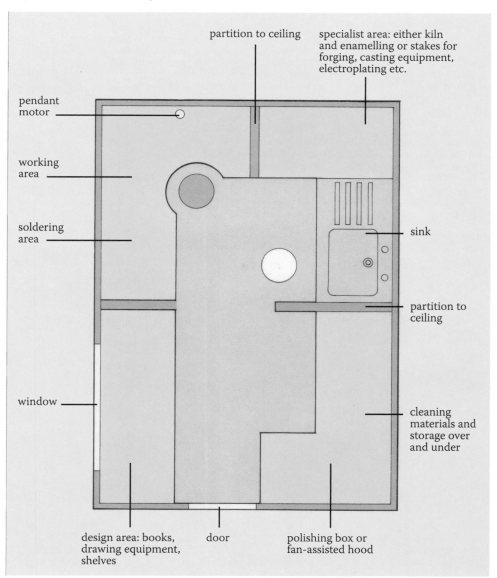

partition to ceiling

specialist area: either kiln and enamelling or stakes for forging, casting equipment, electroplating etc.

pendant motor

working area

soldering area

sink

partition to ceiling

window

cleaning materials and storage over and under

design area: books, drawing equipment, shelves

door

polishing box or fan-assisted hood

Essential tools

YOUR FIRST REQUIREMENT IS A TABLE OR BENCH ON WHICH TO WORK. THE KITCHEN TABLE MAY DO TO START WITH, BUT THE SOONER YOU CAN FIND A LITTLE CORNER OF YOUR OWN WHERE YOU CAN SAFELY LEAVE YOUR WORK UNATTENDED, THE BETTER.

THE WORKBENCH

The recommended height for all benches is about 90cm (36in). This will give support to your elbows while you are sitting in an upright position. Make sure it has sturdy legs.

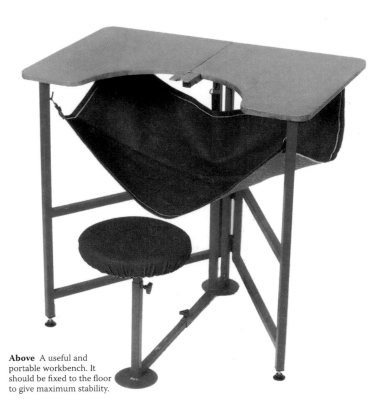

Above A useful and portable workbench. It should be fixed to the floor to give maximum stability.

You can make your own workbench by using a sheet of 25mm (1in) plywood, 120x180cm (48x72in). Cut a semi-circle approximately 60cm (24in) across in the centre of one of the long sides. Anchor the table top to a firm base, making sure that nothing obstructs the semi-circular opening. Fasten a strong piece of muslin or leather around the underside of the semi-circle, holding it in place with hooks. This will catch all the filings and scrap metal pieces, which can be taken to a refiner and sold.

BASIC TOOL KIT

Even for the most basic jewellery-making projects, you are likely to need a handful of essential tools. You can decide whether to collect them gradually, as they come up with each new project, or to invest in the full kit right from the start.

Peg Whether you are working from the kitchen table or have made your own bench, you will need what is called a 'peg' or 'pin'. This is a wedge of wood fitted to the centre of a semi-circle in the bench or held with a G-clamp to a table. Some jewellers cut a 'V' up the middle of the wedge so that the silver can rest on the wood while the piercing saw works up the 'V'. It also supports the work while it is being filed, cleaned, set, burnished and so on. In other words, it is a vital part of your equipment.

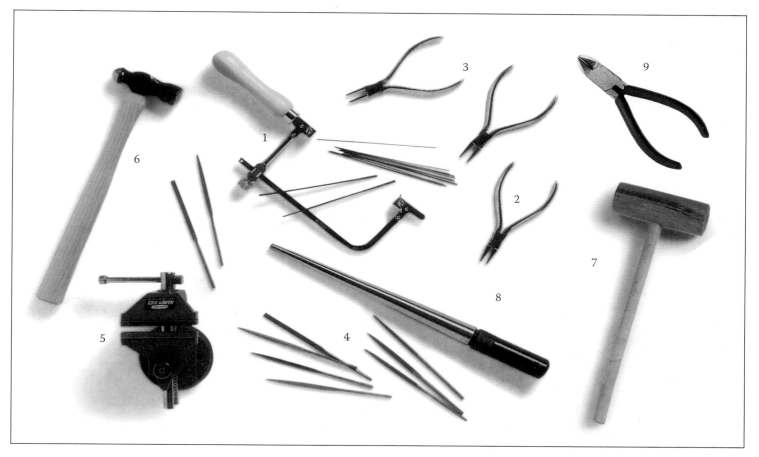

1 Jeweller's piercing saw and blades You will keep this tool forever. The blades come in packs of 12, and it is cheaper to buy a gross. Start off with blade numbers 01 and 02.

2 Flat-nosed pliers It is advisable to buy two pairs of these pliers, either with oval ends or with straight ends. Keep a look out for a very small pair.

3 Round-nosed pliers These are useful for bending wire; you should get a large pair and a small pair.

4 Needle files These are used extensively for refining shapes, removing solder and levelling surfaces, and you will need flat, oval, triangular and semi-circular ones. Needle files are available in packets of eight or ten, and this is a good way to buy them.

5 Small vice There are two different sorts of vice that you will find useful. A jeweller's vice has a ball joint, which means that it can be used in all angles, and 'safe' jaws. A small bench vice is sturdier for most jobs, and you can make your own safe jaws from copper or wood if necessary.

6 Hammer A general-purpose hammer is called a ball-peen (or ball-pein) hammer and is useful for many aspects of jewellery-making.

7 Mallet Wooden, nylon and rawhide mallets are generally used to shape silver because they do not leave marks.

8 Mandrel This tool is a steel rod essential for shaping rings, wires, collets and so on after soldering. It is also sometimes known as a triblet or former.

9 Wire cutters These come in a variety of sizes depending on the thickness of the wire to be cut. Occasionally wire cutters are incorporated within a pair of pliers.

Recommended tools

ONCE YOU HAVE ESTABLISHED YOUR WORKSHOP AND HAVE INVESTED IN A BASIC TOOL KIT, YOU WILL GRADUALLY WANT TO BUILD ON THE EQUIPMENT YOU HAVE. LISTED HERE ARE TOOLS THAT ARE WORTH WATCHING OUT FOR AS YOU PROGRESS WITH YOUR SKILLS.

1 Riffler files These curved files allow you to file in corners, on curves and in generally inaccessible places.

2 Wooden punches Punches are used for all sorts of 'forming' work. Wooden ones shape without marking the metal, and it is useful to have a range of diameters.

3 Ring gauges or sizers These come in sizes A–Z and can be obtained in the form of a sizing card, a ring set of 26 or a set of 52 with half sizes.

4 Doming block Usually brass and available in different sizes, the most useful being a 5cm (2in) cube. This is used for making domes and semi-circles of silver. It should be kept clean and dry. Any specks lying in the bottom of the block will mark the silver.

5 Anvil or flatplate Either of these tools is useful when you are flattening or hammering silver. The size does not really matter, but the surface should be kept smooth, clean and dry.

6 Whetstone You will need to keep your gravers and tips sharp. Keep the stone well oiled when you are using it so that loose particles do not become embedded in the tool being sharpened.

7 Large files You will need oval, flat and half-round files.

8 Drawplates These steel plates have graduated holes, which are used to reduce the diameter or outline of round or sectional wire and tube.

9 Top cutters/side cutters These are useful for cutting up small paillons of solder, for cutting wire and for getting into difficult places.

10 Pliers Half-round pliers (10a) can be used to bend metal into curves without marking the outside; (10b) parallel pliers will grip a piece of silver equally along its length; (10c) serrated pliers are useful for gripping ends of wire when pulling it through the drawplate or straighten it in a vice.

11 Crucible You will need a crucible to melt scrap and pour it into an ingot mould.

12 Scriber This little tool is used for marking a pattern on the silver, and for marking lines and circle centres. It should have a good point.

13 Drills Use an ordinary hand drill to make large holes. When you need to make small holes, use a bow drill (13b), which allows you to hold your work with one hand while the drill is operated with the other. Wind the string around the shaft by twisting the top, and then, with the wooden handle held securely between two fingers, push the drill down. Allow it to rise, which it does because of the tension on the string, then push it down again. You can make fine drill bits (13a) from sewing needles, which are broken in half. Rub two opposite faces flat on your whetstone, and then rub off the other two corners. Small hand vices or drills (13c), which can be used with one hand, are available with different-sized chucks, which will take drills of minute size.

14 Metal punches Used in conjunction with the doming block, metal punches have all of the uses of wooden punches, but are harder and more precise.

15 Swage block This can be used with the handles of your metal punch to shape a strip of silver into a 'U'. The silver should be slightly narrower than the slot into which it is being punched.

16 Burnisher Burnishers are used for rubbing and polishing your finished work. They are also used for setting stones, by rubbing the silver over the stone. They should be kept dry and polished.

17 Suede stick and emery stick Both are used for cleaning and finishing. The emery stick should be used first, and it is possible to dissolve polish onto a suede stick with lighter fluid.

18 Sandbag This provides a good supportive base for silver when it is being shaped with either wooden or metal punches or as a support when engraving.

19 Ring clamp and hand vice A ring clamp can be adjusted by means of a wedge to accommodate a ring of any size, and it will also support your work while you are working. The shank of a ring can be held in the protected jaws of the hand vice while you work on a setting.

20 Jointing tool This tool is used to hold chenier and wire straight while it is cut with a piercing saw.

21 Hammers A selection of hammers will be useful. A ball-peen hammer (21a) is a useful general purpose hammer. A chasing hammer (21b) should be used to strike the heads of repoussé and chasing tools. This type of hammer has a broad head and a rounded handle so that you can deliver rhythmic strokes. A raising hammer (21c) has a round nose, which is used to compress metal, while the flat face is used to extend the metal. Gentle taps with a planishing (21d) hammer will allow you to remove marks made by your raising or ball-peen hammer.

22 Punches and chasing tools These are used for shaping and marking sheet metal. A centre punch has a narrow point and is used for making an indentation in sheet metal before drilling. Punches can be bought in sets, or you can make them yourself from square or round steel stock, tempered and ground or filed to shape (*see page 48*). Always keep your punches clean and dry.

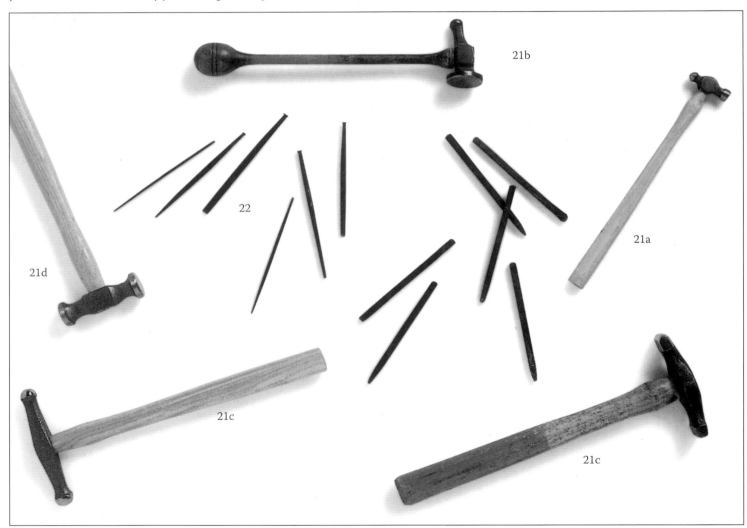

Pitch bowl Jeweller's pitch is used to hold your work firm when you are shaping, engraving, setting stones, chasing and doing repoussé work. It is made from a mixture of asphaltum, plaster of Paris or pumice powder, and tallow or linseed oil. To make a stiffer pitch, add more plaster of Paris; to keep it soft, add more tallow or linseed. Pitch can be removed by being burnt, when it forms ash, or by being dissolved in turpentine. The bowl should rest in a round wooden ring to keep it steady at all angles.

Wire wool This is used for cleaning the surface of sheet metal. It removes grease and dirt, leaving a satin finish.

Tin snips Snips or shears come in a variety of sizes and are used for cutting flat sheet metal in straight lines or simple curves.

ADHESIVES

There will be occasions on which you will want to glue, rather than solder or rivet, components together. There are various glues available, each suited to a different purpose

Resin-based glue A strong bonding glue that requires the mixing of an adhesive and hardener to enable it to work. It is available in tube form or in a syringe. Follow manufacturer's instructions carefully.

All-purpose clear, strong adhesive Useful for sticking non-metal items together, such as wood, fabric and some plastics. It is available in tubes. Always use in a well-ventilated area.

PVA a white non-toxic, water-based glue, particularly suitable for bonding paper, card and fabric. It is available in tubes or plastic bottles and can be applied using a brush. Rinse a brush under water immediately after use.

TIP

It is possible to find a number of good tools in second-hand tool shops. Before you buy, there are a few things to watch out for. Check the tips of pairs of pliers to make sure that they close correctly. Make sure that they are not badly marked, because any dents will transfer to the silver. Watch out for badly marked hammers, stakes and punches. Although they can be reground or polished, it may not be worth it. Remember that most second-hand files have been used for iron, steel or aluminium, and are not recommended for jewellery-making. Second-hand vices, anvils, hand drills and pendant motors, however, are all worth obtaining.

Large equipment

SOME OF THE BIGGER ITEMS OF EQUIPMENT ARE EXPENSIVE, AND IT MAY TAKE YOU SEVERAL YEARS TO ACQUIRE THEM ALL. CONSIDER PURCHASING THEM WHEN THEY ARE ABSOLUTELY NECESSARY, BECAUSE SOME OF THE WORK THEY DO CAN BE DONE VERY SATISFACTORILY BY HAND.

Polisher A polisher in which objects and polished steel shot are loaded into a compartment and vibrated together for several hours. Many objects can be polished at a time, but the process is suitable only for those without flat surfaces or fine protrusions.

Rouge, tripoli and Hyfin These are the three established polishing materials used for making jewellery.

Mops An alternative to a large polisher is to invest in a number of mops for polishing using the pendant motor (*see opposite*).

Scales All sorts of scales are available, ranging from hand-held ones to electronic ones. As long as they are accurate for very small weights, they will be suitable. You might be able to buy a second-hand set.

Ultrasonic cleaner A stainless-steel container is used with an ammonia-based detergent to remove, ultrasonically, excess polish from silver, gold, copper or brass. The work is placed on a rack or on a hook so that is it suspended in the cleaning fluid, through which the sound waves penetrate.

Rolling mill Rolling mills come in a variety of sizes – and prices. Choose the best one you can afford. They are used for reducing the thickness of silver and of sectional and round wire. If you order materials to your precise requirements, you will not need a mill. Use only silver, copper, gold or brass in your mill: steel will leave dents and pits on the rollers, which will then have to be replaced professionally.

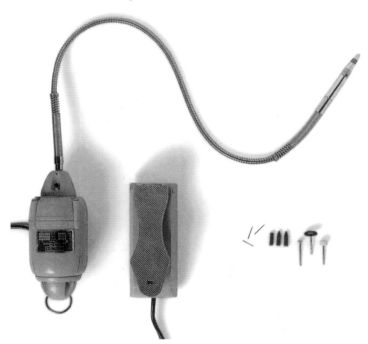

Kiln Either gas-fired or electric, a kiln is used for enamelling, annealing and casting. The same kiln should not be used for both enamelling and casting, because the burnt-out residues from casting would contaminate the enamel, but annealing may be done in either.

Pendant motor with flexible shaft Of all the large pieces of equipment, this is one of the most affordable and is also extremely useful. It is a single unit that comes with a variety of heads that allow you to drill and texture surfaces, to remove solder, to clean inside rings and castings, to polish small areas and to open out settings.

Soldering and pickling tools

SOLDERING IS THE PROCESS MOST JEWELLERS USE FOR JOINING ONE PIECE OF METAL TO ANOTHER. THERE ARE VARIOUS PIECES OF EQUIPMENT AVAILABLE FOR PRODUCING THE HEAT NEEDED DURING THIS PROCESS, AND IT IS WORTH DEDICATING AN AREA OF THE WORKSHOP TO SOLDERING AND PICKLING ALONE.

WHERE TO SOLDER

You will need to set aside an area on your workbench for solder-ing. If you are right-handed, try the area on your left, because you will find it more convenient and practical to have your files, drills, vices and so on, on your right. If you are left-handed, do the opposite. Alternatively, find a completely separate area for your soldering – one in which flames and acids will not threaten your other tools. If you do solder on the bench, make sure that the torch is readily at hand and insert a hook to hang it on.

SOLDERING EQUIPMENT

To guard against accidental burning, protect your soldering area with a heat-resistant mat, an old roasting pan or a revolving soldering stand. You will also need a charcoal block or synthetic soldering block. A charcoal block helps the work heat up quickly if it is left to smoulder. A soldering block is particularly useful when large work is heated because it does not burn through. However, soldering takes a little longer as the block does not reflect the heat.

Keep a good supply of paintbrushes, old toothbrushes, empty jars and an assortment of heat-resistant dishes handy in your workshop. They are always useful for cleaning, pickling, applying borax and many other things.

After heating silver, it is usual to pickle it. For this you need a safety pickle solution, made by adding warm water to shop-bought crystals. Use a glass measuring cup so that you can gauge the correct amount of fluid. You can also use a 10:1 solution of water and sulphuric acid. If you do, be sure to wear good-quality rubber gloves and a heavy apron or smock.

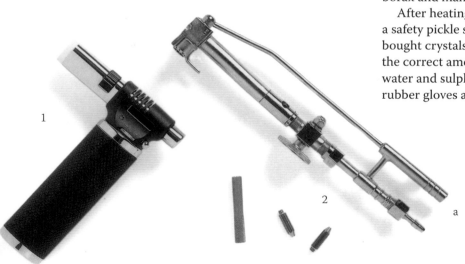

1 Portable torch This is too small for general use, but its small direct flame is useful when soldering small chains, wire rings, etc.

2 Adjustable torch The gas can come either from the main supply or a propane gas canister. The air is introduced by blowing down a flexible rubber pipe attached to the torch at point 'a'. It is a very good multi-purpose torch, but not suitable for very large pieces or prolonged high temperatures.

1 Hard, medium and easy solders **2** Binding wire **3** Flux or borax **4** Insulated tweezers **5** Charcoal block and soldering block **6** Brass tongs or tweezers **7** Stainless steel tweezers **8** Tin snips **9** Spring tweezers **10** Third hand **11** Revolving soldering tray **12** Jeweller's wig

Chemicals

LISTED HERE ARE SOME OF THE ACIDS, CLEANING AND POLISHING MATERIALS THAT YOU WILL NEED. ACIDS AND CHEMICALS MUST BE STORED IN A SAFE, DRY, COOL PLACE. WHEN HANDLING ACIDS AND CHEMICALS, ALWAYS WORK IN A WELL-VENTILATED AREA AND WEAR PROTECTIVE CLOTHING.

ACIDS

Nitric acid is used for etching and for removing fire stain. Use a solution of three parts water to one part acid. When etching, immerse the piece in the solution and 'tickle' it with a feather from time to time to make sure the etch is uniform. Always keep an eye on your work so that it does not etch too quickly. To use nitric acid as a dip to remove fire stain, hang your work by a length of stainless-steel wire for a couple of seconds in the solution. Remove, rinse under running water and clean off the black with pumice powder and water. Repeat until all the oxides have gone.

Safety pickle is used for removing oxides after heating. It comes in a crystal form that dissolves in warm water. It is safe to use and will not damage clothing if splashed.

SODA CRYSTALS

Approximately one spoonful of crystals in 0.5l (½ gallon) of boiling water will neutralise any residue of acid on your work after pickling. Soldering is impossible if there is any acid present, so it is often necessary to boil your work to remove all traces of acid. Rinse your work thoroughly in cold water.

ACETONE

This colourless, volatile and highly flammable liquid is excellent for cleaning off grease and dirt, but it will leave a mark. It also dissolves many types or glue, so be careful where and how you use it. Always store acetone in a tightly closed container and use it only in a well-ventilated working area.

PUMICE POWDER

Keep a container of pumice powder and a toothbrush next to the sink. After soldering and pickling, a quick scrub with pumice and water will help to clean your work. Pumice is abrasive, so do not use it on polished work.

POTASSIUM SULPHIDE

This is used to oxidise particular areas of work. Use one 12mm (½in) cube of potassium sulphide in 0.5l (½ gallon) of hot water.

ARGOTEC

This powder is mixed with water to form a paste that can be painted onto work before soldering to help prevent fire stain.

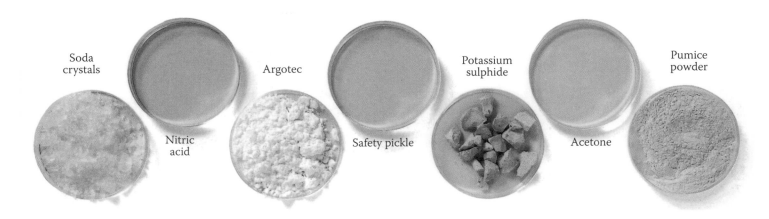

Soda crystals

Nitric acid

Argotec

Safety pickle

Potassium sulphide

Acetone

Pumice powder

Metals

A VAST RANGE OF MATERIALS CAN BE USED FOR MAKING JEWELLERY. THE MAJORITY OF THE PROJECTS IN THIS BOOK USE SILVER – EITHER IN SHEET OR WIRE FORM – WITH A RANGE OF BEADS AND GEMSTONES. YOU CAN FIND A WIDE RANGE OF ADDITIONAL MATERIALS ON *PAGES 58–61*.

Silver, gold and other metals are available in various forms – sheet (which is measured in gauges or millimetres), tube, sectional wire and tube, and rod.

Sheet metal The metals most commonly used in jewellery-making can be split into two main groups: non-ferrous metals, such as copper, brass, tin and aluminium; or precious, such as silver and gold. Copper is a pinkish red colour, is malleable and easy to work with. Brass is pale yellow in colour and a harder metal than copper. Sterling silver is softer than either copper or brass. It is available from specialist refiners or bullion dealers, most of whom will allow you to purchase small quantities at a time. You can often select from offcuts or pieces can be cut to a specific size.

Wire Silver, brass and copper wire are available in a variety of thicknesses. They are often sold in a ready softened or annealed state (*see page 37*) so that they are easy to manipulate straight away.

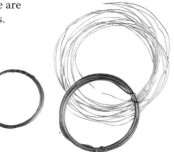

BUYING SILVER AND GOLD

For general-purpose work, standard silver is used. The silver content of Standard or Sterling silver is 92.5 per cent, the remaining 7.5 per cent being copper or other metals. For large pieces, such as bowls and candlesticks, Brittania silver is often used. This has a silver content of 95.8 per cent. Pure silver or fine silver is very soft and is used mainly during enamelling. Before you order, work out the exact measurements of the silver you will need. Silver is sold by weight, and the price varies daily. Collect all the scrap from the bag under the pin on your workbench occasionally, and take it to your bullion dealer once a year. Some jewellers have been known to take their annual vacation on the proceeds!

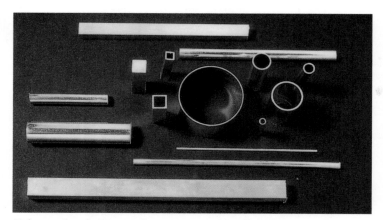

Tubes and rods Pieces of varying size and wall thickness can be found. They have many uses – from producing hollow rings that do not require soldering to making hinge joints and settings for stones.

Basic Techniques

Much of the satisfaction of making your own jewellery is that it usually involves making a number of components, each of which requires manipulation of some kind in order to make it an integral part of the finished whole. Whether you are bending wire, hammering sheet metal or soldering components together, you will need any number of these basic jewellery-making techniques along the way. You can find these, and more, in this section of the book, along with step instruction on how to perform them. You will discover how to transfer designs to your work, how to saw and file metal and how to make your own jump rings and findings. An invaluable investment at this stage is a pendant motor with interchangeable parts. Not only will this speed up essential basic techniques such as drilling, sanding and polishing, but it will allow you to achieve a more professional finish in your work.

Transferring a design

WHETHER A PIECE OF JEWELLERY HAS A SPECIFIC SHAPE, AN INTRICATE SURFACE PATTERN OR REQUIRES A NUMBER OF IDENTICAL PIECES TO BE MADE PRIOR TO CONSTRUCTION, YOU WILL BE REQUIRED TO TRANSFER A DESIGN ONTO SHEET METAL FOR GREATER ACCURACY. THERE ARE A NUMBER OF WAYS OF DOING THIS.

METHODS FOR TRANSFERRING

There are several ways in which you can transfer your design to sheet metal. Try them all until you find the one that suits you best. Of course, if the design is very simple, you can draw or scribe it directly onto the metal.

Things you will need:

Sheet metal

Tracing paper

Acetate or carbon paper

Eraser

Scriber

Pencil

Masking tape

Glue

Dividers

Left A pair of dividers and a good selection of drawing materials, including steel rule, tracing paper, sharp pencils and a craft knife are invaluable to your work.

USING ACETATE

Rub over the surface of the metal with an eraser. Lay a piece of acetate over your design and use a scriber to trace the pattern onto the acetate. Rub soft pencil into the scribed lines, then lay the acetate, scribed side down, on top of the metal, securing it in place with masking tape. Use the blunt end of the pencil to rub over the acetate so that the lines are transferred to the metal.

Remember that your design will appear in reverse if you do this. This may not matter with some designs – a symmetrical pattern will look the same whichever way round it is transferred – or you could turn the sheet metal over after piercing. However, if you prefer, you can transfer your pattern to tracing paper and turn that over before tracing the pattern onto acetate.

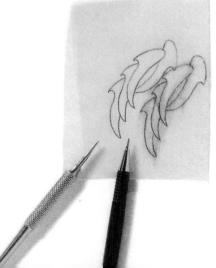

USING CARBON PAPER

Rub over the surface of the metal with an eraser. Transfer your design to tracing paper and attach a piece of carbon paper to the metal, holding it in place with masking tape. Secure the tracing paper in place over the carbon paper and draw over the design, using a fine, hard joint. Remove the tracing paper and the carbon. Use a scriber to go over the lines of your design, making sure that you do not accidentally smudge or wipe off the carbon lines as you work. When you have scribed over the whole design, wipe away any carbon marks that remain before proceeding.

USING TRACING PAPER

Transfer your design to a piece of tracing paper. Cover the back of the tracing paper with adhesive and leave it to dry for a few seconds. Place the tracing paper over the silver and press it firmly into position. Make sure that the paper is securely attached to the silver, then pierce or cut out your design. Peel away the remains of the tracing paper from the silver when you have finished. Any remaining paper can be removed with cotton wool soaked in acetone.

MARKING METAL

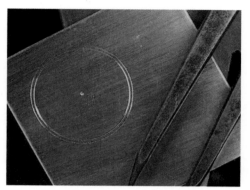

❶ To mark sheet metal with simple lines for piercing, use a scriber and rule for straight lines and dividers for circles. When piercing out a disc, mark a circle to the size you want and then mark a second circle about 1mm (1/32in) larger around it. Pierce between the two lines and file down to the first line.

❷ For more intricate shapes, use a template. Start by cleaning your sheet metal using a fresh piece of wire wool. Cut your desired shape from thin card, place it on your sheet metal and use a pen to draw around it. Cut the shape out using tin snips, and file smooth the sharp edges.

TIP

When you transfer your design, try to use the metal as economically as possible. For example, if your design has a straight edge, use an existing edge of the silver; if you are cutting out more than one piece, do not leave a large space between them, but try to fit them close together.

Sawing and piercing

WHEN YOU CUT OUT METAL WITH A JEWELLER'S SAW, THE BLADE WILL CUT ONLY ON THE DOWN STROKE. DEVELOP AN EASY, RHYTHMIC ACTION AND NEVER FORCE THE BLADE. WHEN THE BLADE GETS STUCK, LIFT UP YOUR WORK AND LET THE SAW FIND ITS NATURAL POSITION. YOU WILL THEN BE ABLE TO CONTINUE.

CHOOSING A BLADE

Saw blades are available in sizes 0/4 (finest) up to 14. For most jewellery purposes numbers 0/4 to 4 will give an adequate range, and number 1/0 is a good one to start with.

Things you will need:

Sheet metal
Jeweller's saw
3 packets of blades, number 1/0
Small hand drill with a 0.5mm bit
Centre punch
Hand drill

FITTING A BLADE

For ease of working, a blade should be firmly fitted before you begin. It is also necessary to know how to fit a new blade when an old one becomes worn and you need to replace it.

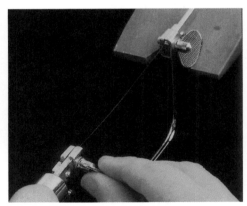

❶ Take a number 1/0 blade, with the teeth of the blade towards you and pointing down, and slot the top end of the blade into the top fastening of your saw. Tighten the screw.

❷ Push the top end of the saw against the bench and slot the bottom end of the blade into the lower fastening of the saw. Tighten the screw. The blade should be firm and springy, with the teeth pointing down towards the handle of the saw.

CUTTING

There is an art to cutting, part of which involves not trying to force the blade through the metal. You should try to avoid pushing too hard, because the thin sawing blades break very easily.

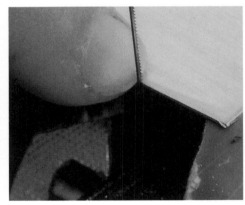

❶ Hold the saw at an angle of 90° to your work. Make the first cut, just touching the blade against your index finger as a guide. Let the blade fall through the metal and continue with a steady up-and-down movement along the line of your pattern.

PIERCING AN ENCLOSED AREA

Cutting a hole within sheet metal does not require a special tool – you can use the same saw that you use for straight-edge cutting.

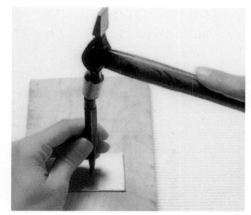

1 Use a centre punch to mark the metal at the edge of the shape you need to cut.

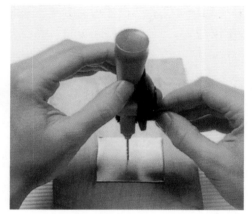

2 Drill a small hole through the metal, at the place marked by the centre punch mark. Make sure it is large enough for the piercing blade to fit through.

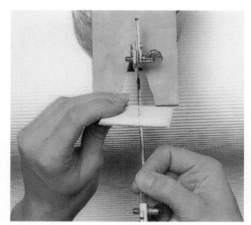

3 Open one end of the piercing saw and thread the blade through the hole. Fasten the blade in position again, making sure it is firm.

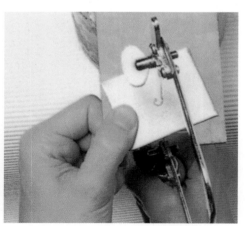

4 Hold the metal firmly against the peg and cut out your desired shape.

TIP

When you reach a corner, rub the smooth, back edge of the blade into the corner you wish to turn, gradually turn the saw frame until it is facing in the new direction. Do not try to move forward until the blade is in the correct position.

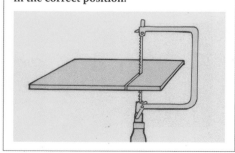

Drilling holes in metal

IT MAY BE NECESSARY TO DRILL HOLES IN METAL FOR A NUMBER OF REASONS, SUCH AS ATTACHING JUMP RINGS TO A PENDANT, FOR MAKING HOLES IN PREPARATION FOR PIERCING (*SEE PAGE 31*) AND FOR FRETWORK (*SEE PAGES 108–109*). YOU CAN DRILL BY HAND OR USING A MOTORISED UNIT.

USING A DRILL

When drilling large holes, begin with a small one, then enlarge it by using a slightly bigger drill bit each time. Drilling a large number of holes by hand can be tedious. A pendant drill – a motorised unit that can be used for drilling – makes the job easier. Always wear safety glasses when using a mechanical drill. The demonstration shown here is worked on a piece to be cut using a fretwork pattern.

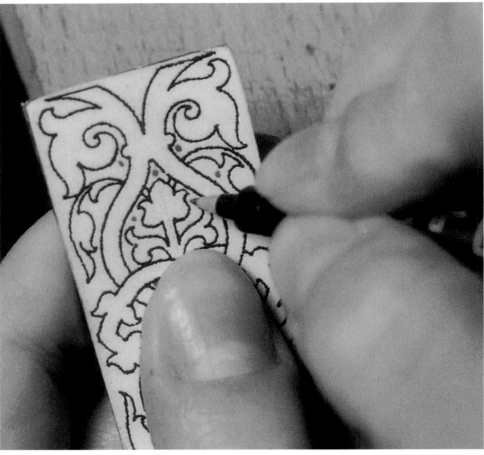

Things you will need:

Pen

Scriber

Archimedes or bow drill, or pendant motor and 1mm (⅓₂in) diameter twist bit

Oil or wax

1 Use a pen to mark a point on your pattern inside a shape to be cut, about 1mm (⅓₂in) away from the pattern if possible. Mark similar points on all the areas to be cut.

2 Load a twist drill bit, ensuring that it is held securely. The tip of a twist drill bit is pointed, so when presented to a metal sheet it can slip. Make an indentation on each pen mark by pushing the tip of a scriber down hard into the sheet to crease an indent on the point marked.

3 Sometimes the friction caused by your drilling heats up and dries the drill bit and the metal sheet. It is a good idea to apply oil or wax to the bit to lubricate it. Lubrication helps to avoid the drill bit getting stuck or breaking – if the bit gets stuck while drilling, the piece can spin out of your grip.

TIP
A twist drill bit is relatively vulnerable and, if possible, should be loaded so that as much of the shank – the smooth area of the drill bit – is held by the chuck as is possible, without covering the spiral section. When drilling, always hold the work firmly against a solid wood surface.

4 If using a hand drill, hold the work firmly on a bench or level bench peg. Position the end of the drill bit in the indentation. Hold the work with one hand while you operate the drill with the other.

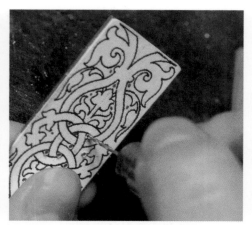

5 If using a pendant drill, hold the work firmly against the bench. Position the end of the drill bit in the indentation. Using firm, but not hard, pressure, push the twist drill bit downwards to drill the hole.

6 If you are drilling using a bow or Archimedes drill, make sure the work is held completely level the whole time.

Manipulating wire

A NUMBER OF PROJECTS IN THIS BOOK ARE MADE USING WIRE. THE THINNER GAUGE SILVER AND COPPER WIRES ARE RELATIVELY EASY TO MANIPULATE WITHOUT ANNEALING (SOFTENING) FIRST, WHILE MOST SUPPLIERS WILL STOCK READY-SOFTENED OR ANNEALED WIRES THAT CAN BE USED STRAIGHT AWAY.

BENDING AND FLATTENING WIRE

With just a handful of techniques at your disposal, you can manipulate softened or annealed wire very easily, adapting it to work with any number of jewellery designs. You can bend and curl silver, gold, copper and brass to make all manner of pretty curls, spirals and zigzags, and you can custom-make your own findings.

Things you will need:

Wire cutters
Round-nosed pliers
Flat-nosed pliers
Hammer

1 To bend wire into a circular shape, first cut the wire to the required length using wire cutters. Grip one end of the wire in a pair of round-nosed pliers and keep a firm hold.

2 Use your free hand to manipulate the wire, wrapping it round the pliers to form a single loop. You can make this loop as tight or loose as you like, depending on the piece you are making.

3 To make a spiral, use a pair of flat-nosed pliers to hold the loop you have made as you continue to bend the wire around itself in a series of rings.

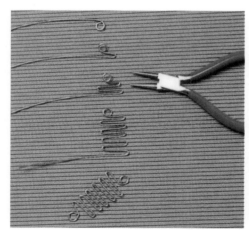

4 To bend wire into a zigzag shape, follow steps 1 and 2 to make a loop. Then use the round-nosed pliers to make a series of bends, back and forth along the length of the wire. For sharper bends, such as a 90° angle, use a pair of flat-nosed pliers to manipulate the wire.

5 To flatten the wire, work on a firm surface and tap the wire gently using a hammer. Make sure you keep the pressure even along the entire length of the wire as you work.

Things you will need:
Wire cutters
Vice
Wire hook
Hand drill
Circular rod

TWISTING WIRE

When twisting wire, you need to bear in mind that the finished piece will be considerably shorter than the length of the individual wires that you start with. Calculate the length of twisted wire you need for the piece you are working on and factor in a 40 per cent increase in length for the pre-twisted wires.

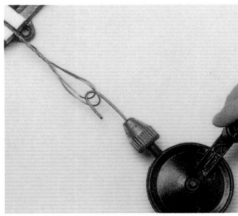

1 Use wire cutters to cut two equal 120-cm (48in) lengths of wire and bend them both in half. Secure the ends in a vice. Take the wire hook and attach it to the hand drill. Hook the looped end of the bent wires onto the hook.

2 Start to turn the hand drill to make the wire lengths twist together. It is important that you turn the drill slowly as you work. This will allow the wires to twist together neatly and evenly.

3 Continue to turn the drill until the wires are tightly and evenly twisted along their length. You can choose how loosely or tightly you want the wire to be. Beware of making it too tight, which may cause the wire to buckle.

COILING WIRE

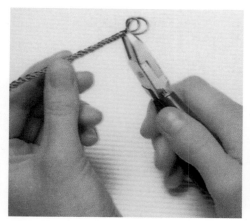

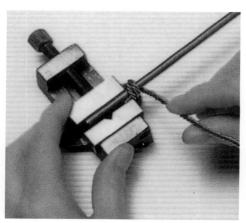

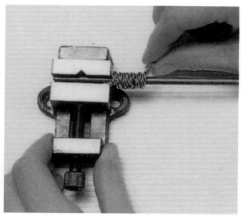

1 Remove the wire from the vice and drill. Using the wire cutters, cut off the looped end so that you are left with an even length of wire.

2 Secure a circular rod and one end of the twisted wire in the vice. Slowly bend the twisted wire around the rod.

3 Continue to bend the twisted wire around the rod until all of the wire has been used and the wires have formed a coil.

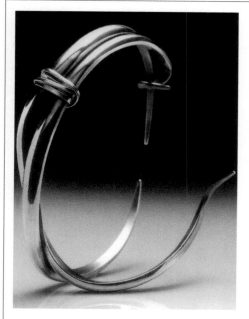

ANNEALING METAL

All but the narrowest gauge and ready-softened wires, rods and sheet metals need to be soft enough to work easily, and this is achieved through a process called annealing. It involves heating the metal gently using a blow torch, or similar. Metals also need re-annealing when they become work-hardened, because if they are too hard they become brittle and are liable to crack.

• Make sure that the area in which you will be working is not in direct light. Put your metal on a soldering block and heat it with a soft flame – that is, in the pale blue area just behind the yellow tip.

• Feather the flame forward and back over the metal until it becomes a dull red. Keep the metal that colour for a few seconds, then put out the flame.

• Pickle the metal (*see page 46*), rinse in water and dry.

Filing

TO ACHIEVE A GOOD FINISH ON SILVER, EVERY SCRATCH THAT IS MADE HAS TO BE REMOVED AND REPLACED BY A FINER ONE. YOU DO THIS BY WORKING SYSTEMATICALLY FROM COARSE FILES, TO NEEDLE FILES, TO WET AND DRY PAPERS, TO THE DIFFERENT GRADES OF POLISH.

Things you will need:
Suitable files
Vice, for holding the work steady

CHOOSING A FILE

A file cuts in only one direction, and there are many different-shaped files that will follow the line of your work. In general, use a flat file on a flat surface; an oval or half-round file inside a curve; a triangular file for grooves and small corners; a rectangular or square file for right angles; and a round file to cut 'U' grooves and open out holes. Some rectangular or flat files have a cutting edge, which is useful for making grooves, and some files have a safe edge, which allows you to file one surface without damaging another that is close to it.

TIP
Filing is a process of gradual elimination. At each stage of filing, you should check that you have erased the scratches made by the previous tool.

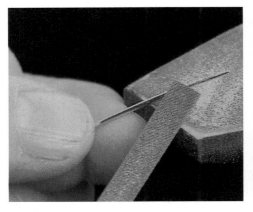

FILING A TAPER

Several projects require you to file a rod or wire to a taper or point. You can do this with a flat file, making long, sweeping strokes and twisting the rod or wire with your other hand to ensure an even taper. Support the end of your rod or wire as you work.

FILING A CURVE

Inside curves, use an oval or half-round file, keeping it straight. Work on alternate sides of the piece to keep the filing even.

FLAT FILING

When you are filing a long edge flat, hold the silver in the vice, parallel to the safe jaws. Holding the flat file in one hand and move it diagonally in long smooth strokes along the silver. Use the index finger of your other hand to keep the file flat and straight.

USING A RIFFLER FILE

This file has a curved tip and a smooth centre that is used as the handle. It allows you to file inside difficult corners and on convex and concave surfaces.

TIP

Files can become clogged as you use them, with metal or wax shavings getting caught between the grooves. In order to get maximum use from your files, therefore, you should clean them regularly. One way to do this is to use a special file brush, always brushing in the direction of the grooves. An alternative is to run a sheet of copper, vertically, along the length of each groove, clearing the debris as you go.

Sanding

BEFORE ANY PIECE OF JEWELLERY CAN BE POLISHED (*SEE PAGES 42–43*) IT NEEDS TO BE CLEANED UP IN ORDER TO SMOOTH OUT SCRATCHES USING EMERY PAPERS OR STICKS, OR SILICONE CARBIDE PAPERS. THIS CAN BE DONE MECHANICALLY OR BY HAND.

ABRASIVE PAPERS

The most abrasive paper, emery paper, is used to remove the marks made by filing. After that, you should use progressively less abrasive papers, each removing the marks from the one before it. Wet and dry papers (as the name suggests, these can be used with or without water) are harder wearing than emery papers. The grade is indicated by the number of grits in a given area; 150 is the coarsest, 1200 the finest. Sanding sticks can be made by attaching abrasive papers to suitably shaped wooden dowel rods or battens. Working by hand allows access to awkward areas. The techniques shown are worked on a ring shank and dome.

Things you will need:

Pendant motor with split pin and abrasive rubber wheel

Emery papers 3, 2, 1, 0, 2/0, 3/0, 4/0 or equivalent wet and dry papers, grades 150, 220, 240, 320, 400, 600, 800, 1000, 1200

Scissors

Masking tape

Grinding stone and grit-impregnated rubber

PENDANT MOTOR SANDING

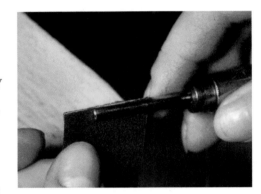

1 Cut strips of wet and dry paper about 25x150mm (1x6in). Load a strip into a split pin by feeding the end into the split with the abrasive surface facing you if the pin is in your right hand. If the paper is loose in the pin, fold the last 5mm (¼in) of the strip over so that it is double the thickness, then load it into the pin. Wrap the paper tightly around the pin so that the abrasive surface is on the outside. Secure the base of the roll with masking tape.

2 When sanding with a pendant motor, keep moving around the area you are sanding. Work from coarse to fine paper, cleaning the form between grades.

3 Alternatively, you can use a grinding stone attachment or grit-impregnated rubber for cleaning up surfaces using a pendant motor. Both are available in a range of shapes.

Things you will need:

Basic tool kit (*see pages 14–15*)

Emery papers 3, 2, 1, 0, 2/0, 3/0, 4/0 or equivalent wet and dry papers, grades 150, 220, 240, 320, 400, 600, 800, 1000, 1200, some made up as sanding sticks

Masking tape

Sheet of polished glass, minimum 5mm (¼in) thick with sanded edges

SANDING BY HAND

1 File where necessary to remove scratches and blemishes or to remove excess solder on the form (*see pages 38–39*).

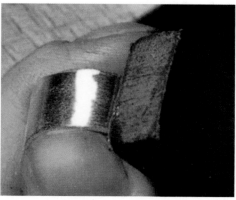

2 Use a sanding stick in the same way as a file to begin to remove the file marks. Begin with grade 3 emery paper or grade 150 wet and dry paper. Use the stick in an opposing direction to the file marks where possible, so that you can see when the file marks are completely removed.

3 Clean away any grit. Repeat step 2 using the next finest grade of paper, working in an opposite direction to the previous sanding. Work through all the grades of paper from coarse to fine, cleaning away grit between grades and changing the direction in which you work by 90° each time so that you can easily see when you have removed the previous set of scratches.

4 To sand flat surfaces, attach a sheet of abrasive paper to a flat surface, such as a sheet of polished glass, using masking tape around its edge. Rub the form against the abrasive paper. Work through the grades of abrasive papers as in step 3.

TIP

When cleaning up sterling silver that has been annealed or soldered you will encounter firestain (an oxide that forms in the top layers of the silver as a result of heating beyond a certain temperature). Sanding and polishing removes the firestain, leaving slightly shadowed areas against the whiter, non-firestained silver. These areas will show up black at the next annealing or soldering, but can be sanded and polished again to remove them. (See also, Soldering and Pickling, *pages 44–46* and Oxidising, *page 47*).

Polishing

POLISHING USUALLY DESCRIBES MAKING A SMOOTH AND GLOSSY SURFACE BY REMOVING MATERIAL IN STAGES OF EVER DECREASING SCRATCHES, UNTIL THE SCRATCHES ARE NOT DETECTABLE TO THE NAKED EYE. THE IDEA IS GRADUALLY TO REMOVE ANY SCRATCHES LEFT BY SANDING USING TRIPOLI AND ROUGE.

Things you will need:

Pendant motor and calico and bristle polishing bobs

Bristle brush

Dishwashing liquid

Tripoli

Rouge

TIP

For projects that require a highly polished finish, use a burnisher as a final stage. Work evenly on the piece applying the pressure firmly to achieve a smooth, uniform finish.

PENDANT DRILL POLISHING

❶ The stages prior to polishing are filing and sanding (*see pages 38–39 and 40–41*). Prepare the piece by washing with warm water, a bristle brush and dishwashing liquid. Load a polishing bob with tripoli. Load the bob into the pendant motor and polish by applying the bob to the surface with a firm downward pressure, keeping the bob moving evenly over the surface.

❷ To access areas that are hard to reach, use different attachments, such as bristle and felt bobs designed for use with the pendant motor. There is a variety of shapes and sizes to choose from, such as fine felt or bristle bobs for reaching tight spots, and shaped felts for polishing awkward shapes.

❸ Clean the piece thoroughly, before repeating the process using rouge. Once all of the tripoli scratches have been removed, give the piece a final clean.

Things you will need:

Bristle brush
Dishwashing liquid
Tripoli
Polishing sticks
Polishing threads
Cup hook
Rouge

POLISHING BY HAND

1 Prepare the piece by washing with a bristle brush, dishwashing liquid and warm water to remove all traces of grit left over from sanding. Rub tripoli polish onto the surface of a polishing stick.

2 Place the polishing stick flat on the surface of the piece at a 90° angle from the previous scratches left by sanding. Using a firm downward pressure, push the polishing stick forward on the surface of the metal. Repeat until all the scratches left from the sanding process are removed, reloading the stick with tripoli frequently.

3 For parts that you cannot reach with a polishing stick, use polishing threads. Tie a loop in the top of the threads and attach them to your bench or other suitable solid surface with a cup hook. Load the threads with tripoli, then run the piece back and forth over the threads. To polish inside a ring, use a round polishing stick.

4 Repeat step 1 to remove any traces of tripoli; this must be done thoroughly to avoid contaminating polishing sticks and threads used with rouge. Load rouge onto a new polishing stick and place it flat on the surface of the piece at a 90° angle from the set of scratches left by the tripoli polishing. Repeat steps 2 and 3 until all the tripoli scratches are removed. Clean the piece once more to remove any traces of rouge.

Soldering and pickling

SOLDERING IS A PROCESS USED WHEN WORKING WITH METALS, AND INVOLVES HEATING THE METAL AND, WHERE NECESSARY, JOINING ONE PIECE TO ANOTHER. PICKLING IS A FINISHING PROCESS THAT IS USED AFTER SOLDERING AND ANNEALING (*SEE PAGE 37*) A PIECE OF METAL.

SOLDERING

Soldering is the process of permanently joining one piece of metal to another. Solder needs a catalyst or agent to make it flow. This is called flux or borax and there are several different types, some being more suitable for high-temperature soldering than others. For most metalwork, a borax cone in a dish is suitable.

Things you will need:

Borax cone

Hard, medium and easy solders

Borax dish

Paintbrush

Tin snips

Divided dish

Charcoal block or soldering block

Gas supply and torch

Insulated tweezers

Binding wire

Flat-nosed pliers

Soldering stick

Pickle

Pickling dish

Brass tweezers

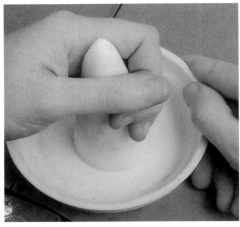

1 To use borax, put a little water in the borax dish and rub the cone in a circular motion to produce a thickish paste. Use a fine paintbrush to apply the borax between the join to be soldered. This process is called fluxing.

2 After fluxing the join apply the solder to your work. Apply it in small pieces called paillons. Cut two or three strips up the end of the solder using snips, and then cut across the solder to make small pieces. When you need thinner paillons, roll or hammer the ends of the solder first. Keep a divided dish near the soldering area for strips and paillons of hard, medium and easy solder.

3 Place the paillons in the borax dish so that they are coated in flux. Use the tip of a paintbrush to pick up the paillons and place them around the join or at the bottom of the join for a ring because the solder will flow upwards. Keep any spare paillons in separate small containers, marked 'hard', 'medium' or 'easy' solder.

4 Place your work on a charcoal block and heat the work gently using a soft flame, adjusting it as necessary.

5 As the water evaporates, the flux will start to bubble, but as soon as all the water has gone, it will settle down. Push any displaced solder back into position with your tweezers. Continue passing the flame over the work until it is heated and has turned a cherry red.

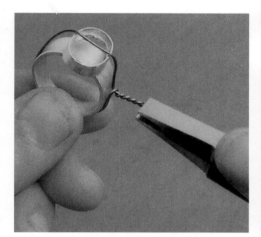

6 When the solder flows and a bright, shiny line appears around the join, turn off the flame. Quench your work in pickle (*see page 46*), using the tweezers to place it in and remove it from the acid. Rinse in cold water and dry.

7 When a join needs a little help to stay together during soldering, fasten binding wire around the work and tighten it by twisting the two ends with a pair or flat-nosed pliers.

8 If your work has other joins, you will need to use different solders. Use the same method as before, but replacing the hard solder with medium, and then the medium solder with easy solder.

TYPES OF FLAME

Above A flame with no added air.

Above A flame with added air, good for soldering.

Above A small, hard flame, good for soldering small areas.

TYPES OF SOLDER

It is often necessary to solder more than once on a piece of work, and there are several grades of solder available for doing this.

- Enamelling solder has the highest melting point; it is used only if the piece is to be enamelled.
- Hard solder is generally the first solder to be used, and it is sometimes used three or four times on the same piece.
- Medium solder is used after hard solder. It does not always flow as easily, so cut it into small paillons.
- Easy solder is used after medium or hard. It is a good, flowing solder, which is often used for findings.
- Extra easy solder is very useful for low-temperature soldering.

For practical purposes, only hard, medium and easy solders are used for the projects described in this book.

TIP

You can deliberately stop solder from flowing onto a previously soldered area by painting the join with a paste of rouge powder and water. However, if the rouge paste has run into the area you want to solder, it won't work, so allow the rouged area to dry before fluxing the joint.

USING A SOLDERING STICK

On a large join that needs plenty of solder, you may find that a soldering stick is the best method.

1 Start by applying flux or borax to the piece in the usual way. Cut a long strip of solder and paint it with flux. Hold the solder in insulated soldering tweezers, then heat the work until it is cherry red.

2 When the correct temperature is reached, feed the length of solder into the join, following the line just behind the flame. You can check that the temperature is correct by placing a paillon of the same solder you are using on the outside of the join. As you see it flow, apply the solder stick.

TIP

Remove any binding wire before immersing your work in the acid. The metal will contaminate the acid and turn everything pink. If that happens dispose of the acid immediately – it is not possible to clean it. Remember: use only brass tweezers in acid.

DIFFERENT-SIZED PIECES

When you need to solder a small piece to a large piece, use the following method.

1 Apply flux and place the solder on the larger piece of work. Hold the smaller piece in soldering tweezers and paint a little flux on the bottom. Add a piece of the same solder and heat the small piece until the solder flows.

2 Heat the large piece until the solder starts to run, and use the tweezers to place the small piece on the work, continuing to heat as you work. Remove the flame, holding the piece steady. Quench, rinse and dry your work.

3 Alternatively, paint flux onto both surfaces to be soldered. Place a small piece onto the large piece, and place paillons around the join. Gently heat the work from underneath or away from the small piece and, as the solder is about to run, bring the heat onto the small piece. Quench, rinse and dry.

PICKLING

This is a process that is used after annealing or soldering, in order to clean the metal and remove any traces of flux. It involves placing the hot silver into a warm solution of safety pickle or alum, which can be bought from jeweller's suppliers in crystal form. Simply add the crystals to warm water according to the manufacturer's instructions, and keep the solution warm while in use. If any of the solution remains on your work after quenching and pickling, rinse it in water and boil the piece in a solution of hot water and a spoonful of soda crystals. Rinse and dry.

1 While silver is being heated, it oxidises and becomes black. To remedy this, place it, still hot, in safety pickle, and the oxides will disappear. If it is left for a few minutes, flux residues will also disappear.

2 Pickling can be done the other way around. After soldering, quench the piece in water and then drop into a warm solution of safety pickle, and hold it at that temperature. This will clean the piece quite rapidly.

Oxidising

COLOURING THE SURFACE OF METALS IS CALLED PATINATION. THE EFFECTS OF PATINATION OCCUR NATURALLY THROUGH EXPOSURE TO THE ELEMENTS, ALTHOUGH THEY CAN BE ACHIEVED BY APPLYING CHEMICALS. OXIDISING IS A FORM OF PATINATION.

HOW IT WORKS

Oxidising causes metal to blacken. This blackening can be washed, but is more suitable for recessed areas. Oxidising cannot withstand heat or abrasion. It is delicate and can be affected by moisture so is an unsuitable treatment for rings. When oxidising, you should wear protective gloves and safety goggles and work in a well-ventilated area away from foodstuffs. The demonstration shows the oxidisation of a formed, sanded and polished piece of jewellery.

Things you will need:

Bristle brush

Dishwashing liquid

Soldering equipment (*see pages 22–23*)

Protective gloves

Safety goggles

Paintbrush

Fine wire wool

Soft brush

Oxidising solution, 15mm (⅝in) cubed piece of potassium sulphide, 275–570ml (½–1 pint) water, and a few drops of ammonia in a Pyrex container

1 Wash the formed piece with a bristle brush, dishwashing liquid and warm water to completely degrease. Rinse and dry. Place the piece on a clean soldering surface, making sure you do not handle the metal directly.

2 Warm the piece with a soft flame from the soldering torch to accelerate the oxidising process. Remove the flame before applying the oxidising solution to the warmed metal, using a paintbrush. Continue until you achieve the colour required.

3 Repeat step 1 to wash the piece. Remove excess oxide with fine wire wool. Repeat step 2 to wash the piece. Remove excess oxide with fine wire wool.

Texturing

YOU CAN ADD AN INTERESTING FURTHER DIMENSION TO YOUR WORK BY TEXTURING ALL OR SOME OF THE SURFACES. THERE ARE SEVERAL DIFFERENT TECHNIQUES TO CHOOSE FROM, DEPENDING ON THE LOOK YOU WANT TO ACHIEVE. JUXTAPOSING PLAIN AND TEXTURED AREAS CAN CREATE A HIGHLY PLEASING CONTRAST.

CHOOSING YOUR METHOD

You can create texture with a planishing hammer, or make your own patterns by filing grooves into the end of a punch; the reverse pattern will appear on your work. The method outlined here allows you to produce a variety of different patterns yourself, although it is possible to buy different patterned punches. If you have a pendant motor, there are all sorts of cutters that can be used to produce different surfaces on metal. Some surfaces can be textured before piercing, while a simple matt finish is added after polishing.

Things you will need:

Basic tool kit (*see pages 14–15*)
Steel stock or selection of punches
Gas supply and torch
Pitch
Polished stake or wooden mandrel
Planishing hammer
Pendant motor with a selection
of burr ends
Steel wool
Wet and dry papers, 240–600
Polishing motor fitted with a steel wheel

USING A PUNCH

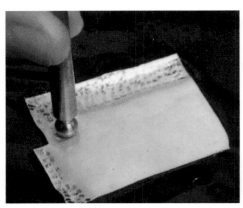

1 Take a steel stock, about 10cm (4in) long and 5–6mm (¼in) square, and slightly taper both ends with your file. File your pattern into one end. Finish the ends by bevelling the corners so that the edges do not drag on your work. Harden the end by heating the punch to cherry red and quickly quenching in cold water. Reheat only the working end with a soft flame until it becomes yellow. Quench again.

2 To add texture with a punch, set your work by gently heating the pitch, dropping the work in it, and, when it is slightly cooler, pushing the pitch up around the edge of the work with your fingers. Dampen your fingertips first.

3 With your punch at an angle of 90° to your work, hit the top with a hammer and work it steadily around the area you want to mark. If the work starts to curl up out of the pitch, remove it, anneal and straighten it before replacing it in the pitch. When you have finished, gently heat the pitch around the work and use an old pair of pliers to prise up the edge of the work and lift it out. Pitch can be burned off or dissolved in turpentine.

PLANISHING

Support your work on a polished stake or wooden mandrel, and work around the piece with your planishing hammer in a smooth rhythmic action. This should be done on your finished piece, because the gentle tapping will slightly mark the surface. Do not hit too hard or you could alter the shape of your work.

PENDANT MOTOR

If using the burrs and cutters on a pendant motor, it is useful to get some practice using the tool before you start to texture a beautifully finished piece of work. There will be a range of different attachments available. Try them out on a piece of scrap metal first to see what effect you prefer.

STEEL WOOL AND PAPERS

If working with steel wool and wet and dry papers, use a regular circular motion or a back-and-forth movement to achieve a matt finish. Try to avoid mixing the two, however, as this will not give a uniform finish. If you have a polishing motor, you can fit a stainless steel wheel, which also gives a matt finish.

PUNCHES AND THEIR USES

Planishing punches are used to smooth and burnish a raised surface.

Hollow-faced punches are used underneath or on top of the metal to create circular rings.

Embossing punches are often used on the reverse of metal for raising ridges, curves and bumps.

Linear or tracer punches are used on the front of work to make lines and curves. They are chisel-shaped and have a bevelled edge, which can vary in width.

TIP

Before you start to texture a jewellery component or piece of sheet metal, always make sure that the surface is clean and free of grease.

Making jump rings and links

JEWELLERY FIXINGS ARE AVAILABLE TO BUY, EITHER AT SPECIALIST SHOPS OR ONLINE. HOWEVER THERE IS A SENSE OF ACHIEVEMENT TO BE HAD IN MAKING YOUR OWN – AND YOU CAN MAKE THEM TO YOUR OWN SPECIFICATION, TO SUIT THE PIECE YOU ARE CREATING.

Things you will need:

0.5–2-mm (7–24-gauge) wire
Basic tool kit (*see pages 14–15*)
Rod or stake
Vice
Serrated pliers
Dividers
Soldering equipment (*see page 22–23*)

MAKING JUMP RINGS

Jump rings are used for joining chains, loops and catches. They are supplied in most sizes, or you could order a selection of sizes. They are also very quick and easy to make yourself.

1 Take a rod or stake of the appropriate size – the shaft end of a drill bit will do – and anneal the wire (*see page 37*). Put the rod in the vice so that it is horizontal, and protecting the cutting edge if you are using a drill bit. Close the vice and grip the end of the wire with serrated pliers.

2 Wrap the other end of the wire around the rod so that each coil fits snugly against the previous one until the wire is finished. Take the rod out of the vice.

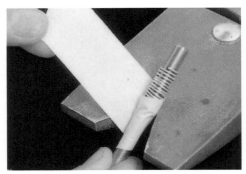

3 Snip off any protruding ends of the wire using wire cutters; wrap a length of masking tape around the entire length of coiled wire while it is still on the rod.

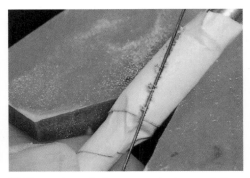

4 Pierce through the tape and wire carefully, making a slightly diagonal line as you work. As you approach the end, take great care not to mark the rod. Remove the tape.

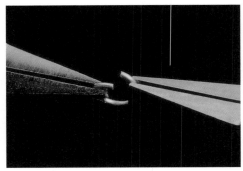

5 To close the ends of a jump ring, hold one side in a pair of flat-nosed pliers and use a second pair to adjust the other side, using a twisting movement to close the ends together.

MAKING LINKS

There are many different chains you can buy from your supplier. They are usually quite fine and, for general purposes, they are difficult to improve upon. However, if you want a chain with larger links or one that is more interesting, try making one yourself. It is important that chain should move freely, so try to make sure that the links are free to move in all directions.

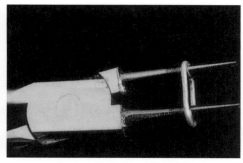

1 To make oval links, cut several lengths of wire the same length – 40mm (1½in), for example – bend up the ends and solder them together (*see pages 44–46*). Make them round by sliding them over a mandrel and tapping them with a nylon mallet.

2 Take a pair of round-nosed pliers. As you remove each loop from the mandrel, place it over the plier ends, with the soldered joint at the side. Gently pull the pliers apart just enough to stretch the wire into an even more uniform shape.

3 To make rectangular links, cut several pieces of wire to length, allowing for the joins to be in the middle of the long sides. Use your dividers to mark on each piece where the bends will be. With a triangular file, make a groove along the marked lines to slightly more than half the depth of the wire. Carefully bend the wire with flat-nosed pliers, apply flux and hard-solder up all the corners.

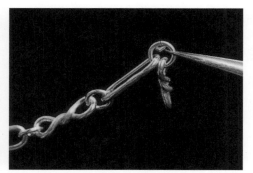

4 To make the links into a chain, pierce through the soldered joint of the links; open up the joint enough to link into the next link. Close the link using flat-nosed pliers. Isolate each link to resolder the joint.

TIP

If you are making several oval links, mark the position on the pliers with tape or a red line so they are the same size.

Findings

FINDINGS IS THE WORD USED TO DESCRIBE THE MECHANICAL FITTINGS THAT ARE ATTACHED TO JEWELLERY AND THAT HOLD THE PIECE ON THE BODY OR ATTACH IT TO YOUR CLOTHING. A WIDE RANGE OF FINDINGS CAN BE SHOP-BOUGHT, BUT YOU WILL SOMETIMES FIND IT MORE APPROPRIATE TO MAKE YOUR OWN.

MAKING THE RIGHT CHOICE

Manufacturer's catalogues include a good choice of findings. Even if you want to make your own, this could be a good place to start in terms of inspiration and suitability. Always take care to position your findings so that your work is balanced correctly.

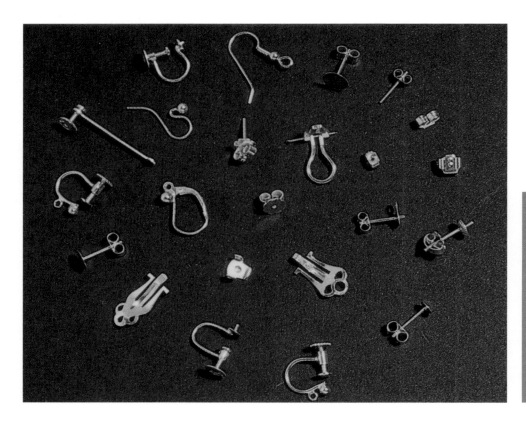

Things you will need:

Round silver or copper wire

Butterfly fittings

Silver sheet

Chain links or belchier chain

Bolt ring

Basic tool kit (*see pages 14–15*)

Soldering equipment (*see pages 22–23*)

Burnisher

Hand drill

Mandrel

FINDINGS FOR PIERCED EARS

Earrings for pierced ears come in several different styles: pin with butterfly clip; wire hooks; and hoops.

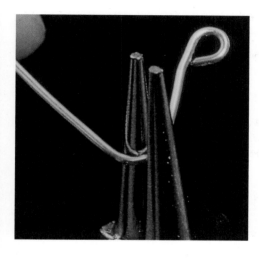

1 To make a pin finding, cut pieces of round wire approximately 12mm (½in) long, file one end straight across, and use easy solder to solder one to each earring (*see pages 44–46*). Taper the other end and, about one-third of the way up the pin, file a tiny groove around the diameter.

2 Burnish the pin after rolling it along a metal surface, gently hammering to harden the silver. Add butterfly fittings.

3 To make hooks for pierced earrings, bend up loops of wire using round or half-round pliers. Avoid soldering if possible, but if it is necessary, solder before bending and harden by tapping with the hammer as above.

4 For hoops, solder a 20-gauge wire to the end of thicker wire, and drill a hole the same size in the other end. Wrap the wire around the top of a mandrel and hit downwards until the hoop is springy and the correct size.

TIP

If you are making earrings for unpierced ears, it is probably easier to buy fittings for clips or screw-type fittings. It is possible to pierce the shape from sheet silver if you need a heavier gauge, and then wire can be bent to fit.

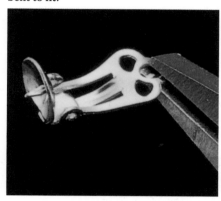

CUFFLINKS

You might find it useful to know how to make findings for cufflinks.

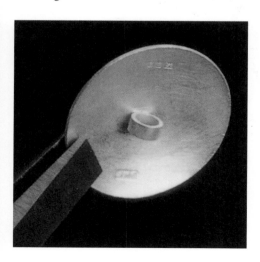

1 To make a chain-link fitting, solder a half-round, using wire or piercing it out from a sheet, to the back of the cufflink and attach five links of chain that you have made or belcher chain. Then attach that to the opposite side of the link. You can combine a T-bar with a chain by attaching the chain to a piece of thick round wire or chenier.

2 These fittings are supplied with the T-bar at the top already soldered on. Solder the bottom face to the cufflink and allow to cool before quenching or pickling.

MAKING A BROOCH PIN

There is a large selection of brooch fittings you can buy. Some of these are very small, and it may be more appropriate to make your own.

1 To make a fichu joint, which is the hinge bracket for the pin to be riveted to: cut out a rectangle of silver approximately 15mm x 5mm (¾x¼in), filing two grooves at ¼in and ½in, and bend it up with flat-nosed pliers. Run hard solder up the grooves before soldering it to your work with easy solder. Drill a hole through the centre of both sides.

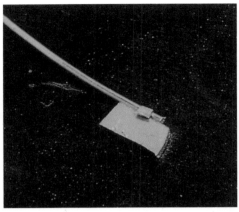

2 Make a silver tag from sheet silver; it should be slightly less thick than the inside of the fichu joint. Solder it to a length of 1.5-mm (18-gauge) round wire. File a groove along the top of the tag to make a good joint.

ALTERNATIVE BROOCH PIN

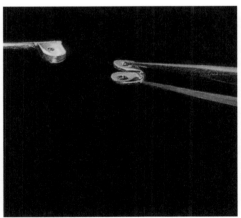

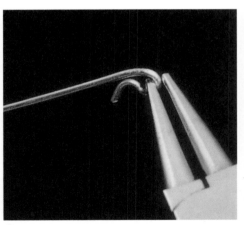

3 Use a piercing saw to cut the wire to size and file the end into a good joint. Gently tap the wire with your jeweller's hammer while you roll it (as far as the tag) on a smooth metal surface. This hardens the pin after soldering.

4 Drill a hole through the tag to align with the holes of the fichu joint.

1 A pin can also be made by simply bending the wire. Do not anneal the wire – it will stay springy if it has not been heated.

ATTACHING A BOLT RING

Bolt rings are the usual way of fastening manufactured chains. They come in different sizes and work well.

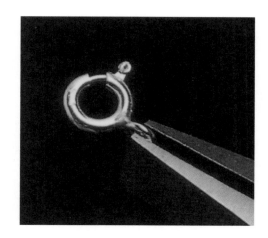

1 To attach a bolt ring, solder, then leave to air-cool, as the spring will become soft if it is quenched immediately.

MAKING A HOOK AND EYE FASTENING

1 To make a simple hook and eye fastening, heat both ends of a length of 18 gauge (1mm) wire, approximately 40mm (1½in) long, so that the ends run up into balls. Hold the wire in your insulated tweezers, flux the ends and concentrate the flame on one end, with a charcoal block behind it. The end will run up into a ball as it begins to melt.

2 Turn it over and repeat the process on the other end. Use round and half-round pliers to bend the wire into a long 'S' shape.

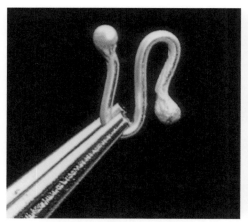

3 Solder up one end with easy solder, and curl the ball on the other end to turn up. Hammer the central area flatter on the anvil to harden it up and improve the appearance.

ALTERNATIVE HOOK AND EYE

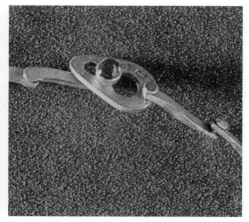

1 To make another version of the hook and eye fastening, pierce out an end tag, with a hole at the chain end going into a slit. Bend up a piece of wire the same diameter as the slit and solder a silver ball to the top so that it will fit through the opposite hole. In this example, a sapphire was set into the end.

MAKING A COILED HOOK-AND-LOOP FASTENING

Things you will need:

Round wire
Round-nosed pliers
Half-round pliers
Wire snips

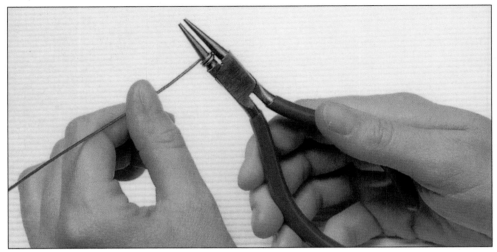

1 Cut a length of wire approximately 30cm (12in) in length. Using a pair of round-nosed pliers, coil the wire, starting from the bottom of the pliers and working upwards.

2 Using the half-round pliers, bend the excess wire at the top of the coil at 90°.

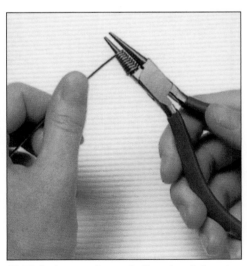

3 With the round-nosed pliers, bend the wire over, forming a loop.

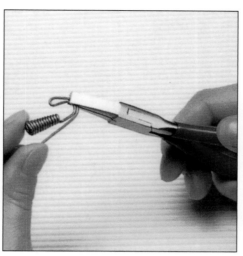

④ Using just the tips of the round-nosed pliers, bend the wire back on itself gently, forming a hook.

⑤ Take the half-round pliers and carefully manipulate the bent back wire so that it follows the first wire.

⑥ When the wire is satisfactorily bent, cut off the excess wire with a pair of wire snips and tuck the end discreetly into the coil.

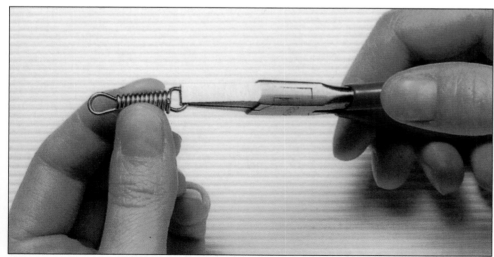

⑦ At the opposite and wider end of the coil, use the half-round pliers to bend the very last coil in half at 90°, again making sure the end of the wire is tucked into the coil itself. This forms the mechanism by which the fastener is connected to the necklace.

Working with other materials

JEWELLERY DOES NOT HAVE TO BE MADE FROM PRECIOUS STONES OR METALS. ANYTHING DECORATIVE OR INTERESTING CAN BE PRESSED INTO USE. WITH A LITTLE INSPIRATION, ALL SORTS OF INTERESTING AND INEXPENSIVE JEWELLERY CAN BE MADE BY COMBINING A VARIETY OF DIFFERENT MATERIALS WITH METAL.

WOOD

Hardwoods are the most suitable to use with metals like silver. Attach wood with rivets (*see pages 110–111*), screws or a good-quality glue. Pierce it out with a jeweller's saw and one of the heavier blades, or a coping saw for a large job. File and sand the edges, and rub beeswax or linseed oil over a finished piece to bring it to life. You can also collect the dust produced by filing and sanding and mix it into epoxy resin. Build up an image with different colours by filling the spaces between wires soldered to a framework with the wood and resin mixture. Leave to dry, level off with a file, then sand until smooth.

NATURAL STONE

A walk on the beach or in the country or a gentle stroll in a park can be not only a source of inspiration, but also an excellent source of natural stone. Some stones and pebbles will be harder and more durable than others, so try flaking and breaking them first to see whether they are worth using. Interesting pieces can be mounted in silver or wrapped in silver or copper wire and then linked up to make an attractive pattern within the overall piece. Alternatively, you can buy wonderful ready-cut pieces of agate from lapidary dealers.

PAPIER MÂCHÉ

Make little papier mâché balls or ovals, paint them, give them a coat of varnish and drill through the middle so they can be hung on necklaces, bracelets or earrings.

TIP

Keep an eye out for any interesting items – wood, pebbles, pieces of glass – and build up a collection of bits and pieces to experiment with in spare moments. Or think of other workable materials, such as leather, papier mâché or acrylics, that can be moulded to shape to create unusual jewellery. The only limitation is your imagination.

Left Rosewood and silver bangle with matching ring, by Jinks McGrath.

Right A finely painted papier mâché ball hung on silk threads, by Paul Vincent.

PLASTICS AND CLAY

These can be used to make colourful pieces with a light, comtemporary feel.

Plexiglass comes in sheets that can be bought in a variety of thicknesses and colours, or you could get scraps from companies that make or use large quantities of plastic. Use a coping saw for cutting, as the heat that is generated will soon clog a small jeweller's saw blade. Plexiglass can be filed, sanded, polished and buffed with metal polishes. It can be set into metal, riveted and screwed, but you will need a special plastic glue, as most ordinary adhesives alter the surface of the acrylic. You can heat it in a warm oven (about 150°C/302°F) and bend it to shape, but take care not to overheat, which will cause air bubbles within the plastic.

Resins are used for cold-cast enamelling. Colours are mixed with the resin and a catalyst, and the liquid is poured into depressions or cells in the silver. If you are casting resin into a framework that does not have a metal back, place the frame on an oiled tray or mould.

Right Cast acrylic on top of a painted base creates these colourful pieces by Rowena Park.

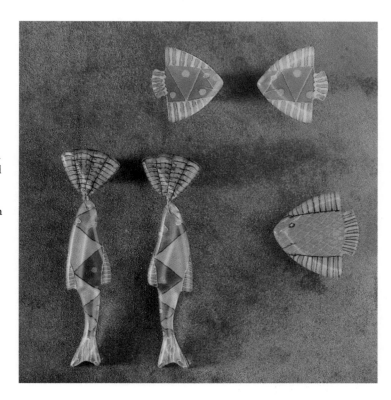

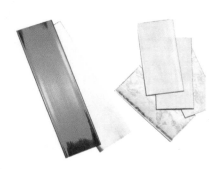

Modelling plastic is available in both strips and blocks and can be found in a range of vibrant colours and finishes. You can buy it at most art shops.

Oven-baked clay A plastic modelling material, which is baked in the oven to harden. It is sold in small blocks of which numerous colours are available.

Self-hardening clay This clay substance hardens on contact with air and therefore needs no baking or firing. It is available in terracotta and white and is sold in art shops.

GLASS

Clear glass or pebbles can be used as the basis for colourful painted designs. Use enamel paints and cover them with a coat of protective varnish. You can make a very original necklace by collecting interesting shapes and holding them in a metal framework. Small pieces of coloured glass can be inlaid and glued into silver cells to build up a mosaic, or use glass beads, mixed in with silver beads, to make attractive earrings and necklaces.

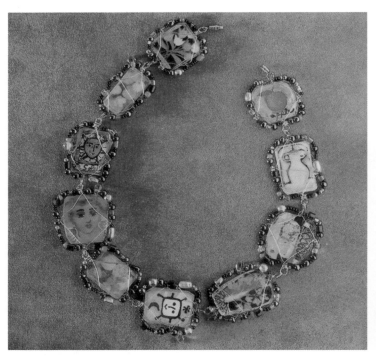

TITANIUM

This light, grey metal produces an attractive range of colours after heat treatment. Because it is so hard, use a strong blade for piercing. You cannot solder, shape or forge titanium, and you should not roll it. Instead, set like a stone into, or rivet it onto, a piece of work. Before heating, clean the surface by rubbing it with wet and dry papers and degrease with an ammonia-based detergent. Apply heat with a torch all over a piece or concentrate it locally to produce a spectacular range of colours. After heating, leave to air-cool. After colouring, scribe designs or lines with a diamond-tipped scriber.

Below Coloured titanium set into a silver brooch, by Brian Eburah.

TIP

Small particles of titanium are combustible, so do not file, saw or clean it near a naked flame.

Above Little paintings on clear glass joined with silver wire and tiny beads, by Nancy Church.

TIP

Findings for use with other materials are much the same as those described elsewhere (*see pages 52–57*). Most will have to be glued or riveted in position. Wherever possible it is a good idea to design your piece so that the fitting can be soldered to the sheet metal first.

NECKLACE THREAD

For a flexible necklace made of different materials, thread is often used instead of wire or chain.

Silk thread is used for stringing pearls, freshwater pearls and semi-precious beads. The drilled pearls or beads are threaded onto silk strands with a fine needle made from a very fine brass wire, doubled and twisted together. After each pearl is added, make a knot in the silk to prevent them from wearing each other away and from all falling off if the threads break. The silk is joined to the catch at the back by threading a fine spring ring over the threads and through the jump ring on the catch; this prevents wear at the point of contact. The silk is then threaded back through the last three or four pearls and knotted again. The knot is coated with transparent glue and made as small as possible so that it does not impede the flow of the pearls.

Nylon is used for threading other beads as long as they are not too heavy. The nylon is knotted at the ends only and held in little findings called crimp beads, which close down over the glued and knotted end of the nylon. The crimp beads are then linked to the fasteners. Nylon threads can also be knotted directly onto the fastener.

Thick linen thread is available in a range of neutral colours that complement natural beads. It is easy to knot and so creates a good base structure for threading beads. You can buy it waxed or unwaxed. The wax provides a protective coating, which makes the thread more durable and it creates a sheen on the surface of the thread, which adds to the effect of the jewellery.

Right A selection of colourful and semi-precious bead necklaces, by Marcia Lanyon. Silk or nylon thread would be suitable for necklaces like these.

Leather thong is used for very large beads. It is available in a range of thicknesses and colours. It is flexible and durable and works well in contrast to lengths of metal tubing and metal beads. Tie the ends together with a bow or knot or fit a coiled loop over the ends.

Tiger tail (very strong thread) is a stronger, but less flexible, way of hanging beads. It has the advantage that it will not lose its shape. It cannot be knotted, so it is looped at both ends, and the loop is kept in place by means of a crimp bead. The loose ends of the thread are then tucked back through the beads. The fastener is attached to the tiger tail loop. If the beads are not heavy enough for tiger tail, it may kink.

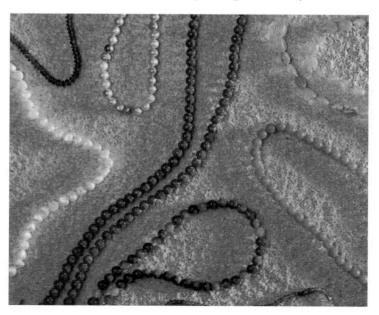

Basic Projects

Ranging from a simple beaded leather bracelet to intricate, textured gold and silver necklaces, the projects in this section of the book allow you to practise the basic techniques demonstrated on the previous pages. Each project is presented as a step-by-step process, enabling you to take each stage of the making up at your own pace. Gradually you will fine-tune your skills at cutting and filing metal wire, snipping and sawing sheet metal, and drilling, soldering and polishing the various components of your works. Among the projects are stylish designs for rings, brooches, necklaces, earrings and bracelets, all of which you can tailor to your own designs as you become more proficient in the art of jewellery-making.

Bead and leather bracelet

IN THIS SIMPLE BRACELET, THE KNOTS USED TO SECURE THE BEADS ARE INTEGRAL TO THE DESIGN OF THE FINISHED PIECE. YOU CAN CHANGE THE 'EARTHY' MOOD SHOWN HERE BY USING COLOURFUL GLASS BEADS OR PAINTED CERAMIC BEADS FROM AROUND THE WORLD.

Knotting is a traditional jewellery-making technique, long associated with stringing pearls. Usually beads are threaded onto twine or cord and a knot tied after each one to hold it in place. In this project, the leather is tied around each bead, as well as above and below it. This creates a more rustic look and adds to the bracelet's visual appeal. Because they are decorative and not purely functional, simple overhand knots are used throughout.

Things you will need:

2.30m (2½yd) neutral leather thong

Two small ceramic beads

Large chunky glass or ceramic beads (quantity depends on the size)

Scissors

Hook

Strong glue

PREPARING THE LEATHER

1 Cut one length of neutral leather thong approximately 46cm (18in) long, fold into two and tie a small loop knot as shown. Use the remainder of the leather to thread through the knot before tightly securing.

THREADING THE BEADS

1 Place the loop over the hook and start by threading a smaller bead onto the shorter pair of strands. Tie the outer strands into a bow knot around the bead, once over the top of the inner strands, once below and again above.

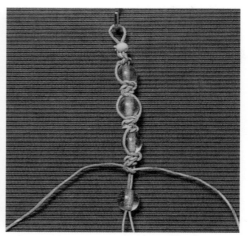

2 Repeat step 1, but with the larger chunky beads. Stop when the bracelet is about 18cm (7in) long.

FINISHING OFF

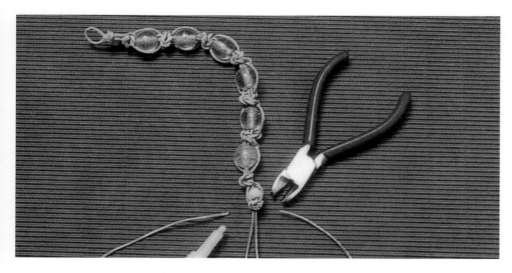

1 Add the second smaller bead, tie the outer strands and glue into place. Cut the remaining outer strands.

Clock brooch

THIS UNUSUAL BROOCH IS MADE FROM A NUMBER OF FOUND CLOCK AND WATCH MECHANISMS. THE SHAPE OF THE PIECE WILL DEPEND ON THE PARTS YOU ARE ABLE TO FIND, SO EXPERIMENT WITH DIFFERENT ARRANGEMENTS OF THE PARTS BEFORE YOU ASSEMBLE THE FINAL PIECE.

You can buy old watch and clock parts but these can cost a fair amount. Because much of the enjoyment of making this brooch comes from using found pieces, keep an eye open for old clocks and watches in jumble sales and other similar sources. If you have a broken clock or watch at home that is beyond repair, this brooch offers the perfect opportunity for some clever recycling.

Things you will need:

Clock and watch pieces

5cm (2in) of 1.1-mm (14-gauge) silver wire

Basic tool kit (*see pages 14–15*)

Resin-based glue

MAKING THE PIN

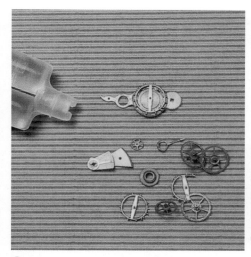

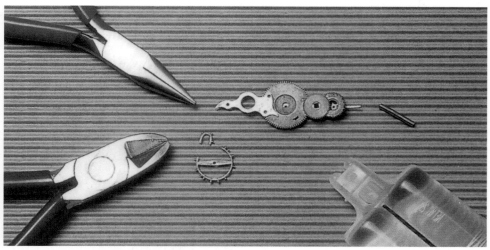

1 Select some interesting pieces of watch mechanism and assemble them in an attractive form, making sure that the piece at the end has a hole in it for attaching the hook. Glue together and allow to set.

2 To make the hook with which to secure the pin, use wire cutters to remove a short section of metal from a wheel or cog, leaving most of the wheel intact. Bend this small section to make a loop shape using half-round pliers.

Now glue this loop into the hole in the end section of the completed piece that you made in step 1. Leave this to dry before gluing a length of clock spring to the opposite end and set aside until this last addition is also dry.

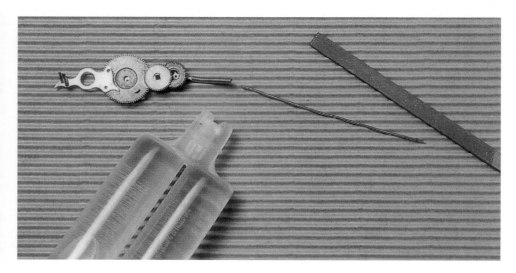

3 Glue the wire to the spring and allow to set. Cut the wire to fit along the back of the brooch as far as the hook. File to a fine point using a needle file. The spring should keep the pin under tension.

Pearl stick pin

SILVER WIRE AND IMITATION PEARLS CREATE A PIN INSPIRED BY NATURAL FORMS. WEAR IT ON A COAT LAPEL, A SHIRT OR A HAT – BUT IT WILL LOOK BEST AGAINST A PLAIN, RATHER THAN PATTERNED, FABRIC AS THIS WILL SHOW OFF ITS DELICATE SHAPE TO GREATEST ADVANTAGE.

The brooch is thought to have evolved from the functional bone or wood fastenings that our ancient ancestors used to secure their clothes. This simple pin evokes some of the earliest forms of brooch, as well as the jewelled pins that became popular in the late 19th and early 20th centuries.

Things you will need:

15cm (6in) of 0.5-mm (7-gauge) silver wire

13cm (5in) of 1.1-mm (14-gauge) silver wire

8 teardrop pearls on stems

Pin stopper

Basic tool kit (*see pages 14–15*)

Resin-based glue

FORMING THE CONE

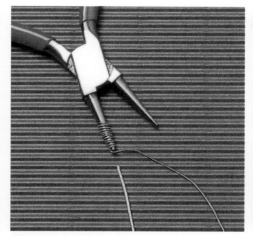 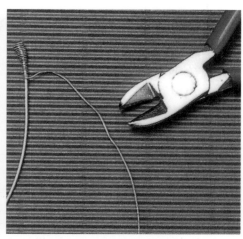

1 Bind the 0.5-mm (7-gauge) silver wire tightly around one point of a pair of round-nosed pliers to form a cone shape. Take the wire around the pliers at least eight times.

2 Take the cone and, using the rest of the wire, bind the cone tightly onto the 1.1-mm (14-gauge) wire until secure. Cut off any excess using wire cutters.

ADDING THE PEARLS

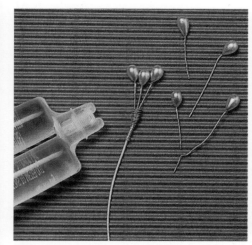 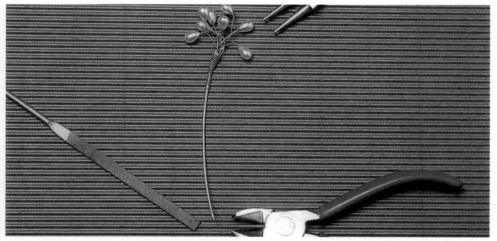

1 Fill the cone of 0.5-mm (7-gauge) wire with resin-based glue. Push the pearls into the cone and allow the glue to set.

2 Curl and twist the pearl stems, some in different directions, to create an interesting arrangement. Trim the pin using wire cutters and file to a fine point using a needle file. Finally, place the pin stopper on the end of the brooch to complete the project.

Free-form wire brooch

ONE CONTINUOUS LENGTH OF SILVER WIRE IS DECORATED WITH BEADS AND MANIPULATED TO CREATE AN ABSTRACT FORM. THIS DELICATE BROOCH LOOKS BEST WORN AGAINST A DARK COLOUR TO PROVIDE A CONTRAST AND THROW ITS FINE, LINEAR FORM INTO RELIEF.

While this brooch is contemporary in style, its delicacy evokes more traditional filigree pieces. Its shape would also lend it to other uses. Thread a chain through the brooch to create a beautiful pendant. Or make two pieces and attach some hooks for a pair of earrings – they won't be identical but that will just add to their charm. And for a perfect gift, pair the brooch or pendant with the earrings to make a matching set.

Things you will need:

90cm (36in) of 1.1-mm (14-gauge) silver wire

8 beads with 1-mm (¹⁄₃₂ in) hole

Basic tool kit (*see pages 14–15*)

SHAPING THE BROOCH

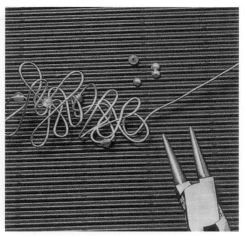

1 Leaving a 2-cm (¾-in) straight piece of wire at the start, begin to curl and bend the remainder of the silver wire into an interesting form, using round-nosed pliers.

2 Thread beads onto the wire as you go to give an even spread throughout the design. This project uses eight beads, but it is up to you to decide how many work best.

FORMING THE PIN

1 Having produced the final design, curl back the remaining wire to form the pin and cut to the right length using wire cutters.

2 Use the 2cm (¾in) of wire at the opposite side of the brooch to make a safety hook. File a fine point for the pin using a needle file. Then,

if you prefer, you can use a nylon mallet to flatten the filed point a little. Simply tap the point gently two or three times.

Spiral pin

THIS ELEGANT AND DURABLE PIN IS MADE BY BINDING FINE SILVER WIRE TIGHTLY AROUND A STRONGER CORE, AND THEN MANIPULATING IT TO FORM THE FINISHED PIECE. DESPITE BEING VERY RIGID, THE DESIGN OF THE PIN IS SUCH THAT IT GIVES IT A 'SPRINGY' APPEARANCE.

Buy ready-softened wire for this project or anneal it before use (*see page 37*). You can easily manipulate the narrow gauge wire by hand to produce the coiled section of this piece. It is a simple technique that brings a sophisticated result. You can use the coiled wire to make any shape you like. Here the form is abstract, but you can also make specific shapes, such as a leaf or heart, for example.

Things you will need:

30cm (12in) of 1.1-mm (14-gauge) silver wire

240cm (96in) of 0.5-mm (7-gauge) silver wire

1 decorative bead

Basic tool kit (*see pages 14–15*)

MANIPULATING THE WIRE

SHAPING THE PIN

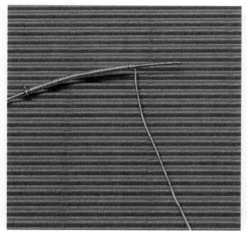

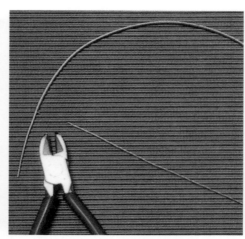

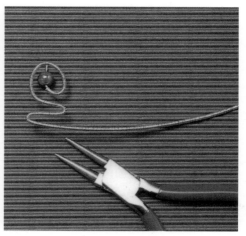

1 Bind the 0.5-mm (7-gauge) silver wire tightly around the 1.1-mm (14-gauge) silver wire, manipulating the wire by hand. Leave at least 6cm (2½in) of the 1.1-mm (14-gauge) wire uncovered at one end and 2cm (¾in) uncovered at the other end.

1 Thread your decorative bead onto the shorter uncovered end of the 1.1-mm (14-gauge) wire and bend back the wire to secure it in place. With this complete, you can cut off any excess 0.5-mm (7-gauge) wire using wire cutters.

2 Begin to spiral the bound wire around the bead. Curl and twist the wire to produce an aesthetically pleasing form, until you get to within 1cm (½in) of the uncovered 1.1-mm (14-gauge) wire. This piece combines spirals with zigzags, but the design is up to you.

3 Turn the piece over. Curl over the exposed 1.1-mm (14-gauge) wire to form a pin, and use the wire bead at the end to form a hook. Cut off any excess wire and file to a point using a needle file.

Spiral silver choker

QUANTITIES OF SILVER WIRE COILED TIGHTLY MAKE A CHUNKY CLOSE-FITTING NECKLACE WITH A RICHLY TEXTURED SURFACE QUALITY. A CHOKER DRAWS ATTENTION TO A BEAUTIFUL NECK SO SHOW OFF THE ELEGANT SIMPLICITY OF THIS NECKLACE BY WEARING IT WITH A PLAIN V-NECK SWEATER.

Necklaces that fit snugly around the throat – commonly known as 'chokers' – have been popular for centuries. A famous portrait of Anne Boleyn, King Henry VIII's ill-fated second wife, shows her wearing her famous choker made of a string of pearls with a pendant 'B' in the centre. Jane Austen's heroines would have worn chokers made from jewels tied on with ribbon, strands of pearls or, more humbly, a simple ribbon tied around the neck. Ribbon chokers might also be accented with a jewelled slide or cameo brooch. This choker is a modern take on a traditional favourite.

Things you will need:

4.6m (5yd) of 1.1-mm (14-gauge) silver wire

Coiled hook and loop fastening (*see pages 56–57*)

Basic tool kit (*see pages 14–15*)

MAKING THE COILS

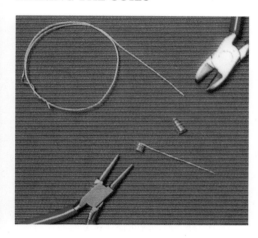

1 Using wire cutters, cut 22 lengths of silver wire, each measuring 17cm (6½in). Grip one end of one piece of wire in round-nosed pliers and wrap it around one side of the tapering nose, starting at the bottom of the pliers and coiling upwards. Repeat on all lengths of wire.

LINKING THE COILS TOGETHER

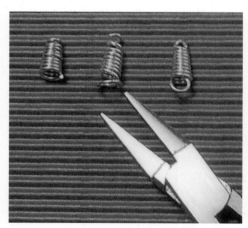

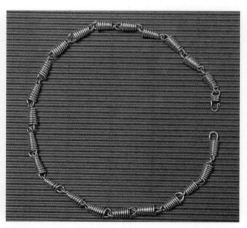

1 To make the linking system, open up the last coil at each end of the spirals, using flat-nosed pliers, and gently bend the single loop at 90°, so that it sits at right angles to the body of the spiral, and repeat.

2 Line up the spirals, the narrow taper facing the widest end of the next spiral. With the flat-nosed pliers, open up the bent links and thread on the next spiral. Close the link making sure it is secure.

3 Link together all of the spirals until they are fastened to one another, end to end, in a chain. Now you can finish the necklace by making and attaching your coiled hook and loop fastening.

Silver-wire flowers

THIS PRETTY DESIGN USES SIMPLE BENDING, SPIRALLING AND HAMMERING OF THE SILVER WIRE TO CREATE A PAIR OF DAINTY DANGLY EARRINGS. THIS IS A RELATIVELY EASY PROJECT TO HANDLE, WHICH MAKES IT ALL THE MORE REWARDING WHEN IT COMES TO WEARING THE COMPLETED PIECES.

Silver is a material that is easy to manipulate; however, you can experiment with other metals such as copper or brass wire, and even combine them to have contrasting colour effects. Instead of flowers, why not try other simple shapes, such as a moon and star, hearts or pieces of fruit with spiral leaves.

Things you will need:

70cm (28in) of 1.1-mm (14-gauge) sterling silver wire
20cm (8in) of 0.7-mm (10-gauge) sterling silver wire
4 silver jump rings (*see page 50*)
Ruler
Basic tool kit (*see pages 14–15*)

FORMING THE FLOWERS

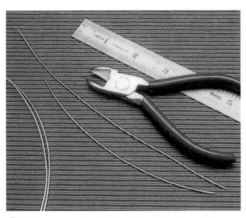

1 Measure and cut the following: two 20cm (8in) and two 15cm (6in) lengths of 1.1-mm (14-gauge) silver wire and two 10cm (4in) lengths of 0.7-mm (10-gauge) silver wire.

FINISHING THE FLOWERS

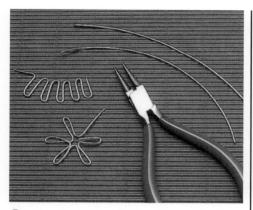

2 Using round-nosed pliers, form each of the 1.1-mm (14-gauge) wire pieces into an even zigzag pattern. Then bend the wire round on each piece, to form the petals of the flower. Leave 1cm (½in) of wire unformed at the end of each flower.

1 Using round-nosed pliers, form a central spiral in each flower from the remaining 1cm (½in) of wire.

2 Using the 0.7-mm (10-gauge) wire, form two spirals, leaving 2.5cm (1in) unformed. Hammer flat, then bend each end into a hook shape to attach the earrings to your ears.

3 When complete, hammer the flowers to flatten them and slightly texture their surface.

3 Using a flat needle file, file the ends of the hooks smooth.

ASSEMBLING THE EARRINGS

1 Use four jump rings, two for each, to connect the flowers and hooks together.

Chainmail bracelet

WHAT A REWARDING BRACELET TO MAKE! FEW METALWORKING SKILLS ARE REQUIRED, BUT PATIENCE IS A MUST. THIS BRACELET SHOULD LAST A LIFETIME – WHY NOT MAKE IT FROM A PRECIOUS METAL? BUT WHATEVER MATERIAL YOU CHOOSE, IT WILL STILL BE A STAR PIECE.

Chainmail – or 'mail' as it is perhaps more correctly known, from the French *maille* meaning mesh – has the advantages of being both highly flexible and easy to repair. As a form of armour, it may have a history dating back more than 2,000 years to pre-Roman times. Once worn by ancient warriors to protect themselves in battle, this traditional metallic fabric shows here that it can look equally good as a fashion accessory. There is no reason why you couldn't start with a line of four or five jump rings and build a more chunky bracelet in the same way. You could also work a longer piece to make a handsome choker. Before getting too ambitious, however, make sure you've had a little practice at making the jump rings so that this part of the process is speeded up.

Things you will need:

Lots and lots of jump rings (*see page 50*) – the quantity required depends on the size of the rings – you can always make more

Two pairs of flat-nosed pliers

Pipe cleaner

Two fasteners

LINKING THE JUMP RINGS

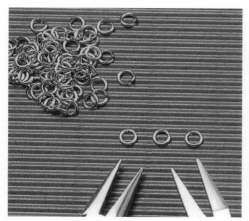

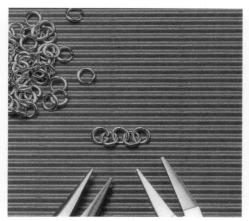

1 Start by lining up three of your jump rings next to one another as shown. Collectively, once joined together, the jump rings become the links in this bracelet.

2 Thread a jump ring through two of the neighbouring links, then close with pliers. Repeat with another ring on the other side, so there are five rings linked uniformly together.

3 Onto this row, link three more jump rings as in step 1. When the piece is placed flat on your work surface, these should lie parallel to the first row of rings.

ASSEMBLING THE BRACELET

1 Continue linking the rings until the bracelet is about 7.5cm (3in) long. Place the bracelet on a flat surface. You are now ready to make the final links down the length of the bracelet.

2 Put a jump ring through the top two side links. Insert the pipe cleaner. Thread a second ring through the first. Thread it through the same two side links as above, then close.

3 Continue to add these final links until you can wrap the bracelet comfortably around your wrist. Add a jump ring and fastener at each end to complete the piece.

Russian wedding band

THIS RING IS MADE FROM THREE INTERLOCKING BANDS, THOUGH IT IS POSSIBLE TO USE MANY MORE. TRADITIONALLY, EACH BAND WOULD BE MADE FROM A DIFFERENT COLOURED GOLD, BUT ONLY SILVER HAS BEEN USED HERE. USE HALF-ROUND WIRE SO THAT ALL THREE RINGS SIT WELL AGAINST EACH OTHER.

To allow the rings to interlock, they need to be three sizes larger than the ring finger size. Remember to add the depth of the metal to your calculations. If you use a strip of paper to measure the finger, refer to the ring size table on *page 246* to figure out the corresponding ring size and the one that is three sizes larger. It is important to make sure the rings are perfectly circular at this stage, because it becomes impossible to reshape the piece once they are linked together.

Things you will need:

3-mm (⅛-in) wide, 2-mm (¹⁄₁₆ in) deep of half-round wire

Ring gauge or paper strip

Basic tool kit (*see pages 14–15*)

Steel ruler

Dividers

Soldering and pickling equipment (*see pages 22–23*)

Mandrel

Flatplate

Sanding equipment (*see pages 40–41*)

MEASURING THE FINGER

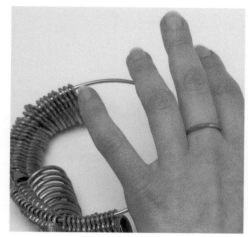
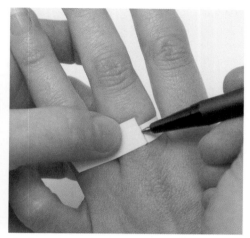

1 Start by measuring the finger on which the ring will be worn. You can use a ring gauge if you have one; the gauge should fit snugly over the knuckles.

2 If you do not have a ring gauge, cut a strip of paper and wrap it around the finger. Mark where the paper overlaps precisely, and cut across the line. Measure the strip of paper.

CUTTING THE RINGS

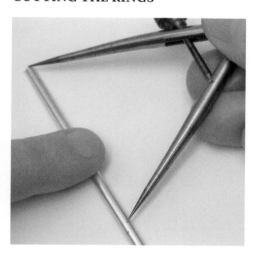

1 Using the measurement you took in either step 1 or 2, you can now calculate the size of the rings. Remember to make them three sizes larger than the measured size and to add on twice the thickness of the metal. Set your dividers to the required length against a steel ruler, and carefully mark the strip of wire to show where to saw.

2 Saw through the wire on the waste side of the line using a jeweller's saw. File off any excess metal up to the line with a flat file.

SHAPING THE RINGS

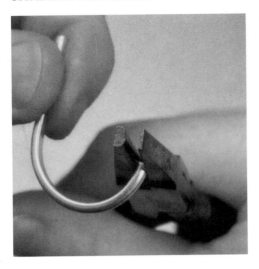

1 Grip one end of the wire in a pair of half-round pliers. Make sure you have the rounded side of the pliers on the flat side of the wire. Bend the rest of the wire around into a semi-circular shape. Repeat this process at the other end of the wire to form a rough circle, annealing the wire if it becomes stiff.

> **TIP**
>
> This piece is made from three identical bands using half-round wire. The simple band is the easiest kind of ring to make and you could try experimenting with different metals, wire shapes and sizes. As long as you remember to keep each band three times larger than the ring finger size, the different variations are innumerable.

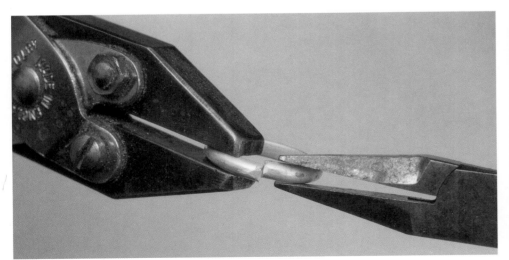

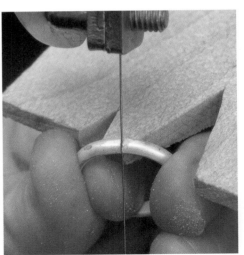

2 Hold the ring between two pairs of flat pliers and maneouvre the ends of the wire towards each other to close the seam. Spring-fit the seam by pushing each end of the wire a little further than necessary; it should spring back just a fraction – enough to create a tight seam that will remain closed owing to the tension in the metal.

3 Now hold the ring tightly against the peg and use a jeweller's saw to saw through the seam to make sure the two faces of the metal fit together very neatly.

SOLDERING THE RINGS

1 Solder the seam shut with hard solder and pickle. Support the ring with spring tweezers while you solder to hold it in place and to make the process easier.

2 File off excess solder from inside and outside the seam.

TIP

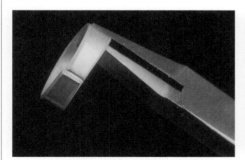

When soldering a ring always make sure the join is properly aligned. Even if the solder were to run in the example here, the join would need so much filing down that it would become very thin.

If the join is incorrectly aligned, as it is on the left, you can adjust it as shown above to allow the solder to flow more easily.

FINISHING THE RINGS

1 Shape the ring into a perfect circle by slipping it onto a ring mandrel and tapping around it with a wooden or hide mallet. Turn the ring over to prevent it from developing a flared shape. If you have any difficulty shaping the ring, anneal it.

TIP

An alternative way to form the simple band is to shape it using a mandrel. With the mandrel held in a vice, hold the wire across its width so that there is a short overhang. Hammer the wire to fit the curve of the mandrel, working your way around and overlapping the wire to form a tight coil. You can now measure the coil and reduce or enlarge its size as necessary. For a smaller ring, remove the coil from the mandrel and place on its side so that you can tap the wire to tighten it further. For a bigger ring, replace the coil on the mandrel and tap it gently on the edge, forcing it further along the mandrel until it is the right size for your finger.

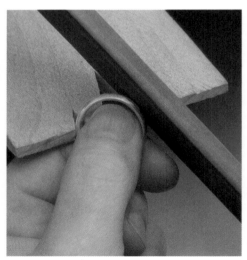

2 To ensure that the ring is flat, place it on a flatplate and tap it with a wooden or hide mallet. Take care not to hammer it too hard in case it becomes misshapen.

3 Emery the inside and outside of the ring using various grits of abrasive paper to remove file marks and to achieve a smooth finish. Repeat the process to make two more rings.

ASSEMBLING THE RINGS

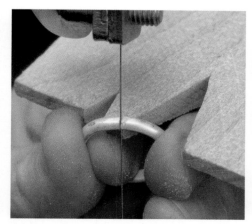

1 Warm two of the rings with a gentle flame to allow you to see the solder lines of the seams. Allow the rings to cool completely and then saw through each one, using the solder line as a guide.

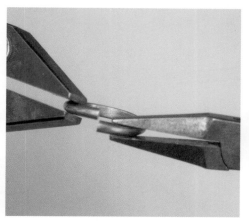

2 Gently open each ring by holding it with a pair of flat pliers either side of the solder line and opening the seam sidewise, using a slight twisting motion. This prevents distortion of their circular shape.

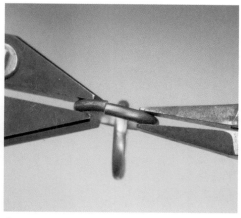

3 Slip the closed ring through one of the open rings. Spring-fit the ends of the open ring back together by pushing them towards each other a little further than necessary, then allow them to spring back into a tight seam.

4 Now you can slip the two linked rings through the remaining open ring and spring-fit the seam back together following the instructions given in step 3.

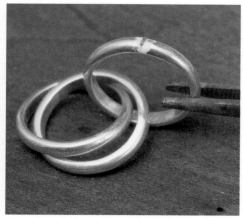

5 Solder the seams of the open rings with hard solder, using spring tweezers to hold each seam clear of the other rings while soldering to reduce the chance of accidental melting.

6 Pickle the completed ring and file off any excess solder, taking care not to change the profile of the wire. Emery both the outside and the inside of the three bands where you have filed and polish with tripoli and rouge.

Chunky glass-bead choker

MORE THAN ONE HUNDRED BRIGHTLY COLOURED GLASS BEADS ARE STRUNG ON WIRES AND COMBINED TO PRODUCE THIS CHUNKY NECKLACE. WEAR THIS STRIKING PIECE WITH AN ETHNIC-STYLE OUTFIT – BUT KEEP THE NECKLINE CLEAR SO AS NOT TO DETRACT FROM THE COLOURS AND SHAPES OF THE NECKLACE.

This necklace may look complicated, but in fact it is relatively easy to put together. All it requires is patience and attention to detail, so don't rush and allow yourself plenty of time to complete the project. This project uses a wide range of beads in an assortment of colours, shapes and sizes, but you do not have to limit yourself to this. Why not make a choker using just greens and blues with a hint of silver or opt for beads that are the same shape but different sizes?

Things you will need:

4.15m (4½yd) of 1.1-mm (14-gauge) copper wire

162 glass beads in an assortment of colours, shapes and sizes

50cm (20in) of black leather thong

29 glass beads which are all the same type (spacer beads)

Coiled hook and loop fastening (*see pages 56–57*)

Basic tool kit (*see pages 14–15*)

MAKING THE BEADED WIRES

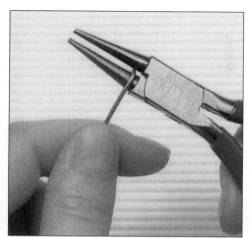

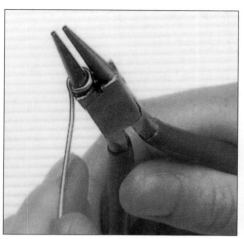

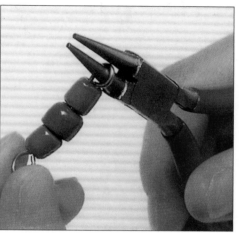

1 Using wire cutters, cut 54 pieces of wire, each about 6cm (2½in) long, although this will depend on the size of your beads. Secure one end of the wire with round-nosed pliers

2 Use the round-nosed pliers to bend the wire carefully to create a loop at the end. Thread three assorted beads onto the wire.

3 Still using round-nosed pliers, make another loop in the other end of the wire to secure the beads. Repeat steps 2 and 3 to make the remaining 53 beaded wires.

THREADING THE BEADS

1 Thread the thong through the loops in the beaded wire, interspersing each series of beaded wires with a spacer bead.

2 When all the component wires have been used, thread 12 spacer beads onto the thong at each end of the mass of beaded wires. Attach a coiled hook and loop attachment to the ends of the leather thong, then tie a knot in the ends of the thong to secure the fastening.

Cluster earrings

A COMBINATION OF DRILLED STONES AND BEADS MAKES UP THESE PRETTY EARRINGS. HERE, FRESHWATER CREAM PEARLS HANG AT THE BOTTOM OF THE CLUSTERS, FOLLOWED BY TURQUOISE BEADS, THEN GREY PEARLS AND LASTLY ANOTHER ROW OF CREAM PEARLS.

The arrangement and combination of stones and beads you use depends on what you have available, but the general shape of the earrings will remain the same. Earring hooks can be bought, but are easy to make and will give the finished earrings an individual touch. Ensure that you make the hooks long enough so that they cannot easily be pushed out of the ear accidentally when worn.

Things you will need:

2 x 50mm (2in) lengths of 1.1-mm (14-gauge) silver wire

40 small drilled freshwater pearls and beads in assorted colours

120cm (4ft) of 0.5-mm (7-gauge) silver wire

2 open and 2 closed jump rings (*see page 50*)

Basic tool kit (*see pages 14–15*)

10-mm (⅜-in) and 20-mm (¹³⁄₁₈-in) diameter mandrels

Top cutters

Steel block

Planishing hammer

Soldering and pickling equipment (*see pages 22–23*)

Dividers

MAKING THE EAR HOOKS

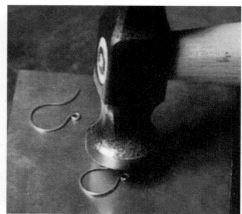

1 Take a 50-mm (2-in) length of 1.1-mm (14-gauge) silver wire and file the end to be passed through the ear smooth. Repeat to make a second hook. Hammer the hooks on a steel block using the planishing hammer to flatten and strengthen them.

2 Bend one end of each wire into a small closed loop using round-nosed pliers. Wrap the wire around the smaller mandrel to make the loop that goes through the ear. Curve the open wire end away from the mandrel over a finger to make the hook end. Trim the ends.

SOLDERING THE HOOKS AND RINGS

1 Rest a closed jump ring on the bottom of an ear hook, paint borax on the seam and apply one paillon of hard solder. Heat until the solder just starts to flow). Repeat with the other ear hook, then pickle and polish them.

PREPARING THE WIRES

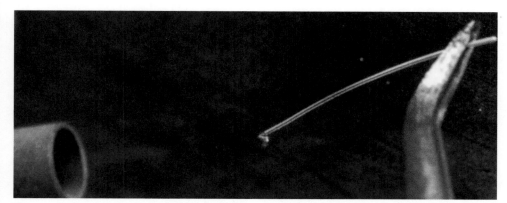

1 Set your dividers to 3cm (1¼in), and mark and cut a strip of 0.5-mm (7-gauge) silver wire using wire cutters. Using the first strip as a guide, cut nine more wire strips. Hold a strip of wire in a pair of spring tweezers and dip one end in borax. Heat the end of the wire with a fine flame until it starts to melt and a bead forms. Withdraw the flame as soon as the bead is evenly formed. Repeat with the remaining strips of wire and pickle them all.

TIP

These ear hooks are extremely versatile and can be applied to a wide range of earring designs. Finished with a freshwater pearl at the end of each hook, as shown here, they make an attractive pair of earrings in their own right.

THREADING THE BEADS

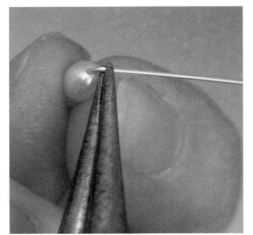

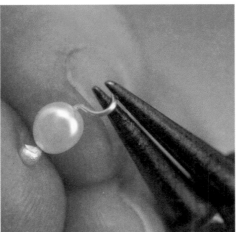

1 Thread your first bead onto a wire and use round-nosed pliers to make a right-angled bend in the wire, close up to the bead.

2 Trim off the wires about 5mm (¼in) from the bend with top cutters. Make a small loop in each wire, using round-nosed pliers and bending the wire back towards the bead.

3 Repeat steps 1 and 2 with the remaining strips of wire. When you have finished this process, you should have ten identical beaded wires that look like this.

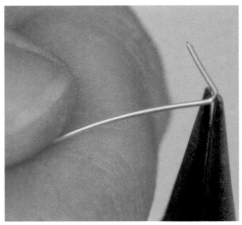

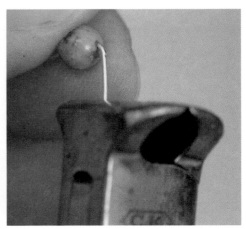

4 Make another loop in the wire by gripping the end in a pair of round-nosed pliers and bending it back towards the bead. Do not close the loop completely.

5 Thread on one of the drops that you made to hang from the bottom of the clusters and then close the loop in the same way that you did in step 2.

6 Repeat this process with the next two beads in the colour sequence. You should now have ten identical strands of four beads each, as shown above.

⑧ Attach an open jump ring to the top loop of both remaining strands, and holding each open ring in a pair of needle-nosed pliers, slip it through the closed jump ring on the bottom of the ear hooks. Position these strands centrally between the strands that have already been attached; they will hang a little lower than the others. Use another pair of flat-nosed pliers to close the jump rings carefully.

⑦ Attach four beaded strands to each of the jump rings on the ear hooks, by opening and closing the top loop of each strand.

ASSEMBLING THE EARRINGS

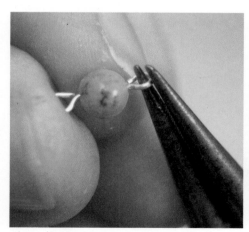

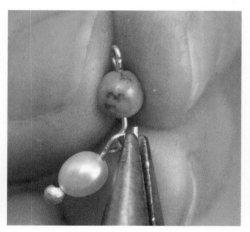

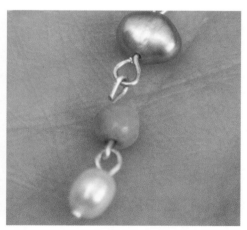

① Cut the remaining 0.5-mm (7-gauge) wire into 3-cm (1-¼in) lengths, but do not solder the end. Make a right-angled bend in each one, about 5mm (¼in) from one end.

② Slip the next bead in your sequence onto the long ends of ten of the wires and make a neat loop with the short bent end, using the very tip of the pliers to bend the wire around.

③ Make a right-angled bend in the wire on the other side of, and close up to, the bead. Trim off the excess wire about 5mm (¼in) from the right-angled bend with a pair of top cutters.

Foiled-bead choker

TINY, BRIGHTLY COLOURED FOILED GLASS BEADS ARE STRUNG VERTICALLY ONTO A THICK FLEXIBLE WIRE CHOKER THAT IS WORN CLOSE TO THE NECK. THE DARK, MATT QUALITY OF THE STEEL WIRE CONTRASTS WELL WITH THE SHIMMERING OF THE MINISCULE JEWEL-LIKE GLASS BEADS.

This is a versatile jewellery-making technique, and one that could be adapted to make a matching bracelet or ankle chain. You could even make drop earrings using a single bead wire. Play around with the bead colours to achieve the look you desire. Here, the beads are chosen randomly, but you could select only greens or blues, golds and oranges, or bright red for a more striking or uniform result. Steel wire can be harder to manipulate than silver wire. If you are unpractised at making jump rings, use silver wire instead.

Things you will need:

5.4m (6yd) of 1.1-mm (14-gauge) steel wire
150 small foiled beads
Clear varnish
Basic tool kit (*see pages 14–15*)
Paintbrush

MAKING THE JUMP RINGS

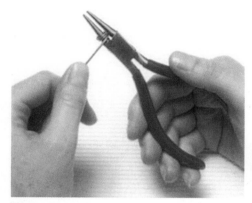

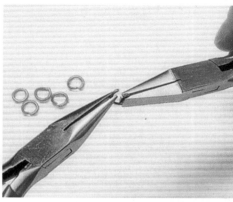

1 Make 132 steel jump rings, using 15-cm (6-in) lengths of steel wire and coiling them around a pair of round-nosed pliers (*see page 50*). As you remove each coil from the pliers, snip up one side using wire cutters.

2 To attach one jump ring to another, or a beaded wire, use two pairs of flat-nosed pliers, and twist the open ends away from one another at the seam. Thread on a jump ring or beaded wire and close up the ring to secure.

MAKING THE BEAD WIRES

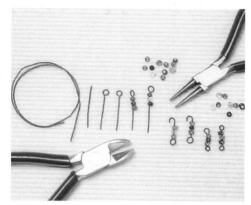

1 Cut 50 2.5-cm (1-in) lengths of steel wire. With the round-nosed pliers, make a loop at one end of each wire. Thread three beads onto the wire and make a loop at the other end of the wire to secure the beads and for fastening.

ASSEMBLING THE CHOKER

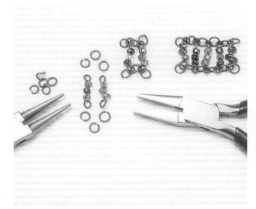

1 Link each beaded wire to the next using a jump ring. Once the jump ring has been threaded on, make sure it is securely closed using the flat-nosed pliers. Repeat until all of the beaded wires are linked together with jump rings as shown.

2 To complete the necklace, make a chain by linking 17 jump rings, using the flat-nosed pliers to open and close the links. Attach each end of this chain to the top and bottom loops of the final beaded wire at one end of the choker. This finishes one end of the choker.

3 Repeat step 2 at the other end of the choker. Now make a hook-and-loop fastening using the remaining steel wire (*see pages 56–57*). Attach one component to each end of the finished choker. To finish, protect the steel wire with a layer of clear varnish.

Textured silver necklace

A SERIES OF TEXTURED WIRES ARE MANIPULATED IN A LIVELY MANNER AND COMBINED WITH GOLD GLASS BEADS TO CREATE A FLAMBOYANT, CLOSE-FITTING NECKLACE. YOU CAN CHANGE THE COLOUR AND QUANTITY OF THE BEADS IN THE PIECE ACCORDING TO YOUR PREFERENCE.

Relatively simple to make, this design is extremely stylish and is best worn against the skin, or with a light top that has a high neckline. It will not sit flat against the body but will rest, instead, on its various curved and twisted edges, because of which it will catch the light brilliantly when worn, casting numerous dancing shadows.

Things you will need:

113cm (45in) of 1.5-mm (18-gauge) silver wire

10 gold barrel glass beads

Silver coiled hook and loop fastening (*see pages 56–57*)

Paper

Pencil

Ruler

Basic tool kit (*see pages 14–15*)

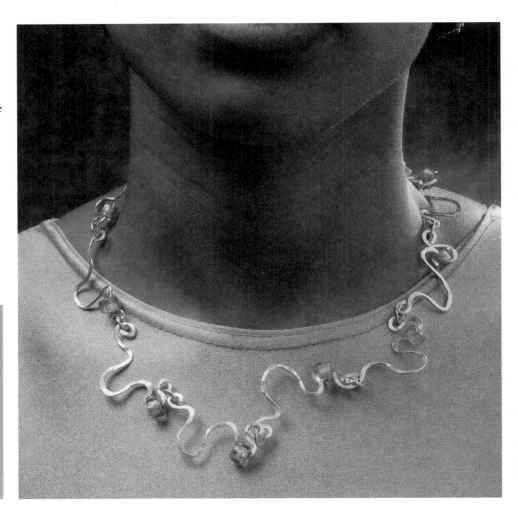

DESIGNING THE COMPONENTS

1 Using a pencil, draw an undulating shape on a piece of paper, making it about 6cm (2½in) long and allowing for a loop at both ends. Keep it fairly simple. This will become the template for the wire components. Cut ten 6-cm (2½-in) lengths of silver wire using wire cutters. Using the round-nosed pliers, manipulate the wires to match the shape on the piece of paper. Make a loop at one end of each wire with the pliers.

TEXURING THE WIRE

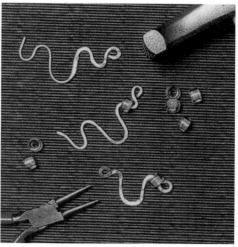

1 Hammer each of the wires until they are heavily textured. Slide on a glass bead at one end of each piece and, using the round-nosed pliers make a loop at the other end of the wire.

ASSEMBLING THE PIECE

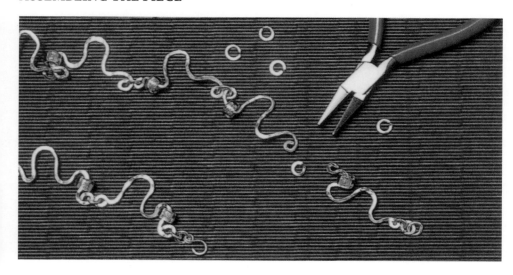

1 Make 14 silver wire jump rings (*see page 50*). Texture them by tapping with a hammer. Thread them through the loops in the bent wire and use the flat-nosed pliers to close them, linking one section of wire to the next. Attach the hook and loop fastening with the remaining jump rings.

Celtic-style brooch

TO WEAR THIS QUICKLY MADE PIECE, YOU SIMPLY THREAD THE WIRE PIN IN THROUGH THE TOP SPIRAL OF THE BROOCH, AND OUT AGAIN THROUGH THE BOTTOM, MAKING SURE YOU THREAD THE PIN THROUGH YOUR CLOTHING AT THE SAME TIME. YOU COULD MAKE THE SAME PIECE USING ALL COPPER OR ALL BRASS.

This design for this brass and copper brooch is inspired by the interweaving decorative patterns used by the Celts from around 450 CE. Known as knots, these stylised, often geometric patterns were used variously to ornament manuscripts, stonework and other crafts. Celtic art has been hugely influential over the centuries, and enjoyed a particularly successful revival towards the end of the 19th century, in the Arts and Crafts and Art Nouveau movements.

Things you will need:

7.5x5cm (3x2in) piece of copper sheet

7.5x5cm (3x2in) piece of brass sheet

12.5cm (5in) of 2 mm (18-gauge) copper wire

Decorative bead with 2-mm (¹/₁₆in) hole

Basic tool kit (*see pages 14–15*)

Wire wool

Pen

Paper

Resin-based glue

Chasing hammer

CUTTING THE SHAPES

1 Start by cleaning the sheet metal using a small piece of wire wool. Cut two same-size rectangles from the paper and draw a spiral shape onto each one. They do not have to be identical. Lightly glue one piece of paper to the copper sheet and one to the brass sheet.

2 Saw-pierce the shapes out of the metal sheets using a size 0 blade. Following your paper template, cut through the paper at the same time. Remove the paper and then file all of the rough edges of the metal spirals using a needle file.

TEXTURING THE METAL

1 Use the chasing hammer to create a textured effect on the copper and brass spirals by hammering the flat metal. Tap the entire surface of each piece until you have achieved the level of texturing you would like. Apply the pressure evenly.

ASSEMBLING THE BROOCH

1 Interlock the two spirals to create a pattern. Bend the piece so that it arches slightly in the centre. Use a little resin glue at the back to hold the pieces in place.

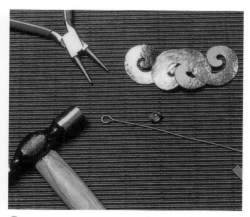

2 Curl the top of the copper wire to form a loop and hammer it flat. Thread on the bead so it is close to the loop. File the other end of the copper wire to a fine point.

Brass necklace

BOLD BRASS GEOMETRIC SHAPES, TEXTURED TO CREATE AN ANTIQUE FEEL AND ASSEMBLED IN A STRONG PATTERN, CONTRIBUTE TO FASHION A NECKLACE THAT IS CONTEMPORARY IN FEEL BUT ALSO EVOKES ANCIENT MEXICAN CIVILISATIONS. YOU COULD MAKE THE SAME PIECE USING SILVER OR BRONZE.

Brass is an alloy of copper and zinc, and is favoured for its gold-like appearance. It does not, however, have the same soft glow as gold and can look rather harsh – hammering the surface creates a texture that both softens its appearance and, here, is an essential element of the design of this necklace.

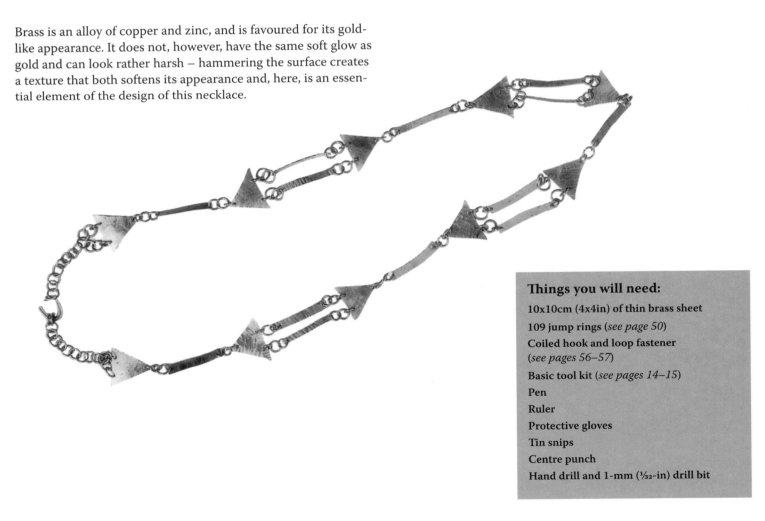

Things you will need:

10x10cm (4x4in) of thin brass sheet

109 jump rings (*see page 50*)

Coiled hook and loop fastener (*see pages 56–57*)

Basic tool kit (*see pages 14–15*)

Pen

Ruler

Protective gloves

Tin snips

Centre punch

Hand drill and 1-mm (¹⁄₃₂-in) drill bit

PREPARING THE PARTS

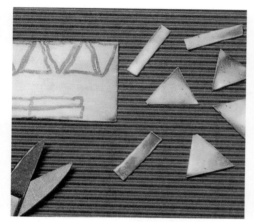

1 With a pen, draw ten triangular shapes approximately 17x17mm (⅞x⅞in) in size and also 13 rectangles 27x5mm (1⅛x¼in) on the brass sheet. Wearing protective gloves use the tin snips to cut out the drawn shapes.

2 Gently tap the surface of the metal shapes with a hammer until they are textured all over. It might be necessary to wear gloves to hold the metal shapes while hammering to protect your fingers from sharp edges.

3 File the edges of the metal shapes smooth. Mark drilling positions using a centre punch: three holes on the triangles and two holes on the rectangles. With a hand drill, make the necessary holes.

LINKING THE PARTS

1 Using the brass wire and a pair of round-nosed pliers, make 109 jump rings. With two pairs of flat-nosed pliers, slightly open the jump rings and, one by one, slip them through the holes drilled in the metal shapes, then close the jump rings. Lay out the metal shapes as shown and attach the parts, with three jump rings between each metal shape.

2 To finish the ends of the necklace, make a chain by linking together 14 jump rings using two pairs of flat-nosed pliers, then attach a brass coiled hook and loop fastener.

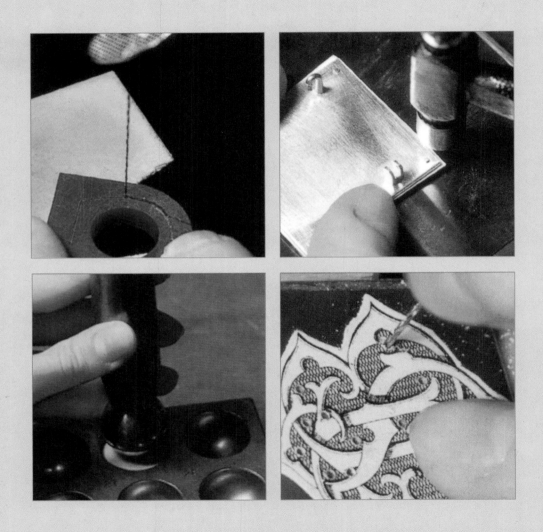

Advanced Techniques

Once you have mastered the basic techniques described on *pages 26–61* and have tried your hand at a number of the projects presented on *pages 62–99*, you will be ready to develop your jewellery-making techniques further, using those included in this section of the book. If your main interest is shaping metal, take a look at the doming, swaging and forging techniques. Or perhaps you would like to branch out in a different direction, such as fretwork, enamelling or etching. You will find all of these in the following pages, as well as techniques for setting stones, for lost-wax casting and for riveting two or more pieces together. Once you have found a technique that you would like to try, there's plenty of scope for putting it to the test using one or more of the various advanced projects that follow.

Drawing and shaping wire

WIRE MAY BE DRAWN TO ALTER ITS SHAPE OR MAKE TUBES. THE PROCESS INVOLVES THE USE OF DRAW PLATES AND IS DONE BY 'DRAWING' OR PULLING THE METAL THROUGH A HOLE IN THE PLATE. DRAWING THICK WIRE TAKES CONSIDERABLE STRENGTH AND MAY REQUIRE A DRAW BENCH.

DRAWING WIRE AND TUBE

To keep the metal workable, anneal the wire before and during the drawing process (*see page 37*). The techniques shown are worked on a swaged strip of wire.

Things you will need:

Basic tool kit (*see pages 14–15*)
Draw plates
Bench vice
Serrated pliers
Oil
Rolling mill, for shaping wire

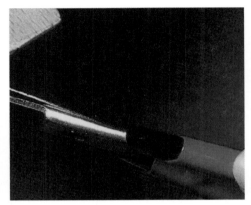

1 Place a draw plate in a bench vice so that the wider, feed-through holes are at the back. Use tin snips to trim the end of the swaged strip into a 'V' shape.

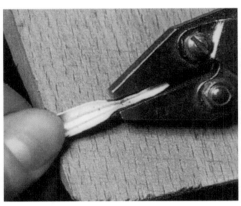

2 Use flat-nosed pliers to pinch the 'V' into a tight taper.

3 Choose a hole in the draw plate by pushing the taper through from the back so that it protrudes through the other side, but so the strip is just too big to be pulled through. Using heavy, serrated-edge pliers, pull the swaged strip through the draw plate. Use a drop of oil to lubricate the work.

4 Repeat step 3 until the seams of the strip join when it is pulled though the draw plate. Use tiny paillons to solder the join.

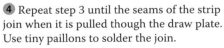

TIP

For drawing wire, file the end to make a taper (*see page 38*).

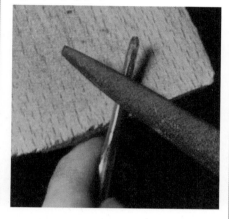

FORMING 'D'-SHAPED WIRE

For this technique the rolling mill must have 'D'-shaped channels on one of the rollers.

1 Anneal, pickle and rinse a length of round wire. To adjust the width between the rollers, turn the handle on the mill so that the wire cannot pass through easily. Then feed the wire through the D-shaped section.

2 Check the thickness of the shaped wire using a vernier caliper. If it is still too deep in section, repeat the process.

SHAPING OR TAPERING A WIRE

For this technique the rolling mill must have rollers with square grooves.

1 Anneal, pickle and rinse a length of round wire. Push the wire between the rollers in one of the square grooves. There should be no gap between the rollers, unless the wire is larger than the largest groove.

2 Holding the wire, turn the handle on the mill so that it draws the wire through the grooved section of the rollers and releases it on the other side. To taper the wire, feed a limited section through the rollers. Repeat as necessary, turning the wire 90° each time.

Shaping metal

THERE ARE VARIOUS SIMPLE PROCESSES FOR FORMING METAL INTO SPECIFIC SHAPES, ALL OF WHICH INVOLVE MANIPULATING THE METAL. IT IS ADVISABLE TO ANNEAL FREQUENTLY SO THAT YOU ARE NOT STRUGGLING UNNECESSARILY WITH WORK-HARDENED METAL. OVERWORKING WILL RESULT IN SPLITS AND BROKEN EDGES.

Things you will need:

Sheet metal
Basic tool kit (*see pages 14–15*)
Doming block
Doming punches
Steel block with curved gullies
Swage block
Mandrel

DOMING METAL

Domed forms are made from sheet metal by hammering a punch into an indent with a disc of sheet between them.

1 Anneal, pickle and rinse a circle of sheet metal. Choose an indent in the doming block that is larger than the metal circle: if the indent is smaller the circle will be marked by the doming process. Choose a punch that is smaller than the indent in the doming block. Try out a range of different punches in the indent to check that there is space for the metal between the two, to prevent thinning of the edges.

TIP

For hollow beads, make two identical domes and solder them together. This can be done by placing each half, dome-side down, on a soldering mat, applying borax around the edge and placing paillons of solder at regular intervals. Heat each dome just long enough for the solder to start flowing. File any bumps of solder down and sit the two halves together. They should sit closely. Flux the join and place one or two pieces of the same solder on it, then solder the two halves together.

② Place the annealed metal circle in the indent. Use a mallet to hammer the punch firmly onto the sheet.

③ Repeat step 2 in smaller indents with the appropriate punch until your dome reaches the required profile.

SWAGING METAL

A steel block is used to make parallel gully or channel forms by hammering a parallel rod into a negative channel. The steel block is useful for creating relief as well as for raising up strip forms when making tubing.

① Anneal, pickle and rinse a strip of metal sheet. Choose a channel in the steel block that is wider than your metal strip: if the channel is narrower the edges of the strip will be marked as it is formed. Choose a mandrel, checking that there is space for the metal between the channel and former, to prevent thinning of the edges. Place the strip in the channel with any overhang at one end only.

② Position the mandrel on top of the strip in the channel and use a mallet to hammer firmly and evenly all along its length.

③ Repeat step 2, working on a smaller channel with the appropriate former until your strip reaches the required profile.

Forging and raising

FORGING AND RAISING ARE BOTH TECHNIQUES FOR RESHAPING METAL WITH CONTROLLED FORCE. RAISING IS A METHOD THAT SILVERSMITHS USE TO 'RAISE' A FLAT SHEET INTO A CURVED, OPEN FORM SUCH AS A BOWL. FORGING USUALLY INVOLVES HEATING, BEATING AND HAMMERING A SOLID FORM.

Things you will need:

100mm (4in) length of 4mm (⁵⁄₃₂in) diameter copper or silver rod or wire

Pickling equipment (*see pages 22–23*)

Steel block

Raising hammer

Planishing hammer

30mm (1³⁄₁₆in) diameter doming punch

Blocking hammer

Vice

It's important to understand what happens to the metal when it is displaced. A cylindrical hammer (curved in one plane) will displace metal at right angles to the curve, while a spherical hammer will displace material evenly all round. A flat support doesn't generally alter the shape beyond the effect of the hammer blow; a cylindrical support will increase the effect of a cylindrical hammer if used in the same orientation.

TIP

To understand the effects of a particular hammer or support on your metal, modelling clay is a useful trial material. To work the clay, use the hammers and supports as you would for the metal; the clay will be displaced like metal, although it will require much less effort.

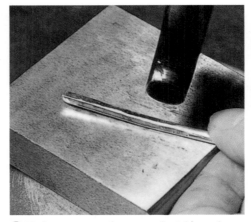

1 To forge a taper, first anneal, pickle and rinse a length of rod. Place the end of the rod on a steel block and hammer along its length with a raising hammer. Ensure that the hammer blow is square to the steel block: if the hammer is tilted the rod will begin to curl to one side. The blows should be at 90° to the rod and be consecutive, so that there is no unhammered metal between blows. The section should now be rectangular.

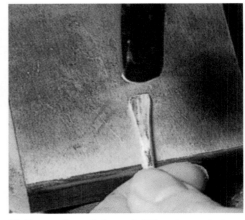

2 Rotate the rod through 90° and repeat step 1. The section should now be square. Anneal, pickle and rinse again. Rotate the rod through 90° and work on the end of the forged rod now, to begin the taper.

3 Keep rotating the rod through 90°, forging from the point forged in the step before each time. Repeat, continuing to reduce the area being forged until the rod tapers to a point.

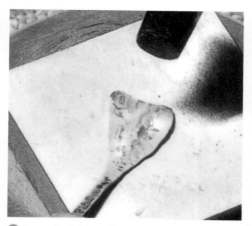

4 Anneal, pickle and rinse again. Planish – that is, flatten and polish – the tapered rod using a planishing hammer with the work supported on a steel block. Work along the full length of one forged face of the rod; repeat for the other three forged faces.

5 Anneal, pickle and rinse again. To raise the metal, spread the unhammered end section by hammering with a raising hammer over a steel block. Begin hammering the end with the hammer face in line with the rod, tilted slightly downwards towards the end.

6 With each hammer blow, change the angle of the hammer slightly so that the far end of the hammer face is radiated in an arc form – the end should fan out, thin and become wedge-shaped in section.

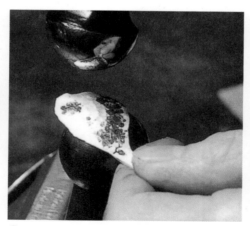

7 Anneal, pickle and rinse again. Tidy the area between the tapered rod and fanned detail by hammering with a raising hammer.

8 Curve the detail by raising. Position the fan end over a doming punch and hammer with a blocking hammer in a circular action radiating from the centre to the edge.

9 Anneal, pickle and rinse. To twist a rod, clamp one end in a bench vice with fibre grips. Hold the form about 5cm (2in) above the vice jaws with parallel pliers. Rotate the form to create a twist. Continue until there are as many twists as desired.

Fretwork

FRETWORK IS THE TERM USED TO DESCRIBE PERFORATIONS IN SHEET METAL THAT FORM A PATTERN OF POSITIVE AND NEGATIVE SHAPES. SOME HIGHLY DECORATIVE EFFECTS CAN BE CREATED THIS WAY, OF VARYING COMPLEXITY – RICH AND SUMPTUOUS OR SUBTLE AND UNDERSTATED.

In order to create fretwork, holes are drilled into the metal to pass a saw blade through, so a negative shape can be cut. There is no simple alternative to piercing, nor is there a simple mechanised method that will do the job as well as piercing, so it is essential to spend time perfecting this advanced skill.

1 Photocopy your chosen pattern so that you can keep the original for reference, adjusting the size on the copier if required. To check that the pattern is suitable for fretwork, colour in the negative spaces on the photocopy and see if the positive spaces are still held in position: for example, to cut an 'O' you need a tab between the centre of the 'O' and the rest of the sheet or you will end up with a hole instead of an 'O'.

2 Completely cover the back of the pattern with double-sided adhesive tape, without overlapping the tape and causing raised areas.

Things you will need:

Photocopied cipher or pattern

2-mm (¹⁄₁₆-in) thick sheet metal, cut to size

Basic tool kit, including 2/0 saw blade

Double-sided adhesive tape

Scissors

Pendant motor and 1-mm (¹⁄₃-in) diameter twist drill bit

White spirit

Soft cloth

Sanding equipment (*see pages 40–41*)

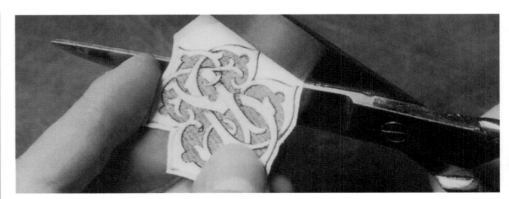

3 Trim around the pattern leaving a 2mm (¹⁄₁₆in) border. Remove the paper backing from the adhesive tape and position the pattern on the sheet metal, placing it close to the edges in one corner so that you don't have far to cut when piercing begins.

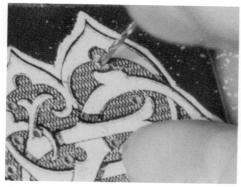

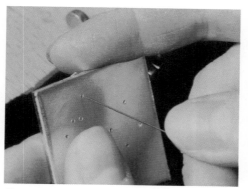

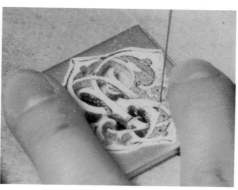

4 Drill a number of access holes inside the shapes to be cut (the shaded areas), about 1mm (1/32in) away from the pattern (the unshaded areas). Position the holes where a line changes direction, such as a corner or the tip of a shape. Avoid positioning a hole halfway along a long, smooth line as you will see clearly the point on the line where you start and finish cutting.

5 Load the saw blade into the bottom knuckle of the saw frame, then pass the saw blade through a hole so the pattern is facing upward in the saw frame. Let the sheet drop to the bottom of the knuckle so that you don't need to support the work. Tense the blade.

6 Pierce the pattern. If you are right-handed, cut in a clockwise direction, so that the pattern is to the right of the saw blade and the line is not obscured by it. If left-handed, cut in an anticlockwise direction.

7 If you happen to break a blade while piercing the pattern, drill another hole nearby and start again. If your blade becomes stuck, raise the work off the bench peg and let go of the sheet. It will spring into a position where there is no resistance on the saw blade. Reposition the work flat on the peg, hold the saw frame at the new angle, and continue cutting until the shape drops out.

8 Repeat steps 5–6 until you have cut out all the negative shapes. Cut out the exterior shape. To avoid obscuring the pattern with the blade, cut anticlockwise if you are right-handed and clockwise if left-handed. Peel off the photocopied pattern. Remove residual stickiness with white spirit on a soft cloth in a well-ventilated area, away from naked flames. Sand away any residue.

Riveting

RIVETS ARE A SIMPLE MEANS OF JOINING TWO OR MORE SEPARATE PIECES BY PASSING SOLID METAL PEGS OR TUBING THROUGH BOTH PIECES AND SPREADING THE ENDS TO SECURE THEM. THE TECHNIQUE IS A USEFUL ONE, PARTICULARLY WHERE DIFFERENT MATERIALS ARE INVOLVED.

Riveting can be used to join metal to materials that can't be soldered, like wood and plastic, or for joining any materials that can't be soldered. Rivets are useful for joining enamelled parts or pieces where awkward stone settings are worked and then assembled post-setting. They are also used to secure fittings where soldering would result in annealing the fitting.

Things you will need:

Basic tool kit (*see pages 14–15*)

Scriber

Pendant motor with a 2-mm (¹⁄₁₆-in) flame burr and 1-mm (¹⁄₃₂-in) diameter twist drill bit

Top cutters

Rivet hammer

Steel block

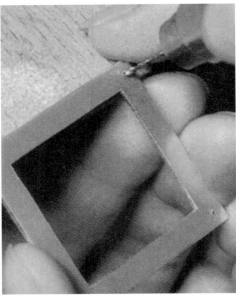

1 Use a scriber to mark the points on the top piece where the rivets are to be located. Assemble the parts and drill a hole on one of the points marked.

2 Using top cutters, cut lengths of round wire 1mm (¹⁄₃₂in) longer than the sum of the parts to be joined. Cut as many lengths as there are rivets needed. Put a gentle taper on the rivet wires by holding them in a pendant drill and presenting a needle file to the wire.

3 Assemble the parts to be joined and peg the drilled hole with a length of the tapered rivet wire. Drill the remaining holes at the points that are marked.

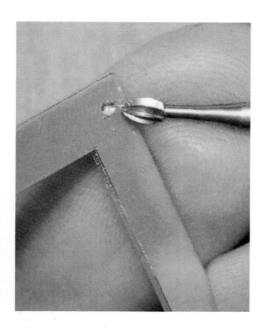

④ Using a flame burr held in the pendant motor, countersink the holes by opening their entry and exit points, rotating the burr in the hole to create a small but wide neck into which the metal rivet will be spread.

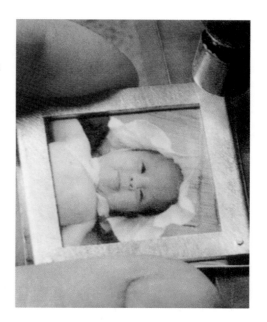

⑤ Insert the remaining rivet wires into the countersunk holes. Using a rivet hammer on a steel block, rivet the piece from the front by tapping a rivet head so it spreads into the countersunk area. Keep the hammer blows square to avoid damaging any of the material around the rivet.

⑥ Turn the piece over and repeat step 5 on the rivet worked in step 5. Repeat for each rivet.

TIP

Turn a favourite photograph into the centrepiece of a brooch or pendant necklace by riveting it in place.

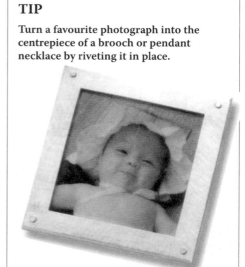

Lost-wax carving

CARVING – USUALLY WITH WAX – IS THE PROCESS OF MAKING THREE-DIMENSIONAL FORMS FOR CASTING. MODERN WAXES ARE ACTUALLY PLASTIC DESIGNED FOR THIS PROCESS. WORKING WAX IS A QUICK PROCESS COMPARED WITH WORKING METAL, SO IT IS EASIER TO SPEND TIME ON A PERFECT FINISH.

The lost-wax casting process is generally a commercial service because the equipment is expensive and the process difficult to perfect. It involves attaching a sprue or feeder wire to the wax form, which is then placed in a tree formation in a plastic base that is covered with an open cylinder called a flask. The tree is then embedded in plaster. The plastic base is removed before the flask is heated in a kiln, burning the wax away to leave a negative space. Molten metal is poured or thrown into the flask by a centrifugal force to fill the negative space. The flask is then plunged into cold water to release the metal forms from the plaster; the individual forms are then cut off the trunk of the tree ready for cleaning up.

Things you will need:

Wax ring blank

Oval template (25° isometric)

Basic tool kit (*see pages 14–15*)

Dividers

Steel rule

Pendant motor and 3-mm (⅛-in) diameter round burr

Wire wool

1 Mark out a semi-circle on a wax ring blank with a pair of dividers set to 2.5mm (³⁄₃₂in), using the inside edge of the wax as the guide for the dividers. Repeat on the reverse side. Mark a line 4mm (⁵⁄₃₂in) above the inside edge of the wax at the top of the ring using a steel ruler and a scriber. Repeat on the reverse side.

2 Join the end of the semi-circle to the straight line to form the taper of the ring. Repeat on the reverse side.

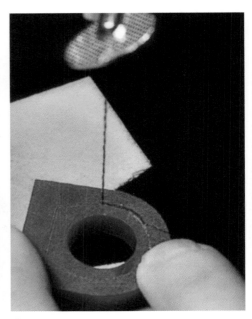

3 Cut away the excess wax using a piercing saw with a spiral saw blade for wax.

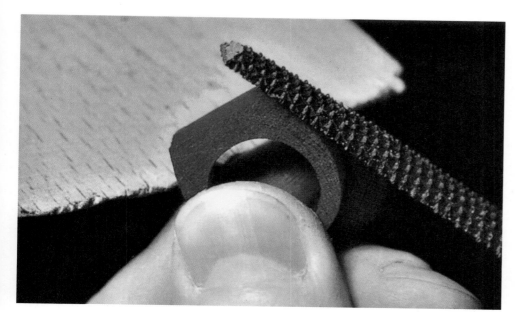

4 Define the profile by filing with a large wax rasp, using the marked lines as a guide. Clean the rasp if it becomes clogged with wax.

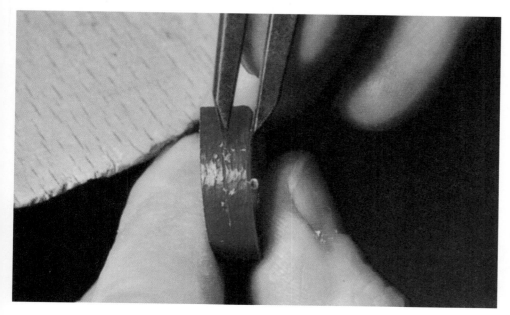

5 On the outside of the ring, mark a central line using dividers, including over the flat face. This will help you to guide the file when you are tapering the shape. You can use the flat face of the ring as a guide for the dividers.

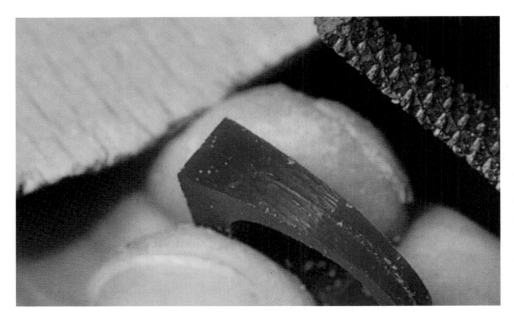

6 Taper the ring by filing the face at an angle from the base of the ring using a large wax rasp. File so you don't get too close to the guideline at the base of the ring or reduce the width at the top of the wax by breaking the top edge. The top face of the ring should now be a rectangle. Mark an ellipse on the face using an oval template.

7 File the rounded form of the ring using a wax rasp, tilting the angle of the file to achieve a 'D'-shaped section and remembering to file with the curve. Take care not to break the centre guideline marked earlier or you will thin the profile of the ring. File the profile at the top of the ring with care so that you define the ellipse without breaking the guideline marked in step 5.

8 Tidy up and smooth the form with hand files once the basic shape has been established. Make sure you clear the wax regularly from the file's cutting face, or it will clog.

9 Polish the surface by rubbing with fine wire wool to soften any remaining ridges left by the filing process.

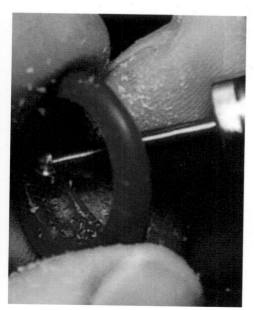

10 To reduce the weight of the wax ring, hollow it out under the ellipse area using a 3-mm (⅛-in) diameter burr in a pendant motor: practise on scrap wax before working on the finished ring. Present the wax ring to a casting company for casting.

Setting stones

WHEN YOU WANT TO SET A STONE IN YOUR WORK, YOU MUST MAKE A MOUNTING TO HOLD IT SECURELY. THIS MOUNTING CAN BE AN INTEGRAL PART OF THE PIECE, OR IT CAN BE MADE SEPARATELY AND SOLDERED INTO POSITION. QUITE OFTEN THE TYPE OF SETTING YOU USE WILL DEPEND ON THE SHAPE OF THE STONE.

SETTING CABOCHON STONES

Cabochon stones – which are shaped and polished rather than cut with facets – are usually displayed in a rub-over, or bezel, mounting. This forms a collar around the stone and shows it to its best advantage.

Things you will need:

Sheet silver

Basic tool kit (*see pages 14–15*)

Dividers

Soldering and pickling equipment (*see pages 22–23*)

Mandrel

Ring vice

Burnisher

MEASURING UP

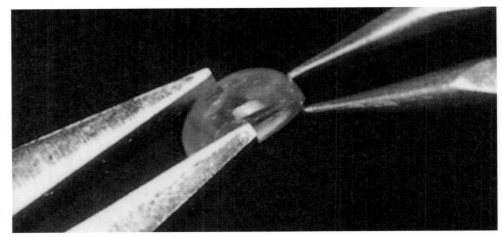

1 Measure the diameter of your stone and use the 2πr to find its circumference (π =22/7 or 3.141). Say your stone is 9.5mm (⅜in). You would use the calculation 2 x 22/7 x 4.75mm = 29.84mm (2 x 22/7 x ³⁄₁₆ = 1⅛in). The silver surrounding the stone is called a bezel. Choose a thickness of silver that is appropriate to the size of the stone. In the example given above, a thickness of 0.6mm is about right. To calculate the length of the bezel add together the circumference of the stone and 1½ times the thickness of the silver. Measure the height of the stone with a pair of dividers. Mark the height on your silver.

2 Mark out the length you need, pierce out the silver and anneal it. Use half-round pliers to bend the two ends of the bezel up so that they meet exactly. To keep the shape tight for soldering, push the two ends past each other and then spring them back into position. Solder the ends together using hard solder.

MAKING THE BEZEL

1 Make the bezel round by tapping it on your mandrel or in your pliers. File of any excess solder from the inside. Check that the stone fits; it should just slip in.

2 Rub the bottom of the bezel on a flat file to make sure it sits perfectly straight, then place the bezel on a piece of silver between 1 and 1.5mm thick. Flux the silver and solder it with medium solder. Place the paillons around the outside edge of the bezel and heat the surrounding silver before bringing the heat into the bezel.

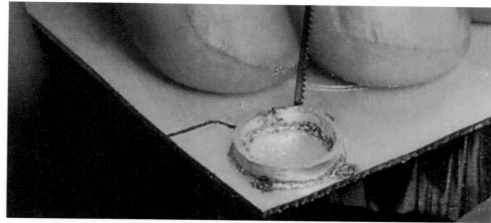

3 After pickling and rinsing, carefully cut away the excess silver from the outside of the bezel. File the outside edge neatly and clean it thoroughly using wet and dry papers. The bezel is now ready to add to a piece of jewellery, following a design of your choosing.

4 If you need an open setting so that the light brings out the best qualities in your stone, cut away most of the back. Place one side of the dividers on the outside of your setting and the other side inside the bezel. Scribe a line around the circumference, leaving a margin of about 2mm (¹⁄₁₆in) of silver on the inside. Drill a hole in the centre of the setting and pierce up to the line to cut away the inside. Neaten the edge with a needle file.

TIP

To find the length of bezel required for an oval stone, add together the length and width of the stone, divide by 2 and multiply by π. Add the length of the bezel to 1½ times the thickness of the silver.

117

SETTING THE STONE

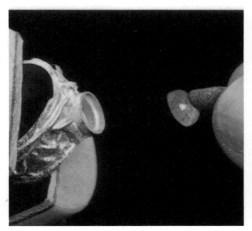

① Hold the ring in a ring vice. File the top edge of the bezel so that it is smooth and flat, and clean off any file marks with wet and dry paper. Use either a stone holder or a small piece of plasticine to hold the stone and place it securely in the setting.

② Using a straight or curved highly polished burnisher, press over the edge of the setting at 12 o'clock, move down to 6 o'clock, then across to 9 o'clock followed by 3 o'clock. Continue pressing with a smooth motion all the way round until the whole circumference is pressed down onto the stone.

③ On heavier settings it is necessary to use a small punch with a hammer. Work in the same order as with a burnisher, gently tapping the punch at an angle of about 45° until all the bezel is resting on the stone.

SETTING FACETED STONES

Faceted stones have flat surfaces cut at different angles to reflect and transmit light. For setting purposes, a faceted stone has three important parts – the table, the girdle and the culet. A flush setting is one of several different ways in which faceted stones can be successfully mounted.

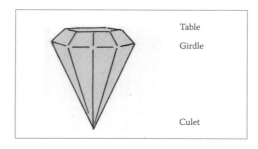

Table

Girdle

Culet

1 Drill a hole through the silver; the hole should be about 1mm (⅓₂in) smaller than the diameter of the stone.

2 Use a pendant motor with a burr attachment to remove enough silver for the stone to sit in the hole. Alternatively, you can use a small hand drill.

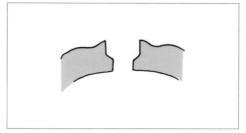

3 File away the silver around the top edge of the bezel. Place the stone in the setting and burnish the bezel onto the stone. Polish the piece to finish.

FACETED STONES: CHENIER (TUBE) SETTING

Use chenier that has the same diameter as your stone or a fractionally larger diameter.

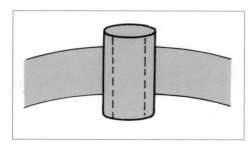

1 Drill a hole in your work that is the same size as the chenier. Solder the chenier into place, leaving the top proud so that the stone will appear to sit on the top edge of the ring.

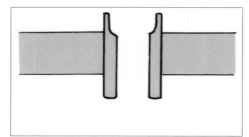

2 Use a pendant motor with a burr attachment or a small hand drill to remove the inside of the chenier to fit the stone as far as the top edge of your work.

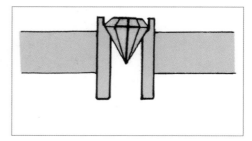

3 Gently file around the top outer edge of the chenier. Set the stone in the tube and burnish the edges of the tube over the stone. Polish and finish.

MAKING A COLLET USING WIRE

This basic technique can be applied to any shape of stone by altering the shape of the rings – to fit an oval, for example – and by changing the number of wires or claws.

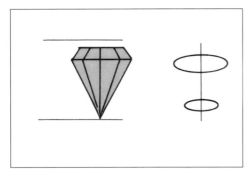

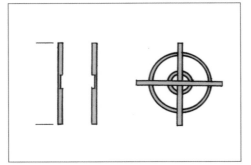

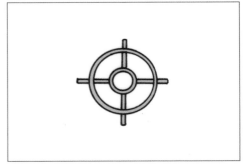

1 Measure the diameter of the stone at a point slightly below the girdle and at a point just above the culet. Make two rings of the diameters above from 0.75-mm (20-gauge) wire (or thicker if your stone is large).

2 Cut two pieces of wire that are longer than the height of the stone. Solder the wire together by filing a notch in the centre of each length and placing them at right angles, one on top of the other.

3 Solder the smaller wire ring centrally under the wire cross, with the larger ring on top. Pierce away the wire of the cross pieces at the points where they cross the lower wire ring.

4 Measure the point where the girdle of the stone will lie on the wires and use a triangular file to make a groove. Bend the wires upward. Solder the collet to your work, and use a needle file to finish the edges of the wire. Set the stone in the collet and use a burnisher to rub the wires over the stone.

USING A COLLET

When you have made your collet, set your stone in it in the following way.

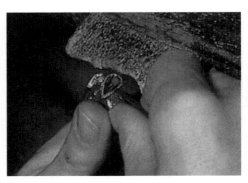

1 Adjust the claws for the stone, then push them down onto the stone.

2 Clip off the excess length with side cutters then burnish to a thumbnail finish.

TAPERED RECTANGULAR OR SQUARE SETTING

This is an alternative setting for square or rectangular stones.

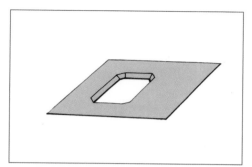

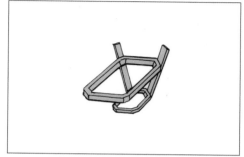

1 Use 1.1-mm (14-gauge) silver sheet and measure the width of the stone at the girdle and 1mm (¹⁄₃₂in) below the girdle. Mark on the silver the outline of the girdle and then mark the lower outline. Pierce out from the inner line to the outer by holding your saw at an angle between the two lines as you cut.

2 Mark an edge approximately 1mm (¹⁄₃₂in) away from the outer cut edge and pierce, using the same technique with the saw. Alternatively, pierce out the shape straight and file the taper. Cut claws out of the same sheet and file a groove so that they fit each corner.

3 Solder the setting and claws to a base and then pierce away the inside at a similar angle so that the stone sits comfortably. Before setting the stone, file the top edge of the claws to make a neat rub-over setting.

MAKING A COLLET WITH SHEET SILVER

This classic setting forms a cup in which to set the stone.

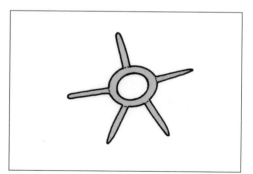

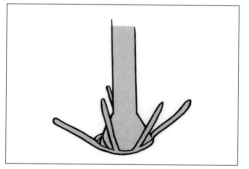

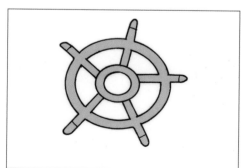

1 Pierce out a suitable shape for an oval or round stone and file a small groove in each claw where it will turn down onto the stone.

2 Place the collet on the pitch and gently hit a doming punch held in the centre, which will allow the claws to come up.

3 Make a wire circle or oval that fits just under the girdle and solder it onto the frame. Set the stone in position and turn the claws in.

Etching

THE ETCHING TECHNIQUE USES ACID TO CORRODE METAL. AN ETCH RESIST IS USED TO PROTECT OR MASK AREAS THAT YOU DO NOT WANT ETCHED SO THAT PATTERNS CAN BE FORMED. AREAS PROTECTED WITH RESIST WILL REMAIN RAISED, EXPOSED AREAS WILL BE RECESSED.

Things you will need:

Nitric acid
Etch-resist film and thinner
Safety glasses
Protective gloves
Pyrex container
Plastic tongs
Feather
Cloth
Iron
Craft knife
Fibre-tipped pen
Bristle brush
Dishwashing liquid
Etch-resist paint and paintbrush
Etch-resist pen

ETCHING THE METAL

The solutions used for etching metals vary: for silver, copper, gilding metal and brass you should use one part nitric acid to three parts water; for steel use one part nitric acid to six parts water. Always add acid to water, not water to acid, and mix together wearing safety goggles and protective gloves.

1 Wearing safety glasses and protective gloves, slowly add nitric acid to water in a Pyrex container in the correct ratio for the metal you are etching. Using plastic tongs, gently lower the metal sheet or form into the etch solution. Ensure that the metal is immersed completely to achieve an evenly etched surface.

2 Occasionally brush the surface with a feather to help distribute the etch solution. Check the depth of the etched area after about five minutes. If it is not deep enough, return the metal to the solution for a further five minutes. Repeat the process until the required depth is achieved.

3 Use the plastic tongs to remove the metal from the etch solution and rinse thoroughly in cold water. Remove the etch resist according to the manufacturer's instructions. This is normally done with a thinner.

4 Use a cloth to rub away the etch resist and reveal the etched pattern.

USING ETCH-RESIST FILM

This specialist resist film is ironed on and needs to have high-contrast black and white images photocopied or laser-printed onto it. It can be used only on flat sheet metal. Photocopy or print your design onto the resist film according to the manufacturer's instructions.

> **TIP**
>
> **Masking out completely with resist can be difficult. You will also find that the edges of the sheet you are working on may be partially etched, so consider etching your pattern on a sheet slightly larger than the size required, so the excess material can be cut away after etching.**

1 Degrease the sheet as in the etch-resist paint instructions. Place the film emulsion-side down against the clean metal sheet on a surface suitable for ironing. Transfer the image to the sheet by dry ironing it from the centre outwards, using an iron set for 'cotton'.

2 Using a circular motion, iron the film from the edges towards the centre. The image should appear progressively more pronounced through the film. Iron until the image appears dense black rather than blue. Leave to cool. Release and peel away, using the craft knife.

USING ETCH-RESIST PAINT OR PEN

Etch resists can be painted on as a liquid stop-out varnish or drawn on using a fibre-tipped pen containing a resist ink.

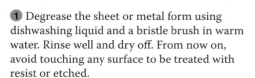

1 Degrease the sheet or metal form using dishwashing liquid and a bristle brush in warm water. Rinse well and dry off. From now on, avoid touching any surface to be treated with resist or etched.

2 Paint a pattern onto the surface of the metal using a clean paintbrush. If the resist is too thick it can be thinned, so check the manufacturer's instructions before use. Leave to dry according to the instructions.

3 Another way to draw a pattern onto the metal surface is by using an etch-resist pen. You need to make sure the ink is not too thin, as this may prevent it from resisting the etch solution adequately.

Enamelling

ENAMELLING IS THE ART OF FUSING GLASS TO METAL. THE PROCESS IMPARTS A WHOLE NEW DIMENSION TO JEWELLERY BECAUSE IT IS POSSIBLE TO ADD SO MUCH VARIED COLOUR. APART FROM A KILN AND THE ENAMELS THEMSELVES, YOU WILL NOT NEED MUCH EXTRA EQUIPMENT.

TYPES OF ENAMELLING

Work that is to be enamelled must be very carefully constructed because it has to undergo extremely high temperatures in a kiln. There are several different methods of enamelling, all of which depend on how the silver has been worked in order to receive the enamel. The simplest method is simply to apply enamel directly onto the silver. It can be taken right up to the edge, or a little border of silver can be left. It should be counter-enamelled, and depth of colour is added with every additional layer of enamel. It does not usually need stoning down.

The champlevé process, from the French for 'raised field', lays the enamel in etched-out or engraved-out areas of silver and 'raises' or builds it up until it reaches the same height as the remaining silver.

The cloissonné method, from the French for 'partitioned', describes how thin silver or gold wires called cloisonné wires are laid onto or into the silver to form a pattern or picture. The cells are filled with different coloured enamels.

The baisse-taille or 'deep cut' technique can be used with champlevé or when enamelling straight onto the silver. The background silver is engraved or chased to show an outline or pattern beneath the transparent enamel.

Pliqué à jour enamel is said to resemble a stained-glass window. The enamels are suspended between silver 'walls' and the piece is fired without any backing so that the light can shine through both sides.

Painted enamels are usually applied onto a slightly domed surface, which has been enamelled with white before painting. The very finely ground painting enamels are mixed to a workable paste with lavender oil or water on a flat glass sheet and applied with a brush.

The grissaille technique is similar to painting enamels, but it uses only black and white.

FINDINGS

Whenever enamelling a piece of jewellery, it is best to make sure all the findings are in place before you start, in order to avoid cracking or discoloration of the enamel. Make sure you take care to use findings that will be safe in the kiln. If you prefer to solder after enamelling, you can do so with easy solder in the kiln, or after firing on a soldering block, but take care to protect the enamel. You will find more information on findings, including instructions on how to make some of them in the Basic Techniques section of the book (*see pages 52–57*).

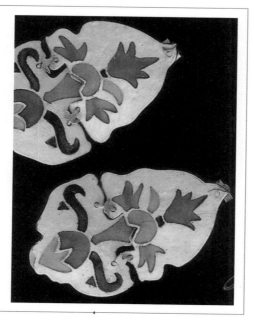

Things you will need:

Assortment of transparent, opaque and translucent enamels

Basic tool kit (*see pages 14–15*)

Soldering and pickling equipment (*see pages 22–23*)

Glass brush

Mortar and pestle

Palette

Paintbrush

Mica

Long fork

Kiln

Carborundum stone

Wet and dry papers

Below A selection of coloured transparent enamels in lump or 'Frit' form, together with an opaque white enamel.

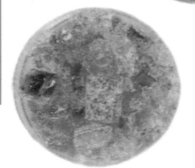

TIP

You should try to set aside a special area in your workshop for enamelling, as far away from your polisher as possible.

PREPARING THE ENAMELS

Enamels are supplied in lump or powder form. Both need grinding and washing before they are placed into or onto the silver.

PREPARING THE SILVER

Silver needs to be very clean and free from grease for the enamel to adhere well.

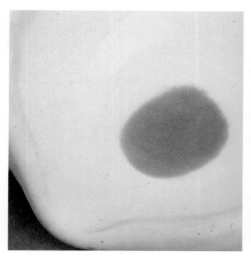

1 Place the enamel in the mortar and pestle, add water and grind until it is very fine. Swill away the water and add fresh water, which is swirled around and thrown away.

2 Repeat this process until the water is absolutely clear, then give the enamels a final rinse with distilled water. Note that powdered enamels do not need so much grinding as they are already fairly fine but the washing should be just as scrupulous. After grinding, keep the enamels under water to stop dust and dirt from getting into them. Any dirt that gets fired into enamel will show up as an ugly mark.

1 Pierce your design or make your shape on the silver, anneal, pickle and rinse.

2 Make sure you wash the silver very thoroughly under running water and brush the whole surface with a glass brush. You should aim to reach a stage where the water will the stay on the surface of the silver without running off to form little globules.

DOING A TEST FIRING

Always fire a test piece first. It is a good idea to keep the results of each of your samples as a reference.

1 Most enamels will fuse at temperatures of 790–890°C (1450–1650°F). The kiln should be up to temperature before you begin firing. If you have no temperature gauge on your kiln, a good red heat will generally be sufficient to fire painted enamels and possibly some reds. A cherry red will fire most fluxes, many transparent enamels, and opaque and opalescent enamels. A bright orange, being very hot, will fire some hard transparent enamels and overfire others.

2 Use a piece of properly prepared silver, and try firing your selected colours at different temperatures. Watch to see how and when each one fires and, from the results, work out the order of firing the piece. Fire colours directly onto silver and on top of a clear flux, and onto silver and gold foil to assess whether you need to use flux on your piece.

APPLYING ENAMEL

It is better to add five thin layers of enamel than two thick layers, because it is easy to trap air in thick enamel, which results in pits in the surface that can be difficult to fill. If this does happen, drill out the pit completely and fill the hole with two or three new layers of enamel. When enamel is overfired, it looks rather mottled and develops black lines around the edge; transparent enamels can look dull and lifeless. This can sometimes be rectified by refiring at a lower heat, but overfiring and underfiring should be avoided by good testing methods.

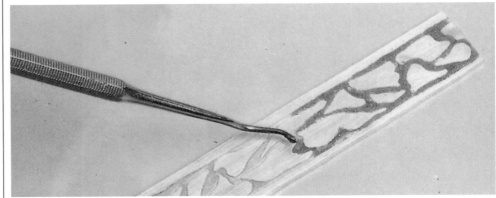

1 After all your enamels are ground and washed, place them wet into a palette ready for use. Use either the end of a quill, a small rubber spatula or a paintbrush to place a thin layer of flux or enamel on your piece. If necessary, suck up excess water with the edge of a clean tissue. This is helpful when you are laying one colour close to another. Lay the enamel on a sheet of mica, or use a support and place it on a steel mesh tray. Allow it to dry either on top of the kiln or nearby.

2 When the enamel is completely dry, place the mesh tray on a long fork, and put it in the centre of the kiln. At first, the piece will darken as the metal oxidises, then the enamel will start to resemble orange peel, then suddenly it will begin to shine. The enamel can now be removed from the kiln and left to cool once more. If it is cooled too quickly, however, it may crack. Repeat this process until the height of the enamel is the same as the cloisonné or the silver surrounds.

FINISHING

When the enamel is just higher than the surface of the silver, it should be ground down ready for finishing, using a carborundum stone.

1 Hold the work under running water and grind until the enamel is level. Any depressions can be filled up, fired and then ground down again.

2 After the carborundum stone, use wet and dry papers to give a finer finish to both the enamel and the silver. Then refire the piece at a slightly higher temperature and for a shorter time to restore the shiny surface. Surfaces can be left matt by omitting the final firing.

3 Once the final firing has been carried out, the work can be polished as for silver (*see pages 42–43*), but some enamels absorb dark polish, so it is always wise to try the polish on the test piece to see if your enamel is suitable. Pumice paste will give a good finish to enamels. Silver will be oxidised after enamelling, and although it is usually possible to pickle the piece to get rid of it, some enamels are sensitive to acid, so once again experiment with a test piece first.

COUNTER-ENAMELLING

Because enamel expands and contracts at a different rate from silver, it is often necessary to counter-enamel the back of your piece to avoid chipping and cracking on the front. If a piece is not counter-enamelled, it tends to bend backwards, although this can be partly avoided by using a thicker-gauge silver. Counter-enamelling can be done at the same time as the first firing as long as you support the work without anything touching the enamel.

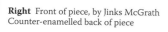
Right Front of piece, by Jinks McGrath
Counter-enamelled back of piece

Working with gold

GOLD IS A BEAUTIFUL METAL TO WORK WITH. IT HAS A SPECIAL QUALITY AND REALLY COMES ALIVE AS IT IS BENT, STRETCHED AND MOULDED INTO SHAPE. GOLDS ABOVE 14 CARAT ARE BOTH MALLEABLE AND RESILIENT, AND THE QUALITY OF COLOUR MAKES THEM UNSURPASSABLE.

Pure gold, like pure silver, is generally too soft to use for any practical purpose in jewellery, and in order to make gold more workable, other metals are alloyed with it. The proportions of these other metals determine the carat, the colour, the melting point and the hardness of gold. Pure gold is 24 carat. Other workable golds are 22 carat, 18 carat, 14 carat and, in Britain, 9 carat. In general, yellow gold is the easiest to work. White gold, if it is not kept properly annealed while it is being worked, tends to become brittle. Green gold is usually fairly soft, and red gold needs to be kept reasonably soft for working. Gold of 10 carat and below is less malleable and does not have such good colour quality as higher carats.

TYPES OF GOLD

Gold can be:

Yellow – alloyed with silver/copper/zinc.

Green – alloyed with silver/copper

White –alloyed with silver/platinum/palladium/nickel/zinc

Red – alloyed with copper

Given as a proportion of 24 carats, each figure represents the ratio of gold to alloy. So 24 carat is pure gold, while 10 carat is 10 parts gold to 14 parts alloy, and so on.

| 24 carat |
| 22 carat |
| 18 carat |
| 14 carat |
| 10 carat |
| 9 carat |

Left Assorted cufflinks set in 18-carat yellow gold. Gerald Benny

ANNEALING

Yellow and green golds should be heated to dull red and either quenched hot or allowed to air-cool. Red gold is also heated to dull red, but it is quenched while it is hot to avoid hardening. White gold is heated to cherry red – a little higher than the others – but is left to cool for a while before quenching, or it can be left to air-cool (*see also Annealing, page 37*).

FLUXING

A flux of borax will sometimes burn out before gold solder flows, and more suitable fluxes, with a longer life at high temperatures, are used for gold. These are available in powder form and are mixed with water to form a creamy paste. Gold joints are fluxed in the same way as silver (*see page 44*).

Above Gold bracelet with emerald, amethyst and topaz. Simon Benny.

Left Handmade chain in 18-carat gold with diamonds. Alexandra Coppen.

TIP

Store different carat golds separately, and when you are ordering gold, ask the suppliers for their technical information sheets, which will give all the information about each type of gold – the melting, annealing and soldering temperatures, for example (*see also pages 245–246*), and also the correct time to quench each one and the best fluxes to use.

SOLDERING

Gold solders come in small, thin rectangles, which are printed with the carat, whether they are hard, medium or easy. The same carat and colour solder should be used as the carat and colour of the gold. Work through the solders as for silver (*see pages 22–23*). When you are soldering gold, the areas to be joined should be clean, grease-free and lined up exactly. Gold solder does not run in the same way as silver, and only very small paillons should be used. After soldering, check with a loupe glass to see if the gap is completely filled. If it is not, add a tiny sliver of gold and solder again. Take care with the flame: gold gives little colour warning when it is getting too hot.

PICKLING

Gold can be pickled in the same sulphuric acid solution as silver (*see page 46*), although it can pick up a rather silvery hue. A different pickle, of 8 parts water to 1 part nitric acid, can be used for gold instead.

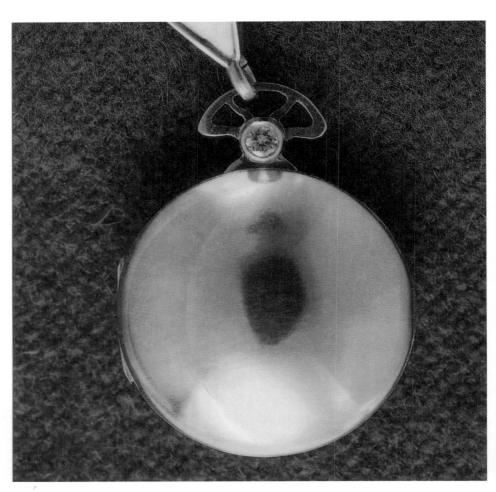

Above This 18-carat gold locket is made from red, white and yellow golds and set with a diamond. Jinks McGrath

Left Silver locket with gold inlay. Jinks McGrath.

TIP

Take great care not to leave any deposits of lead, brass or aluminium on gold work. Avoid using a file or saw blade which has been used on these metals, and make sure that punches and hammer heads are clean before you use them on gold. If they are heated together with gold, deposits of these metals will collapse and burn holes in the surface of the gold – a calamity!

ENAMELLING

Special gold alloys for enamelling come in 18 carat, 14 carat and occasionally in 9 carat. However, the best gold for enamelling is 24 carat (very soft) or yellow 18 carat. It is possible to enamel 24 carat and set it into an 18 carat setting. Gold foil is also used. The foil is 23.5 carat and gives a wonderful base for transparent colours. To cut foil to fit a pattern, draw the outline on the paper and cut through all three layers. Lift the foil with tweezers or a paintbrush with a dab of enamelling and position it on the base coat of the enamel. Use a pin to prick little holes in the foil so that air bubbles are not trapped, and fire it into place. Enamel over the top. (*See pages 124–129.*)

ETCHING

To etch gold of 18 carats and lower, use one of the following solutions:

Hydrochloric acid	2 parts
Nitric acid	1 part
Water	10 parts

or:

Nitric acid	1 part
Hydrochloric acid	3 parts
Iron perchloride	1 part

PIERCING AND FILING

Gold can be pierced and filed in much the same way as silver (*see pages 30–31 and 38–39*). Because it is such an expensive metal, practise any bending with copper or silver first, and if necessary make a jig, to guarantee that the first bend of the gold is the right one. When you are making a larger piece, remember that gold weighs more than silver, so make sure that your proposed size is appropriate. Larger, heavily contoured pieces can be cast – it will be less expensive and there will be less waste.

SETTING STONES

Collets and bezels can generally be thinner than their silver counterparts (*see pages 116–121*). White 18-carat gold is often used for setting precious stones because it remains hard even if it is thin. Avoid using gold which is too thick for the setting, because it will be hard to coax down onto the stone.

Above Gold and silver brooch. Pat McAnally.

Advanced Projects

Having practised the basic techniques and made several of the accompanying projects, you will doubtless be keen to develop your jewellery-making skills one stage further. Ranging from intriguing fold-formed earrings to a jewel-like enamelled pendant, the ten projects in this section of the book make wide-ranging use of the advanced techniques demonstrated on the previous pages. Here you'll find intricate designs for a bracelet using twisted silver wire, a delicate, beaded filigree necklace and an elegant fretwork hair ornament. A couple of the projects employ traditional stone-setting techniques, while others focus on careful doming and forging processes to manipulate sheet and rod metal to striking effect.

Fold-formed earrings

FOLD-FORMING INVOLVES MINIMAL EQUIPMENT AND JUST A FEW SKILLS, BUT THE RESULTS ARE BOTH VISUALLY APPEALING AND TECHNICALLY INTRIGUING. IT IS AN IDEAL TECHNIQUE FOR ELABORATE EARRINGS, AS FORMS CAN BE MADE THAT ARE QUITE LARGE YET STILL LIGHT.

Earring hoops can be bought, but they are also easily made. Bought findings can cheapen the overall look of a pair of earrings, but, with a little time spent with wire, pliers and a mandrel, they can be made to look individual.

Things you will need:

60x20mm (2⅜x1³⁄₁₆in) piece of 0.4-mm (¹⁄₆₄-in) thick sheet silver

0.9-mm (12-gauge) silver wire

Basic tool kit (*see pages 14–15*)

20mm (1³⁄₁₆in) diameter mandrel

Soldering and pickling equipment (*see pages 22–23*)

Steel block

Dividers

Blunt knife

Scriber

Steel ruler

Tin snips

Creasing hammer

Polishing equipment (*see pages 42–43*)

MAKING THE EAR HOOPS

1 Coil 0.9-mm (12-gauge) wire around the mandrel to make a hoop. Don't cut the wire too short, but test the fit of the hoop and the mandrel and adjust if necessary. Remove the hoop from the mandrel and use round-nosed pliers to turn a closed loop on one end.

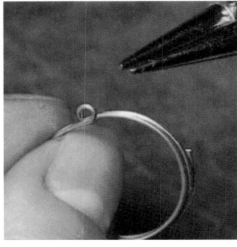

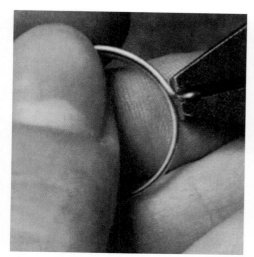

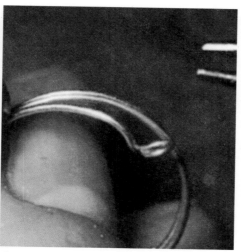

④ Cut the hoop off the coil beyond the loop so that the wire can be secured through the loop. File the end to be passed through the ear so there is no sharp point or edge. Hammer on a steel block with a planishing hammer to strengthen the hook. Repeat steps 1–3 to make a second hook.

② Use a pair of flat-nosed pliers to turn the loop through 90°.

③ Use round-nosed pliers to make a kink at the base of the loop to lower it, so that when the end is cut, it can be secured through it.

MAKING THE SEMI-CIRCLES

① Anneal, pickle and rinse the strip of sheet silver. Pierce the sheet in half to make two 30x20mm (1³⁄₁₆x¹³⁄₁₆in) pieces. Mark a line down the centre of each sheet using dividers set to 15mm (⁹⁄₁₆in). Place one of the sheets in a bench vice with fibre grips so that the line is level with the top of the jaw of the vice. Bend the sheet at the point of the marked line by levering it over the vice jaw by hand. Hammer the fold with a nylon mallet to define it.

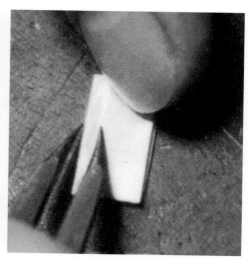

② Remove the metal from the vice and complete the fold by hand. Flatten the form by hammering with a mallet over a steel block.

③ Using dividers, mark a line on the flattened metal, approximately 3mm (⅛in) from the folded edge.

④ Place the sheet in the vice so the new scribed line is level with the jaw, then prise the folded sheet open using a blunt knife.

⑤ Lever the two sides of the sheet over the vice jaws by hand.

⑥ Hammer the sheet with a mallet to define the folds.

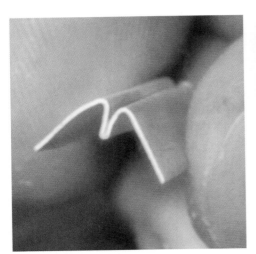

⑦ Anneal and pickle. Rinse again, then complete the fold by hand.

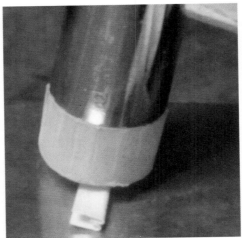

⑧ Flatten by hammering with a mallet over a steel block.

⑨ Using a scriber and steel ruler, mark a tapered line on one side of the folded form. Start just above the fold at one end and end 4mm (⁵⁄₃₂in) from the open edge at the other.

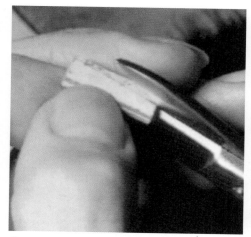

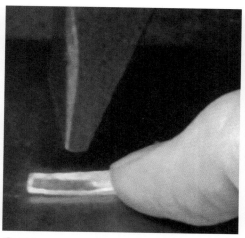

10 Cut along the marked line using tin snips. Anneal, pickle, rinse and dry thoroughly.

11 Using a creasing hammer on a steel block, forge along the folded edge beginning at the narrow end of the form. Hold the hammer face level with the work, at 90° to the fold.

12 Hammer all along the folded edge so that the sheet curves into a semi-circle. Anneal, pickle, rinse and dry the form thoroughly whenever it becomes hard to hammer.

ASSEMBLING THE EARRINGS

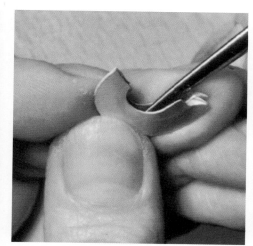

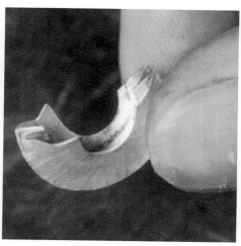

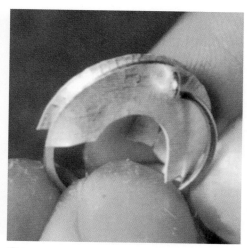

13 Carefully prise the centre fold and the sides at one end of the form open using a blunt knife. Continue prising the form open along the rest of the centre line.

14 Prise the form open by hand until it is the shape required. Repeat steps 4–15 with the second strip of sheet, this time turning the folded piece over before forging.

1 Use a pendant motor with mops and polishing compounds to polish the forms. Assemble the forms and hoops, as shown.

Spiral filigree necklace

THIS DELICATE NECKLACE IS MADE FROM THREE DIFFERENT SILVER FILIGREE PANELS AND IS INTERSPERSED WITH FACETED GLASS BEADS IN ASSORTED SIZES AND COLOURS. THE FINISHED NECKLACE SIMPLY SLIPS OVER THE HEAD WHEN WORN, SO NO CLASP AND CATCH IS REQUIRED.

Filigree jewellery is a delicate kind of jewel work made with twisted threads usually of gold and silver of the same curving motifs. It reached the height of its popularity during the Art Deco period of the 1920s and 1930s when it was made with bright colours and straight lines, its delicate detail evoking romance, love and affection. There are intricate examples of this kind of jewellery in the great museum collections of the world; in the Louvre in Paris and the Victoria and Albert Museum in London. This design has been taken from the earlier Edwardian era with its intricate links, light colours and flowing lines. Once the technique has been mastered, have a go at designing your own necklace, perhaps in the Art Deco style.

Things you will need:

120cm (48in) of 0.8-mm (12-gauge) silver wire

30 closed silver jump rings (*see page 50*)

10 round solid silver balls, 1.5mm (³⁄₄in) diameter

5 flat-bottomed solid silver balls 3mm (⅛in) diameter

4.6m (15ft) of 0.5-mm (7-gauge) silver wire

30 small faceted beads

20 large faceted beads

Basic tool kit (*see pages 14–15*)

Flatplate

Planishing hammer

Dividers

Steel ruler

Top cutters

Charcoal block

Soldering and pickling equipment (*see pages 22–23*)

Polishing equipment (*see pages 42–43*)

MAKING THE A PANELS

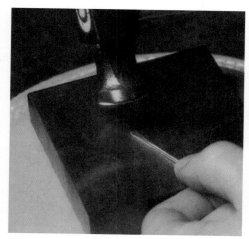

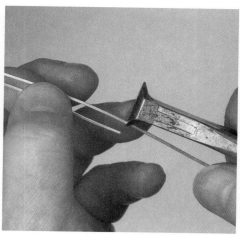

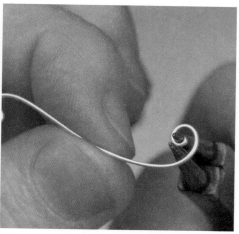

1 For the large (A) panels, cut a length of 75cm (30in) of the 0.8-mm (12-gauge) silver wire and flatten it by hammering it on a flatplate with a planishing hammer. Anneal the wire to soften it.

2 Using dividers and a steel ruler, measure and cut five sets of each of these lengths of the 0.8-mm (12-gauge) silver wire: one x 55mm (2⅛in), one x 37mm (1½in), two x 25mm (1in). Cut the lengths with top cutters.

3 Bend the two longer strips of wire into S-shaped spirals. Hold one end of the wire firmly in a pair of round-nosed pliers, and coil the long end gently around to make a spiral.

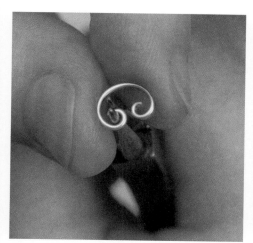

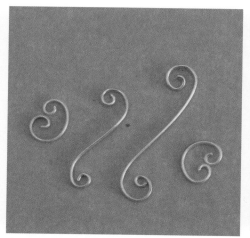

4 Bend the smallest strips of wire into heart-shaped spirals by curling each end in towards each other.

5 Once all the wires have been bent as in steps 3 and 4, you should have a set resembling the above. Place the wires on a charcoal block.

6 Assemble as shown. Paint borax where the wires touch. Solder, pickle and polish. Repeat to make five A panels.

MAKING THE B PANELS

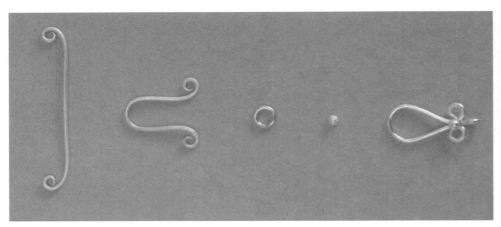

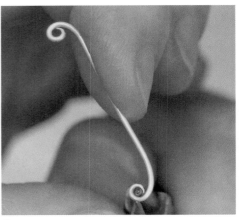

1 Using the remaining 0.8-mm (12-gauge) silver wire, cut enough wire for ten B panels. Each panel is made from one 40-mm (2½-in) strip of the wire, one closed jump ring and one small round solid ball. It is a good idea to anneal the wire to soften it before cutting it to length. Now file a neat taper on each end of the ten wire strips.

2 Holding one end of a wire strip with round-nosed pliers, wrap the rest of the wire around to create a small curl. Repeat at the other end; the curls should face in the same direction. Repeat for the remaining nine strips.

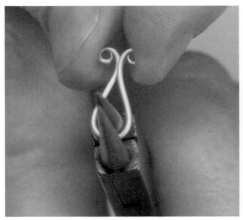

3 Holding each wire strip with the round-nosed pliers, ease the ends together. Solder the seam where the two ends meet and solder a tiny ball on top.

4 Holding the piece upside-down with the spring tweezers, solder on the jump ring with the seam pointing in towards the ball. Make nine more panels, then pickle and polish.

MAKING THE C PANELS

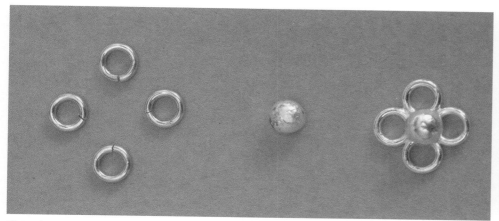

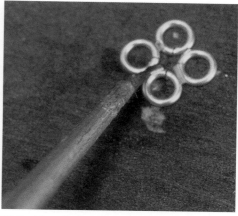

1 Each C panel is made from four closed jump rings and one flat-bottomed ball. You will make five of these C panels in total, each with the jump rings radiating out from the silver ball to make a symmetrical floral shape. Assemble the parts you need, as shown.

2 Position the jump rings in groups of four with the seams all facing inwards. Paint a thin line of borax where they touch and position a tiny paillon of hard solder at each seam.

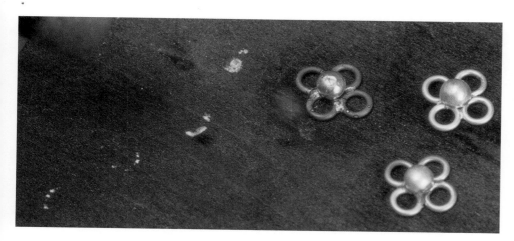

3 Solder all the seams with a gentle flame, nudging the rings together with fine tweezers if they move apart. Solder the ball in the middle of each panel, flat side down, with easy solder. Pickle and polish each piece.

4 Next, prepare the wire for joining the parts together. Snip the 0.5-mm (7-gauge) silver wire into 8cm (3in) lengths, in the same way as in step 2 on page 141. Do not anneal the wire.

ASSEMBLING THE NECKLACE

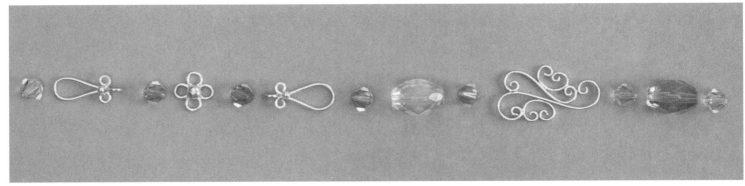

1 Lay the parts out in your chosen sequence on a piece of paper. Here, it is: small bead, B panel, small bead, C panel, small bead, B panel, small bead, large bead, small bead, A panel, small bead, large bead, small bead. Repeat the sequence from the beginning.

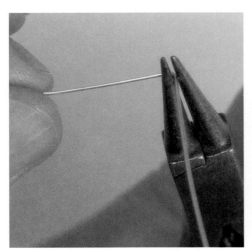

2 Using the round-nosed pliers, make a right-angled bend about 3cm (1in) from the end of one of the strips of joining wire. Then fold the wire firmly over the edge of the pliers with your finger.

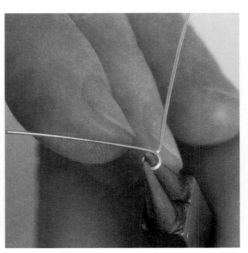

3 Now hold the wire in the pliers slightly to one side of the bend, and use your other hand to cross the shorter end of the wire over the longer end to form a loop.

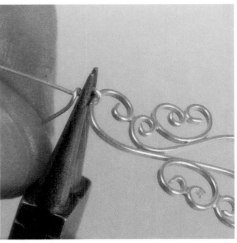

4 Slip the first panel in the sequence onto the loop. Hold the loop gently with the pliers and twist the short end of the wire around the long end a couple of times. Snip off the remaining short end of the wire.

5 Thread the first bead onto the wire. Make a loop a little way from the bead by holding the wire in the round-nosed pliers and bending it at a right angle. Hold the wire in the pliers just past the right-angled bend and lever the other end around to form a loop.

6 If the next piece in the sequence is another bead, close the loop by twisting the long end of the wire a few times around the short end, then cut off the excess wire with top cutters.

7 When adding the next bead, make a loop in a new strip of wire as in steps 2 and 3, and thread it onto the chain. Thread on the next bead. Holding the loop in the round-nosed pliers, wrap the end of the wire around itself towards the bead. Snip off the excess wire.

8 Make a loop at the other end of the bead as before. If the next piece on is a bead, close the loop as in step 5. If it is a panel, slip the panel onto the loop before closing it.

9 Continue adding pieces in the correct sequence. Finish by joining the last piece of the necklace to the first piece.

Hair ornament

THIS PRETTY HAIR ORNAMENT IS MADE FROM 0.75-MM (20-GAUGE) SHEET SILVER, WHICH MAKES IT LIGHT ENOUGH TO STAY IN THE HAIR WHEN WORN, BUT HEAVY AND DURABLE ENOUGH NOT TO BEND WHEN IT IS IN USE. THE TWO HOLES FOR THE PIN ARE INTEGRAL TO THE DECORATIVE DESIGN.

This piece uses fretwork techniques described on *pages 108–109* to pierce out a design from sheet silver. The decorative pattern is a relatively simple and geometric one, and is symmetrical to the horizontal axis. Once you become adept at using the piercing saw, you can apply designs of your own in the same way.

Things you will need:

90x50mm (3½x2in) of 0.75-mm (20-gauge) sheet silver

30x15mm (1¼x⅝in) of 1.1-mm (14-gauge) sheet silver

90mm (3½in) of 2.5-mm (10-gauge) silver wire

Templates

Basic tool kit (*see pages 14–15*)

Scriber

Sandbag or lead block

Doming equipment (*see pages 104–105*)

Wet and dry papers

Soldering and pickling equipment (*see pages 22–23*)

Drilling equipment (*see pages 32–33*)

Anvil

TEMPLATES

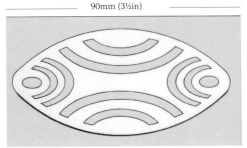

90mm (3½in)

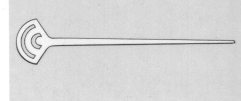

Enlarge pin template so the head fits your forged metal.

PREPARING THE SILVER

1 Draw or scribe the outside outline of the hairpiece onto your 0.75-mm (20-gauge) silver sheet and pierce out. Anneal, pickle and dry. Use a wooden hammer or dome to shape the piece on a sandbag or lead block.

2 Dome the piece by placing it on the doming stake and shaping it downwards all around with a wooden mallet. Note that, if you try to dome, shape or bend the silver after piercing, the corners will bend differently and the edges will tend to rise.

TRANSFERRING THE DESIGN

1 Use the template to transfer the design to the shaped piece and pierce it out from the inside. Clean all edges with needle files and wet and dry papers.

2 Use an oval needle file to flatten the entrance and exit areas to make them ready to accept the pin. Polish and finish.

MAKING THE PIN

1 Take the 1.1-mm (14-gauge) piece of silver and place flux and paillons of hard solder over the top side. Run the solder on it. Pickle the piece, rinse and dry.

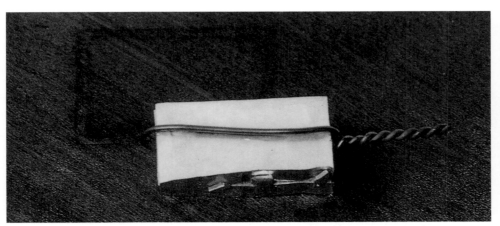

2 File the solder flat and cut the piece in half. Now flux the soldered sides, place them together and hold in place with binding wire.

Place a little hard solder around the outside edges. Solder it all together. Pickle and dry. File one edge straight.

3 Hold the piece in the vice and drill a hole in the centre of the straight edge, beginning with a 1-mm drill bit and finishing with a drill that just allows the 2.5-mm (10-gauge) wire to fit snugly in. Use easy solder to solder the wire into the silver head to make the pin.

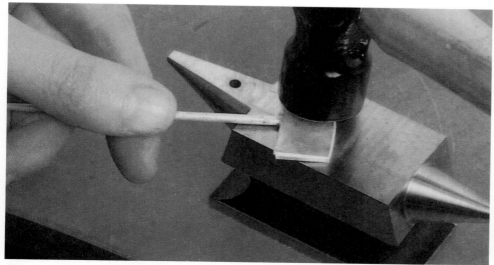

4 Forge out the silver head on the anvil, using a heavy flat-faced hammer. Continue until it is large enough for the pattern on the template to fit and until it is about the same thickness as the pin. It will need annealing once or twice during forging to keep it soft enough to work.

5 Now transfer the pattern to the head. Pierce out the inside areas first and then the outline. File both sides smooth.

6 Shape the pin by filing and then hammering it to a point. Roll the pin along the anvil while you gently hammer to harden it. File the edges, clean the whole pin with wet and dry papers and finally polish.

Lapis lazuli ring

LAPIS LAZULI IS A RICH MID-BLUE GEMSTONE WITH OPAQUE QUALITIES THAT MAKE IT IDEAL FOR A RUB-OVER SETTING LIKE THIS ONE. THE PRETTY, OVAL STONE HAS BEEN HIGHLY POLISHED AND HAS FLECKS OF BRIGHT YELLOW PYRITE SHIMMERING ON THE SURFACE.

This ring is made using the instructions for stone-setting on *pages 116–121*. Round and oval stones are easiest to make such a setting for, but you could also use an irregularly shaped stone, as long as it has smooth surfaces. You simply make a bezel to fit the shape of the stone, solder the bezel to a base and cut away as much of the base as possible to leave just enough for the stone to be supported.

Things you will need:

80x20mm (3¼x¾in) of 1.2-mm (16-gauge) sheet silver

Ring template

Basic tool kit (*see pages 14–15*)

Ring gauge or sizers

Mandrel

Ruler

Soldering and pickling equipment (*see pages 22–23*)

40x5mm (1½x¼in) of bearer wire

14x10mm (½x⅖in) piece of lapis lazuli

Polishing equipment (*see pages 42–43*)

Stone-setting equipment (*see pages 116–121*)

Burnisher or punch and hammer

Wet and dry papers

TEMPLATE

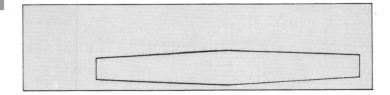

MAKING THE RING SHANK

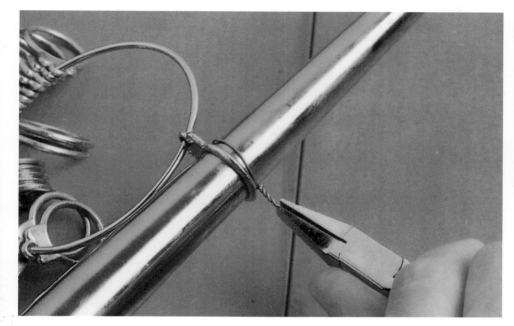

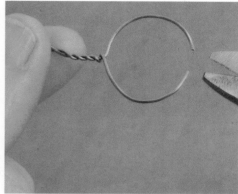

1 Measure the finger with ring sizers: this example is size 0. Slide your ring sizer over the mandrel. Cut a length of binding wire, wrap it around the mandrel next to the ring sizer, and twist it firmly.

2 Take the wire off the mandrel, make a cut in it and straighten it out.

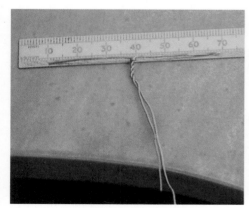

3 Measure the length of the binding wire against your ruler. Try to be as accurate as you possibly can.

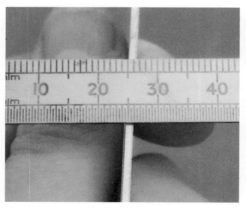

4 Add to the length of the wire 1½ times the thickness of the silver you are going to use for the ring shank.

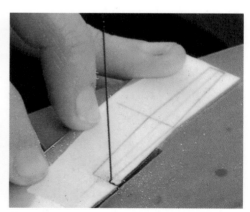

5 Trace the pattern for the ring shank using the template, adjust the length to fit, and transfer the design to the silver. Pierce it out.

SHAPING THE RING SHANK

1 File off the square edges on both the inside and outside of the ring shank. Use a flat file to begin with, and then move on to an oval, file. Leave both of the ends flat.

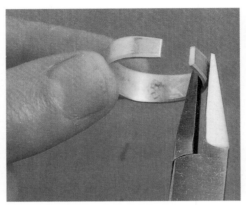

2 Anneal, pickle, rinse and dry the silver. Bend the ends of the shank and fit them closely together, although it is not necessary for the ring to be round at this stage.

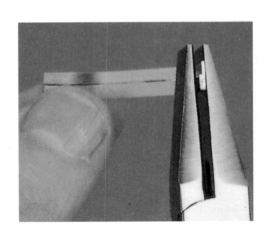

3 Flux the joint and solder with hard solder. Pickle, rinse and dry.

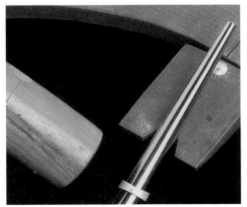

4 File off any excess solder from the inside of the ring. Make the ring round on the mandrel and file off excess solder from the outside.

MAKING THE SETTING

1 The bezel must be made to fit both the stone and the curve of the ring. Calculate the length of bearer wire required for the bezel, using the formula on *page 116*.

2 Cut off the required length of wire. Anneal, pickle, rinse and dry. Bend up the ends to fit, flux the joint and solder using hard solder. Pickle, rinse and dry. Make the setting oval. Check that the stone fits and make any necessary adjustments.

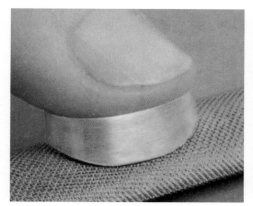

3 Use an oval file to file the base of the setting (where the wire is thickest) to fit the curve of the ring shank, until it sits snugly on top.

4 Make sure the ring and setting are clean, flux the bottom of the setting, and secure it to the ring with binding wire. Solder the two together with easy solder. Pickle and rinse. Clean the ring with pumice paste.

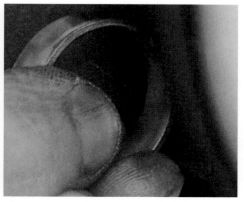

5 File away any excess solder with a needle file, then work down through grades of wet and dry papers. Polish the ring, first with tripoli, then with Hyfin. Polish the inside of the ring by hand or on a ring cone. Hold the ring in both hands while you polish it.

SETTING THE STONE

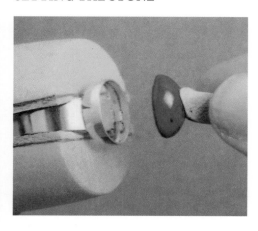

1 Hold the shank of the ring in a ring clamp or in the safe jaws of the vice. Place the stone in the setting.

2 Use the burnisher to push down on the two longer ends and then at the two sides. Continue rubbing all around the setting until it rests snugly over the stone. If you find that the silver is too hard to push over with a burnisher, use a punch and hammer in the same sequence. Clean the setting and then polish the whole ring with jeweller's rouge, taking care not to get polish on the stone.

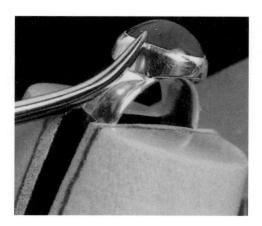

Wax-carved ring

WAX CARVING IS A FUN, RELATIVELY FAST WAY TO ACHIEVE STRONG SCULPTURAL SHAPES THAT CANNOT BE CREATED FROM SHEET METAL. THIS RING IS FIRST CARVED FROM A BLOCK OF WAX, AND THEN CAST BY A PROFESSIONAL IN YOUR CHOSEN METAL, READY TO BE FILED AND POLISHED BY YOU.

The design for this ring is simple, having a slightly greater depth at the back of the ring, where the piece meets the palm, than at the front, where the ring stands proud of the finger.

It is a traditional design that has been used for many centuries.

The example shown here has been gently textured and polished, although there are various ways in which to finish the piece, as described on *page 155*. You could make the same ring using aluminium, platinum, silver or gold, the choice is yours.

Things you will need:

4cm (1½in) square of 1cm (⅜in) deep carving wax in blue or green

Basic tool kit (*see pages 14–15*)

Ring gauge

Ruler

Dividers

Hacksaw

Scriber

Spiral saw blade for your piercing saw

Old coarse hand files and needle files

Sanding equipment (*see pages 40–41*)

Polishing equipment (*see pages 42–43*)

Glass brush and pumice powder (optional)

Ball-end hammer

MEASURING THE FINGER

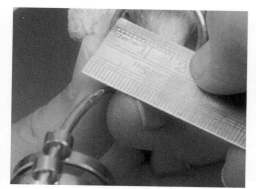

1 Measure the ring finger using your ring gauge; choose one size larger than the finger, as the wax shrinks slightly when cast. Measure the diameter of the chosen ring size with a ruler. Halve this amount to calculate the radius and set your dividers to this figure.

2 With a ruler and a scriber, draw a horizontal and vertical line across the centre of the circle, on both the front and back of the wax block. Open the dividers another 3mm (⅛in) and draw an arc across each side of the horizontal line. Repeat on the back of the block. These arcs mark the sides of the ring.

3 Open the dividers another 4mm (⁵⁄₃₂in) and draw an arc across the remaining end of the vertical line. Do the same on the back of the block. This arc marks the top of the ring. Draw smooth curved lines between the arcs to create the outline of the ring, as shown on the right.

PREPARING THE WAX

1 If you are starting with a large block of wax, cut it to the required dimensions using a wax blade in your hacksaw. Then use a coarse flat file to even out each face of the block, so that you have a smooth surface with square edges and straight sides.

RING OUTLINE

SHAPING THE RING

1 Thread the wax blade through the drilled hole and saw out the central circle of wax, taking care to keep the blade upright and not to wander across the line. File the inside of the circle with a coarse half-round file. File the circle from both sides to avoid a tapered edge and to maintain the circular shape.

2 Place the ring on the appropriate finger to check the size. Saw around the outline of the ring, keeping well away from the drawn lines as the blade removes a lot of wax.

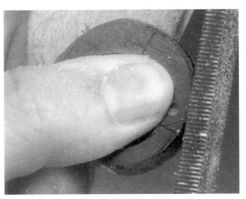

3 File carefully around the outline with a coarse flat file, until you are left with the drawn shape and it is the same on both sides.

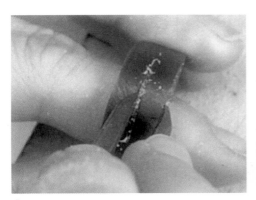

4 Set your dividers to 5mm (³⁄₁₆in), which is half the depth of the wax block. Rest one point of the dividers at the edge of the wax ring and draw a central line around the outside of the ring with the other point.

5 File the front and back of the ring with a broad flat file, until the bottom of the ring is 6mm (¼in) deep and the top of the ring remains 1cm (⅜in) deep. Shape the ring into the profile shown on the right.

RING PROFILE

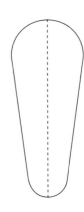

FILING THE RING

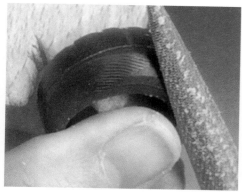

1 File around the edges of the ring at an angle with a coarse, flat file; you are, in effect, filing off the corners. Be sure not to go over the central line. Once you have filed off the corners, continue to develop a more rounded shape. Work on one section at a time to make sure the shape is balanced and symmetrical.

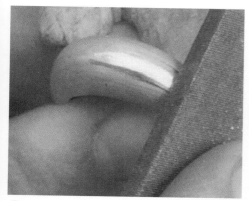

2 File the ring to remove any air bubbles and to achieve a smooth surface. Emery with a buff stick on the inside and outside until it is completely mark-free.

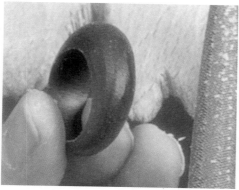

2 Use the edge of an old needle file to smooth the surface of the wax and to make final adjustments to the shape. Emery the surface gently, until it is smooth and scratch-free. Do the same thing on the inside of the ring.

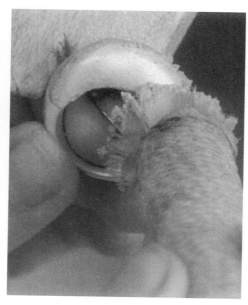

FINISHING THE RING

1 Ask a caster to attach a sprue to the base of the ring (this will create the opening in the mould through which the metal is poured) and to cast the ring. When you have the cast ring, saw off the sprue with a coarse blade.

3 Choose a surface for finishing the ring. You could polish it to a mirror finish or, as shown here, create a matt sheen by rubbing the metal with a glass brush dipped in pumice and water.

Nine-stone bracelet

THIS PRETTY BRACELET USES A DELICATE SUNFLOWER MOTIF AS A MOUNT FOR DIFFERENT-COLOURED CABOCHON STONES. CLEAR STONES ARE PREFERABLE, SINCE THEY ALLOW THE BEAUTIFULLY TEXTURED CENTRE OF THE SUNFLOWER SETTINGS TO SHOW THROUGH WHEN CATCHING THE LIGHT.

Delightfully feminine, this delicate piece evokes Victorian jewellery. If you need to make it longer to fit the wearer's wrist, simply add more rings between the flowers, but take care not to extend the length too much or the design will not work.

MAKING THE FLOWER SETTINGS

1 Trace the outlines above. Transfer the round-petalled sunflower shape onto the thicker silver sheet, and the spiky-petalled sunflower design onto the thinner sheet. You will need nine of each size. If your stones are larger or smaller than those used here, simply adjust the size of the sunflowers accordingly.

Things you will need:

12x2cm (4¾x¾in) of 1.5-mm (³⁄₆₄-in) thick sheet silver

12x2cm (4¾x¾in) of 1-mm (¹⁄₃₂-in) thick sheet silver

9 round flat-back cabochon stones, 5mm (³⁄₁₆in) in diameter

18 closed and 12 open jump rings made from 1mm (¹⁄₃₂in) round silver wire (*see page 50*)

A catch and clasp – a small hook clasp is used here with a catch made from twisted wire

Basic tool kit (*see pages 14–15*)

Sanding equipment (*see pages 40–41*)

Soldering and pickling equipment (*see pages 44–46*)

Polishing equipment (*see pages 42–43*)

Stone-setting equipment (*see pages 116–121*)

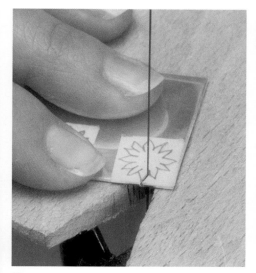

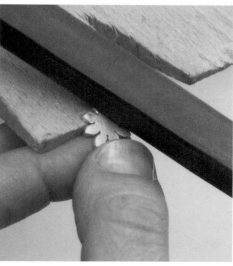

2 Use a jeweller's saw to saw carefully around each flower shape, taking care to saw on the waste side of the line.

3 File the sides of the sunflowers to neaten the outline, then file the edges at an angle to round them slightly.

4 Emery the surface of each flower, both back and front, until both sides are nicely smooth and free of marks.

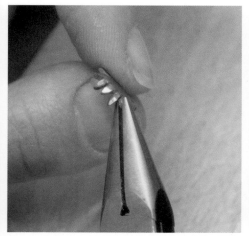

5 Use a pair of round-nosed pliers to grip the end of each petal on the spikier flower shapes and turn them up one by one.

6 Solder the spiky flowers to theirs bases. Heat two small paillons of hard solder onto the base of each spiky flower until they run. Pickle, then file down any bumps of solder until they are almost completely flat. Flux and place each on its base with a tiny pile of solder so that you can be sure to see when it runs. Pickle and clean the flowers under running water.

7 Next, hold a closed jump ring in a pair of flat-nosed pliers and file a flat edge on the side where the seam is. Use a needle file and keep a firm grip of the jump ring as you work.

8 File two small flat edges on each of the sunflowers, on opposite petals. This is where the jump rings will be soldered. Place the flowers on a charcoal block.

9 Add the closed jump rings so that the flat sides of the rings and flowers are touching. Paint a little borax onto each seam, then a paillon of medium solder.

10 Heat the flowers and rings; the flowers need to be heated more than the rings since the rings need very little heat to reach soldering temperature. You may need to nudge the rings towards the flowers as the solder melts with some tweezers. Pickle and clean all the flowers.

11 Use a centre punch to create the texture in the base of each flower. Place the flowers on a steel block and tap the end of the punch with a hammer. Move the punch across the centre of the flower until the indentations cover the base of each flower.

ASSEMBLING THE BRACELET

③ Paint a little borax onto each seam and position a small paillon of easy solder on top. Solder the rings shut one by one with a small, controlled needle flame. Attach the catch and clasp at each end of the bracelet with jump rings. Solder these rings shut in the same way. Pickle the bracelet, clean and polish before setting the stones, using a bristle brush. Make sure you remove all traces of polish before setting the stones.

① Link the flowers together using the open jump rings, taking care to close the rings tightly together. Use two pairs of flat pliers to do this.

② Solder the jump rings shut to provide extra strength. Stretch the bracelet out on a mat or charcoal block, and manoeuvre each ring so the seam is uppermost.

④ Set the stones one at a time. Here, the petals are levered over the stones instead of a bezel. Hold the bracelet firmly and push the petals in with a setting tool. Alternatively, secure each flower in setter's cement on a wooden block while setting the stones. When all the petals are folded over, use a burnisher to bring up the shine on the petal tips.

Twisted-wire bangle

THIS ELEGANT BANGLE IS MADE USING THICK-GAUGE WIRE AND HOLLOW BEADS. A TWIST IN THE FINISHED DESIGN, AS WELL AS IN THE LENGTHS OF WIRE THEMSELVES, MAKES THIS A SIMPLE PIECE TO SLIP ON AND OFF WITHOUT THE NEED FOR A CLASP, MAKING IT AN IDEAL DESIGN FOR A YOUNG CHILD.

The design for this bangle uses wire twisting and doming as its principal techniques. It can be adapted by using different combinations of wire instead of the ones shown here – silver with gold, for example, or copper with silver and brass.

Things you will need:

75cm (30in) of 2.1-mm (24-gauge) silver wire

4-cm (1½-in) square 1-mm (¹⁄₃₂-in) thick silver sheet

Basic tool kit *(see pages 14–15)*

Vice

Draw tongs or large pair of pliers with serrated jaws

Bangle mandrel

Dividers

Sliding caliper (optional)

Drilling equipment *(see pages 32–33)*

Doming equipment *(see pages 104–105)*

Soldering and pickling equipment *(see pages 22–23)*

Sanding equipment *(see pages 40–41)*

Polishing equipment *(see pages 42–43)*

TWISTING THE WIRES

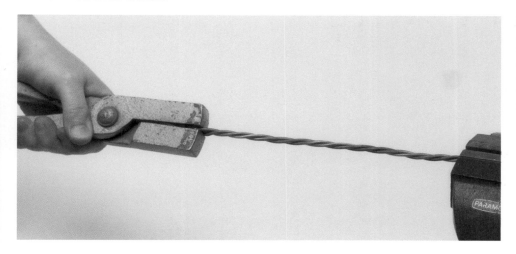

1 Saw the wire into three equal lengths. Anneal each piece, then secure them at one end in a vice. Grip the other ends in a pair of draw tongs and twist the wire evenly in one direction. You will probably need to anneal the wire several times before the twist achieves the desired tautness.

SHAPING THE BRACELET

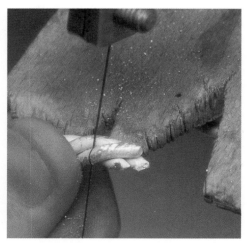

1 When the wire is twisted sufficiently, anneal it again. Bend it around a bangle mandrel, overlapping the ends slightly. Tap it with a mallet to make sure it is perfectly round.

2 Saw off the ends of the twisted wire to remove the section that has been in the vice. You may need to adjust the overall length of the bracelet a little more so that it will fit the wearer's wrist comfortably.

TIP

When curving thick wire or rod, it is a good idea to allow a little extra length. This gives you greater leverage. You should be able to manipulate the wire around a mandrel using your hands and then tap it with a mallet for a better shape.

MAKING THE DOMES

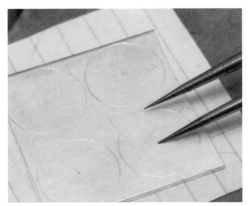

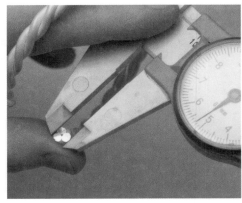

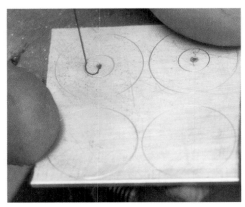

1 Set a pair of dividers to a radius of 8mm (⁵⁄₁₆in) and draw four circles on the silver sheet.

2 Measure the width of the twisted wire with a sliding caliper or your dividers. Halve this measurement, set your dividers to this figure, and draw a small circle centrally inside two of the large circles.

3 Drill a small hole in the centre of the two small circles. Saw out the inside circles, taking care not to wander over the line.

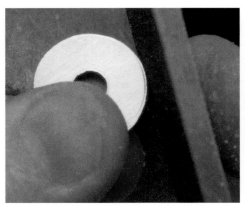

4 Support the circles against a slot in your pin and saw around the four large circles, just outside the scribed line. File around the outside edges of the circles, up to the scribed line, with a flat file.

5 Check the twisted wire will fit tightly into the sawn-out holes in two of the circles. Open the holes if necessary with a round file. Anneal all four circles, then dome them in a doming block with a large punch.

6 The circles should be domed until they form a softly rounded shape when they are put together. They should be roughly the same depth as each other. Follow the directions for making a hollow bead (*see page 105*).

ATTACHING THE DOMES

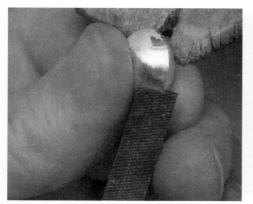

1 Remove any excess solder with a flat file, taking care to maintain a crisp line around the centre. Emery both domes carefully.

2 Slot one end of the twisted wire into a hole in one of the domes. Balance the bangle in a pair of spring tweezers so the dome is supported on the soldering block. Paint plenty of borax around the seam between the wire and the dome.

3 Solder the dome and wire together. Place paillons of easy solder around the seam and be ready to apply more as they melt – you will need to aim a lot of heat at the join. There may still be tiny gaps, but as long as the dome is firmly soldered, this is fine. Pickle the bangle.

4 To position the second dome on the other end of the wire, hold the bangle upright between two soldering blocks, with the unsoldered dome sitting firmly on top of one of the blocks. Solder this dome, then pickle.

5 Complete the bangle by filing off any excess solder from the outside of the domes with a flat needle file and emery them to smooth away any scratches or file marks. Polish the bangle or apply a matt finish.

Evening earrings and brooch

CURVES, BOLD SHAPES AND SIMPLE OUTLINES GIVE THIS JEWELLERY SET AN ART DECO FEEL AND MAKE IT PERFECT FOR SOMEONE WITH CONTEMPORARY TASTES. CREATED FROM SILVER SHEET AND MOONSTONES, IT IS ELEGANT ENOUGH TO GRACE THE SMARTEST EVENING OUTFIT.

Things you will need:

0.5x30x35mm (³⁄₁₆x1³⁄₁₆x1⅜in) sheet silver

1x50x65mm (⅜x2x2½in) sheet silver

0.5x10x80mm (³⁄₁₆x⅜x3⅛in) sheet silver

18mm (¾in) moonstone

2 x 12mm (½in) moonstones

Ready-made ear studs, for earrings

Ready-made fichu joint, for brooch

Ready-made safety catch, for brooch

Basic tool kit (*see pages 14–15*)

Texturing equipment (*see pages 48–49*)

Scriber

Doming equipment (*see pages 104–105*)

Drilling equipment (*see pages 32–33*)

Soldering and pickling equipment (*see pages 22–23*)

Sanding equipment (*see pages 40–41*)

Polishing equipment (*see pages 42–43*)

Stone-setting equipment (*see pages 116–121*)

You can make either the earrings or the brooch using textured silver domes, as in the brooch below, or set them with moonstones, as in the earrings. As an alternative to making the brooch, suspend the same piece from a chain for a matching pendant.

MAKING THE TEXTURED DOMES

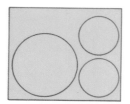

Templates for domes shown at 100%

1 Texture the first silver sheet by hammering it on a steel flatplate.

2 Using the templates as a guide, mark three circles on the reverse side of the sheet, one (A) with a diameter of 18mm (¾in) and two (B) with diameters of 12mm (½in). To make the piercing easier, scribe a slightly larger circle around the outside of each one and pierce between the lines. File to the inner line. Anneal, quench, rinse and dry.

MAKING THE STONE SETTINGS

3 Place the larger circle, textured side down, on your doming block. Punch down until it measures 18mm (¾in) across. Repeat with the smaller circles until they measure approximately 12mm (½in) across.

1 Use the second silver sheet to cut out three strips for the settings. These should be about 38.5mm (1½in) long for the 12mm (½in) moonstones and 57.5mm (2¼in) long for the 18mm (¾in) moonstone. To determine the width that the settings need to be, measure one-third of the height of each stone – that will provide a slight bezel.

MAKING THE SURROUNDS

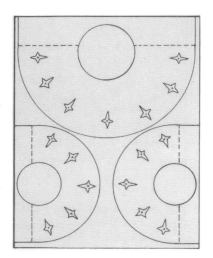

templates for surrounds shown at 100%

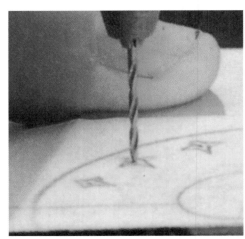

1 Using the templates as a guide, transfer the pattern of the earrings and brooch to the third silver sheet. Drill small holes in the centre of each star and pierce out.

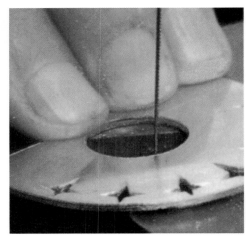

2 If making textured domes, pierce out the shape of the surrounds, leaving the bottom edges straight. Place the domes on the pierced-out pattern, scribe around the outside, then scribe another line approximately 2mm inside the first line. Pierce out that circle, file and clean the edges.

SOLDERING THE PARTS

1 If you are setting moonstones, place the bezels on the surrounds. Flux, solder with hard solder, pickle, rinse and dry. Pierce away the backs of the settings to make open settings for the stones.

2 Place the domes in position. Working on the larger surround first, flux and solder with hard solder.

3 Repeat for the other two surrounds. Pickle, rinse and dry before cleaning with pumice powder. Now pierce along the bottom straight edge and close round the domes or bezels. File the edges neatly.

ATTACHING THE FINDINGS

1 To attach an ear stud, find the balancing point by placing an earring (and stone or textured dome) on the edge of a metal ruler or file. Mark the position. Place flux and a paillon of easy solder on the marked position. Place the earring on the soldering block. Hold the wire stud pin with insulated tweezers and bring it down into position as the solder runs on the earring. Hold it steady and remove the flame. Pickle, rinse and clean with pumice powder. File the wire to a point, clean with emery papers and burnish. Repeat for the second earring.

2 To attach the brooch fittings, place the fichu joint in position. Flux the join and place paillons of easy solder at each corner. Flux the underside of the safety catch and run a paillon of easy solder onto it. Place some flux and a paillon of easy solder where the safety catch will go. Flux the bottom again. Heat the work slowly on a charcoal block. As the solder runs for the safety catch, lower it onto the work and hold it steady. Remove the flame, then pickle. Rinse, dry and clean. Make the tag of the pin to fit the inside of the fichu joint (*see page 54*), and rivet in place.

SETTING THE STONES

1 Gently heat some pitch or jeweller's wax and place your work in it to hold it in place. Allow to cool slightly, then gently work it up around the edges of the piece. Lower the stones into place.

2 Set the stones using either a punch and hammer or a burnisher.

3 Gently heat the pitch or wax around the edge of your work to soften it, and carefully prise up the piece with tweezers.

OXIDISING THE DOMES

If you want to oxidise the domes, protect all the other parts of the work with beeswax or stop-out varnish. Immerse all the pieces in a hot solution of potassium sulphide for about a minute, suspending them on fine silver wire attached to the fittings. If oxidisation occurs on areas that you had hoped to keep shiny, heat the whole piece up gently and quench in acid. However, you will have to start again with the potassium sulphide. Small areas of oxidisation may be removed by polishing.

Mixed bead necklace

THIS NECKLACE HAS AN EARTHY, TRIBAL APPEAL. IT USES A COMBINATION OF SILVER, GOLD, COPPER, LAPIS LAZULI, PEARLS AND TURNED WOODEN DISCS TO ACHIEVE THE LOOK. THE COMPONENTS ARE STRUNG ON TIGER TAIL, WHICH IS BETTER SUITED TO HANGING HEAVIER PIECES LIKE THESE.

The beads used for this project were selected and made from a personal stash, but you could use any that work together well. The silver and copper beads were made from sheet metal: silver for the largest bead; copper and silver for the others. They are all made in the same way, so you could use a combination of your own. You could also texture the surfaces of the metal if you like. If you prefer to use wood, look in your local bead shop or haberdasher's for suitable alternatives. If you have the time, you could even make a handful of painted wood or decorative papier mâché ones yourself.

Things you will need:

300mm (12in) of 2.5–3mm (⅒in) silver chenier

10mm (⅜in) of 1.5mm (¹⁄₁₆in) silver chenier

45x40mm (1¾x1½in) of 0.5-mm (24-gauge) sheet silver

35x35mm (1⁵⁄₁₆x1⁵⁄₁₆in) of 0.5-mm (24-gauge) sheet copper

approx. 60mm (2½in) of 1.1-mm (14-gauge) gold wire

approx. 50mm (1½in) of 1.1-mm (14-gauge) silver wire

approx. 40mm (½in) of 1.1-mm (14-gauge) copper wire

Jump rings (*see page 50*)

'S' fastener

1m (1yd) tiger tail

8 pearls approximately 3mm (⅒in) across

8 lapis lazuli beads approximately 3mm (⅒in) across

Wooden disks or beads

Templates

Basic tool kit (*see pages 14–15*)

Jeweller's pitch or beeswax

Jointing tool

Polishing equipment (*see pages 42–43*)

Doming equipment (*see pages 104–105*)

Rolling mill or anvil

Soldering and pickling equipment (*see pages 22–23*)

Drilling equipment (*see pages 32–33*)

Pliers

Fine wire wool

BENDING THE CHENIER

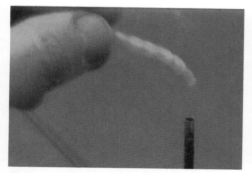

1 Anneal the full length of the 2.5–3mm (¹/₁₀in) silver chenier. Pickle, rinse and dry. Plug one end of the chenier and fill the entire length with heated pitch, melted beeswax, salt or a wire that fits snugly in the tube. Plug the other end of the tube.

2 Gently bend the chenier. Begin with a curve that is tighter than you need and take the curve right to the ends. Gently tap it to the right shape with a wooden mallet. Remove the beeswax or pitch by heating it gently, or pull out the wire or empty the salt.

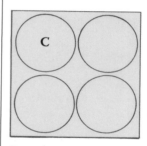

3 Use a jointing tool to cut the piece of chenier into four equal lengths. File away any rough edges and polish each piece if you want a shiny finish.

TIP

If you are using beeswax to fill the chenier, it helps to keep the chenier warm using a small flame. This allows the beeswax to stay molten, so filling the tube with ease. Do not try to bend chenier unless you have filled up the interior: the inside curve will crumple and the outside will kink.

TEMPLATE FOR THE SPHERES

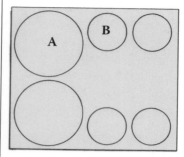

Silver shown at 100%

C

Copper shown at 100%

CUTTING THE SHEET METAL

Cut two circles (A) with diameters of 18mm (⅜in) and four silver circles (B) with diameters of 10mm (⅜in) from the sheet silver. Cut four circles (C) with diameters of 16mm (⁵/₁₆in) from the sheet copper. Anneal, rinse, and dry all the circles.

SHAPING THE SPHERES

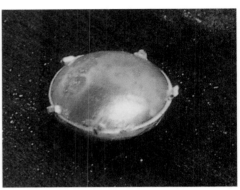

1 Dome each circle until the largest are approximately 16mm (⁵⁄₁₆in) in diameter, the middle are about 14mm (½in) in diameter, and the smallest are about 8mm (⅓in) in diameter. Flatten the top and bottom of the gold, silver and copper wire pieces by passing them through a rolling mill or gently hammering on your anvil. Anneal the wire lengths, pickle, rinse and dry.

2 Use each length of wire to make a ring that fits the circumference of a corresponding domed sphere (the inside diameter of the ring should be smaller than the dome, but the outside should be larger than the dome). Solder each of the rings with hard solder. Place a domed sphere on top, flux and using hard solder again, place paillons on the outside edge. Solder up the dome.

3 Drill a 0.5mm hole in the centre of the soldered dome. Scrape out an area in your charcoal block for the soldered dome to sit in and place the other half of the sphere onto the ring. Flux and place paillons of easy solder around the joint and solder. Drill a hole in the centre of this side.

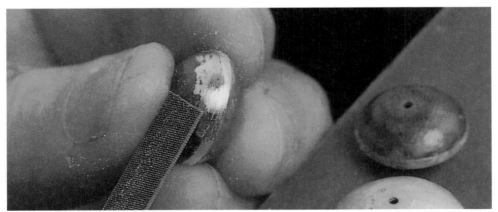

4 File away excess metal from the centre of the spheres. Clean and polish the spheres. Take care after pickling the spheres that you remove all the acid before working on them further. Boil them in a solution of soda crystals and water, rinse and let them sit on paper towels to make sure they are thoroughly dry. All of the components are now complete.

ASSEMBLING THE NECKLACE

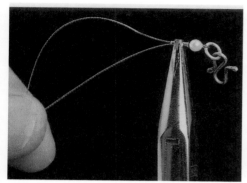

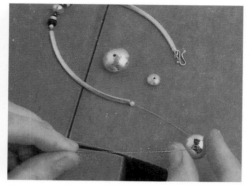

1 Solder two jump rings, attaching an 'S' fastener to one of them. Thread the soldered jump ring with the fastener onto the length of tiger tail, followed by a pearl and then by a 5-mm (¼-in) length of the 1.5mm (¹⁄₁₆in) chenier. Make a loop in the tiger tail and push the short end back through the pearl and chenier. Squeeze the chenier together with serrated pliers.

2 Thread on the 2.5–3mm (¹⁄₁₀in) chenier, followed by a pearl, wood, lapis, sphere, lapis, wood and pearl. Continue threading until everything is on your necklace, finishing with a 5-mm (¼-in) piece of chenier, a pearl and the jump ring. Thread the tiger tail back through the pearl and chenier, pull it all tight, and squeeze the chenier together. Tuck the remaining tiger tail back through the necklace.

3 Finish the silver chenier by rubbing with fine steel wool along each length. If your prefer a polished finish, it is best to polish the silver before assembly.

Springtime pendant

THIS PROJECT INVOLVES ETCHING AND ENAMELLING PLUS MAKING A CHAIN OF HAND-FORMED SIVER WIRE LINKS. IF YOU DO NOT HAVE ENAMELLING EQUIPMENT YOU COULD ETCH OUT THE PATTERN OR SOLDER WIRES IN POSITION AND THEN OXIDISE THE BACKGROUND.

The silver wire chain links shown in this project can be used as the basis for simple bracelets and pendants with different links and embellishments. In this example the centrepiece of the design is etched onto a silver sheet before being enamelled. Enamel is an excellent material to use in jewellery-making because it is chemically resistant, durable, scratch-resistant, colour-fast and easy to clean. Try creating different designs for the centrepiece using different shapes and colours.

Things you will need:

3.5cm (1⅛in) of 1.65-mm (20-gauge) silver wire

50cm (19½in) of 0.7-mm (10-gauge) silver wire

Jump rings

7.5-cm (3-in) square of 1.3-mm (³⁄₆₄-in) thick sheet silver

Roll of 0.3-mm (6-gauge) cloisonné wire, flattened in a rolling mill

Enamels: transparent blue flux, transparent golden brown, transparent rich pink, transparent walnut, transparent crystal blue, opaque white

Basic tool kit (*see pages 14–15*)

Forging equipment (*see pages 106–107*)

Soldering and pickling equipment (*see pages 22–23*)

Polishing equipment (*see pages 42–43*)

Burnisher

Etching equipment (*see pages 122–123*)

Enamelling equipment (*see pages 124–129*)

MAKING THE CHAIN

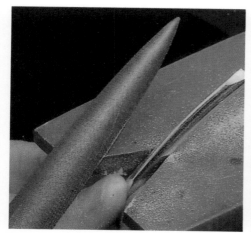

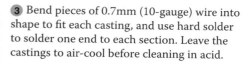

3 Bend pieces of 0.7mm (10-gauge) wire into shape to fit each casting, and use hard solder to solder one end to each section. Leave the castings to air-cool before cleaning in acid.

1 File the thick silver wire into a suitable shape for model link. Use a pendant motor to remove any excess silver if necessary, and spread the ends flatter by forging.

2 Hold one end of the piece in the safe jaws of a vice and twist through 360°. Solder on a sprue and polish. Send this model away to the casters, specifying how many pieces you need. When the pieces are ready, pierce away the remaining sprue. File and clean each one. Alternatively make all of the links for the necklace in the same way.

4 Turn each piece upside down and solder the wires onto the other ends with medium or easy solder. For a secure join, run some solder onto the wire ends as well as placing paillons on the casting.

5 Solder the chain together with jump rings and easy solder, isolating each link before soldering. Make a strong fastener for the chain out of slightly squared wire, tapered at each end and twisted in the middle. Bend it into an S-shape and solder it to the last link. Clean and finish each link, burnishing the high spots.

ETCHING THE CENTREPIECE

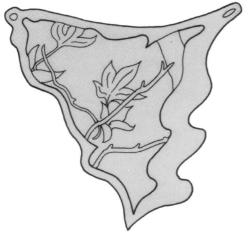

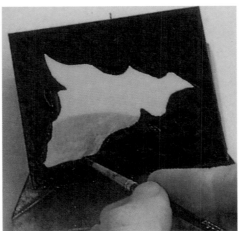

1 Take your silver sheet and, using this template as a guide, transfer the inner outline of the design to the silver sheet.

2 Paint up to the outline from the edge of the silver sheet with stop-out varnish. Wait until dry, then turn over silver sheet and repeat this step on the back of the silver sheet. Immerse the sheet in a solution of nitric acid (four parts water to one part acid) for about 40 minutes. Tickle with a feather from time to time.

3 Once the acid has etched away about 0.3mm of the sheet, remove it from the acid. Rinse in water and turpentine to remove stop-out varnish. Pierce out the final shape of the piece and file the edges smooth. Remember to include a border around the outline of your design. Clean the sheet under running water using a glass brush. Leave to soak.

ENAMELLING THE PENDANT

1 First do a test piece, using all the colours on top of the transparent flux. Wash the enamels, then grind them until they are fine and place them one at a time into the palette. Cover the whole of the etched-away area of the centrepiece with a thin layer of transparent blue flux. Place your work on the wire mesh tray and leave to dry. Fire at about 830°C (1500°F), or when the kiln is bright red, for approximately 2 to 3 minutes. It may not take this amount of time. Keep an eye on it and remove when the flux has fused. The silver should be a soft pink, while the blue flux should look whitish-blue after firing.

2 Bend the flattened cloisonné wire to fit the picture exactly. Place the wires in position with a pair of stainless steel tweezers, using a dab of colourless enamelling glue if necessary. Try to avoid using straight lines because cloisonné wire falls over easily. When all the cloisonné wires are in place, refire the piece for the same time that it took to fire the blue flux.

3 Now fill in the colours, taking care not to spill one over into another. Fire at the temperature your test showed to be most suitable. It will probably be similar to the flux firing and take a similar length of time, but keep checking to see when the enamels flow.

4 Remove the piece from the kiln and wait until it is cool before putting in the next layer of enamel. Continue firing, cooling and putting in more enamel until you have built up to a level just higher than that of the surrounding silver.

5 Under running water, rub a carborundum stone over your piece until the enamel is level and all the cloisonné wires are exposed. Dry, and refill any low areas with enamel. Refire. Rub down again under running water, this time working down through the wet and dry papers from numbers 280 to 600. Fire again, slightly hotter and quicker than previous firings. The silver will probably have oxidised. It is usually safe to immerse the piece in a pickle of sulphuric acid. If you cannot pickle it carefully, remove the oxides with 600 wet and dry papers or use wet pumice powder on a felt mop, taking care not to touch the enamel.

6 Finish the silver by polishing or leaving a satin finish. Drill holes at the two top corners and loop through a jump ring, which is attached to the chain. Using easy solder and taking care not to let the flame stray onto the enamel, solder the jump rings in place.

Designing your own Jewellery

By now, you will have practised your favourite projects in the book — basic and advanced. You will have established your own way of working, mastering a good number of the jewellery-making techniques along the way. Now you can really start to think about designing and making jewellery of your own. This can be a daunting process, and tips for success first focus on basic design theory: the inspiration behind a piece; sketching ideas that might give shape to the concept; brainstorming and researching techniques that can help develop a concept and give it greater strength. Then the focus shifts to the finer details: shape and form, texture, colour and function. Through considering these aspects of jewellery-making you will be encouraged to turn your theory into a reality in creating unique pieces of your own.

Inspiration

INSPIRATION CAN COME FROM AN OBJECT, AN EMOTION, A PERSON, A PLACE OR A FORM. IT CAN EVEN COME FROM A PROCESS, TECHNIQUE OR SMELL – IT COULD BE ANYTHING. THERE ARE NO RULES, AND WHERE YOU SEEK IT DEPENDS ON YOUR INTERESTS.

DISCOVERING AND UNDERSTANDING INSPIRATION

Inspiration is simply that which stimulates a reaction, anything that drives and motivates. Often we are unaware of what really inspires us, as we tend to take a great deal for granted. We are inclined to react subconsciously to something we see or feel without really focusing on it, let alone taking the time to analyse the initial reaction. Getting to know what really inspires you as an individual involves being able to stand back from a subject and look at it both subjectively and objectively at the same time. You need to learn to think about what you are confronting and then ask yourself exactly what it makes you feel, and why. With a greater understanding of inspiration, designs can gain a clear and confident voice, and more accurately express intentions. Without this understanding, the development process and finished designs can be rather bland and uneventful, and will almost certainly lack genuine character or individuality.

Left and above In these striking rings, the structure of a sea urchin can be seen as the original inspiration behind the design.

Left The notion of chillies being too hot to handle is used as inspiration for pieces where the wearer is protected from the chillies' potential heat.

IDENTIFYING THE PARTS

To start to form a design based on your inspiration, it helps to examine the constituent parts so that you are familiar with each and every component. You will then need to consider how many of these elements can be removed from the equation before the inspiration becomes simply ordinary. For example take a bird or chicken. Consider its shape in profile as a two-dimensional image, its form as a three-dimensional object, its internal skeleton or structure, skin texture, feather colour and movement. Depending on your intentions, the profile of the bird alone may be all that is necessary to relay your concept, but if you need to show the beauty of a bird then perhaps colour, texture and an accurate form are also required. There is a great deal that is inspiring in the most unlikely objects if you know how to look.

CONSIDERING THE EFFECT

By abstracting information we can decide what really attracts us to a subject. One aspect of the inspiration might be its ability to give a feeling of comfort – for example, evoking calm, ease and perhaps complacency. A design could be given a tactile quality, like a weather-worn pebble, that invites one to handle and caress it.

Surprisingly, however, what inspires us or draws us to something may well be that which makes us feel uncomfortable. Our state of awareness is heightened when we are consciously or subconsciously put on our guard. A piece that exploits subject matter that is generally considered unpleasant is likely to attract attention because most people have a morbid desire to be shocked.

INDIVIDUAL AND UNIVERSAL APPEAL

Once you have these answers, you can begin to consider how to translate the properties of the inspiration into a design in an evocative way so that it provokes similar reactions in others. In some cases this is relatively simple. People tend to share many criteria of beauty, as well as having certain experiences, prejudices, interests and viewpoints in common. There are many things, such as a beautiful shell, a flower or a sublime landscape, that have universal appeal.

However, on occasions the source of a jeweller's inspiration may be quite unexpected, and not at all obvious to others. This presents the designer with another challenge; to pass on their own inspiration to a wider audience by emulating its characteristics in their designs. The secret lies in being able to abstract its essence, the thing or things, the quality, that defines the inspiration.

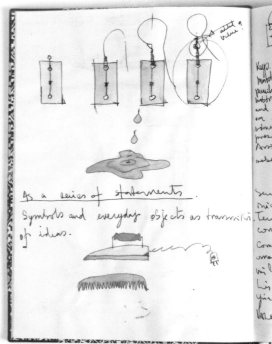
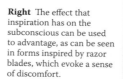

Right The effect that inspiration has on the subconscious can be used to advantage, as can be seen in forms inspired by razor blades, which evoke a sense of discomfort.

Below A collection of inspirational images is collated so that the connection between them is obvious – this grouping also enriches the individual images, resulting in a more impactful display.

Sketching

ARTISTS AND DESIGNERS ARE VISUAL PEOPLE WHO SEE IDEAS AS IMAGES RATHER THAN WORDS. THEY USE SKETCHING AS A SHORTHAND OF DRAWING. SKETCHES CAN BE QUICK DRAWINGS USED TO NOTE AND OUTLINE AN IDEA, OR STUDIES OF A MORE FINISHED PIECE OF WORK.

VISUAL IDEAS

If you see something that stimulates you, being able to note it down as a quick sketch will enable you to recall it with greater clarity at a later date. Sketching is used both before and throughout the design process to explore and record images and ideas. Just as a writer may make quick notes of phrases or snatches of overheard conversation, a designer should be ready to note down an image. This should ideally be an ongoing process. It is often difficult to hold the thread of a long conversation, and, in the same way, it is hard to keep track of the numerous images that fly around in our minds as a train of thought progresses. Sketches keep track of images and ideas in much the same way that minutes record a meeting.

Making a visual record of the progression of an idea enables you to return to a particular image or idea to develop it further. It also helps to keep your mind focused and uncluttered so that you don't waste energy trying to memorise information.

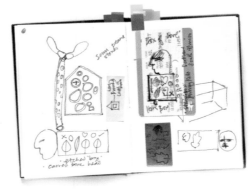

Left A designer may have to make use of whatever is available to quickly record an idea, and collate it in the sketchbook later; here a train ticket has been used.

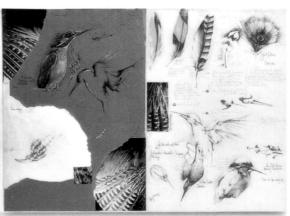

Far left This atmospheric sketch is made up of layers of photocopied images, silhouettes, lettering as well as pencil line, colour and stitchwork.

Left Different features of a bird are examined in detailed sketches that focus on colour, structure, pattern and movement.

DEFINING THE INTENTION

Unlike artists' sketches, those made by designers are not simply concerned with composition, tonal balance and so on. There are any number of things you might want to record or explore, and to do so quickly and efficiently, it is necessary to decide what exactly it is that you want to achieve. It might be the texture that interests you, or possibly the mechanics. The area of your focus will dictate how much of the image needs to be detailed. For example, to indicate context or form, a simple outline might be all that is required.

FORM A HABIT

Like many things in life, sketching becomes easier the more you do it. Initially your sketches may appear crude to you, but with practice you will gain confidence and purpose, and the sketches will be less self-conscious and more useful. Try not to be overly concerned with making a pretty drawing, as this might cause you to expend too much energy on looks. Accurate description should be the main concern.

Try using different drawing materials to enliven your sketches and widen your range, so that you can focus on and define detail. Using a pen or pencil alone is fine, but the addition of colour and visual texture not only provides relief to the eye but may also help you to explore your ideas in more depth. In addition, it can lift a sketch so that it becomes less mundane and more likely to stimulate further ideas.

Above An extravagant colour sketch is used to create a fabulous abstract composition that invites the viewer to consider a personal interpretation of the subject.

Right Even quick sketches can be highly individual and informative; this faithful hound has purpose and is clearly on a mission.

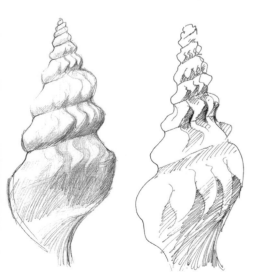

Left These two sketches of a shell focus on different aspects of the form, resulting in sketches that convey specific information such as surface detail and tonal contrast.

Right The beauty of a city skyline is captured in a sketch that suggests the exotic character and flavour of the culture and its inhabitants.

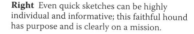

Concept

THE NOTION OF A CONCEPT IS SOMETIMES VIEWED WITH SCEPTICISM AND SEEN AS AN UNNECESSARY
ELEMENT, BUT IN FACT IT IS OF PARAMOUNT IMPORTANCE. A CONCEPT IS THE IDEA BEHIND A DESIGN,
THE INTENTION OF THE PIECE. IT IS WHAT YOU INTEND TO SAY TO YOUR AUDIENCE THROUGH YOUR WORK.

THE NEED FOR A CONCEPT

Design begins with inspiration (*see pages 180–181*), but without a
well-defined concept and a firm idea about how to translate or use
the inspiration, the design process will tend to be more accidental
than intentional, imparting a similarly accidental character to the final
design. That is not to say that a piece made without a deliberate concept
will fail, but a little thought and analysis will identify a concept behind
the vast majority of good pieces of design.

Defining the concept clearly at the start allows the design process
to be decisive and well focused so that you can find the most relevant
solutions and reach more exact and exciting conclusions.

Right There is a clear
intention to relay specific
geographical information
in this series of design
development sketches
for a brooch intended to
commemorate Christmas.

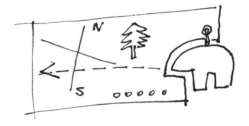

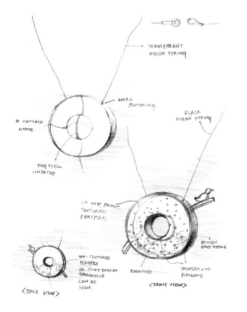

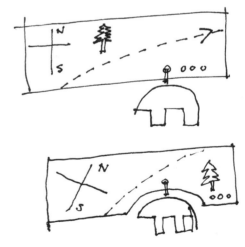

Left These two pendants are based on the concept of emotional frailty. In one,
the concept is communicated through the egg in its centre, which represents
the fragile human ego and potential growth. The other pendant reaches a more
optimistic conclusion; with the self-assurance that comes with maturity, the
fledgling is ready to leave behind the naivety of youth.

KEEPING IT SIMPLE

Many designers will tell you from experience that a simple concept is often considerably more successful than a complex one. The main reason for this is that it is less likely to tax the imagination or intellect of your audience, and so will probably reach a greater number of people. A concept can easily be overworked, sometimes without the designer being aware of the fact, and might become so convoluted that it is unintelligible to all but the designer. A concept that is not carried through well enough may be the result of relying too much on tenuous connections rather than concentrating on the central idea. Similarly, if a design concept is so exclusive that it can only reach an audience of one, it is highly probable that the work will not have the appeal that the designer wants or intends.

In such cases it would be advisable to rethink the design and content with a view to making it more intelligible, which may involve simplifying and clarifying the concept. It is important to retain the main focus throughout and not to clutter your ideas with non-essential peripheral information. A good test is to try to clearly articulate your concept. If you find you cannot explain it well verbally, the chances are that others will not understand your intentions, in which case further refinement is necessary.

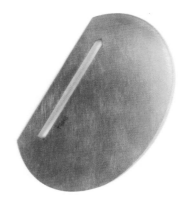

Above The wearer of this piece is invited to interact with the pendant form; the arrow hints at a direction and a base, but the piece dictates that the wearer be the decision-maker.

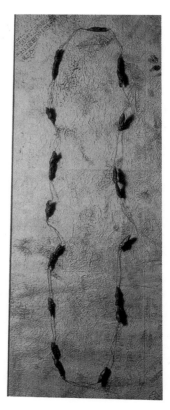

Right 'Eternal Life', the unbroken form relays a sense of continuity, while the carefully crafted natural materials refer to the endless cycle of life.

Above This piece expresses an emotional state – if you are feeling too emotionally fragile the piece can be worn as a warning to those who may otherwise be heavy handed.

Below The idea of something being too hot to handle is explored with images of a chilli that has been wrapped for our protection; in some of the designs wording is used as a decorative device that also compounds the concept.

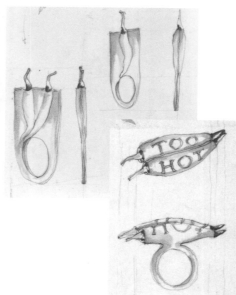

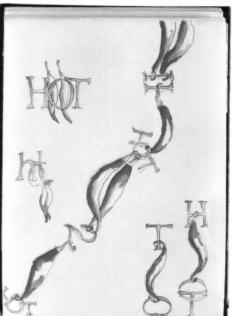

Brainstorming

BRAINSTORMING IS ABOUT CONSIDERING EVERY OPTION – THRASHING OUT AN IDEA SO THAT EVERY POSSIBILITY IS CONSIDERED AND THE DESIGN PROCESS CAN REACH ITS FULL POTENTIAL. YOU NEED TO CONSIDER, FIRST, WHAT IS OBVIOUS, BUT ALSO THE SUBTLETIES THAT MAKE A CONCEPT MORE INTERESTING.

OPENING UP THE MIND

To ensure that your designs are not based only on the most simplistic ideas, you need to look beyond your initial ideas to find solutions that are more sophisticated.

First impressions of a subject are usually based on purely instinctive reactions, but after this you need to scrutinise your inspiration and concept, and enquire further. Brainstorming is a process of opening up the mind to all the possibilities by intensive exploration and

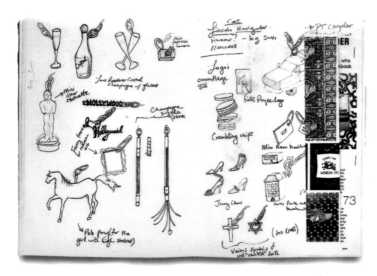

Above A variety of icons for wealth is brainstormed before a shortlist is made and a design is developed based on the concept of oppulence.

Right A variety of interpretations of a simple circular form are noted so that the designer can focus on the different associations, with the form as part of the design process.

examination – it is about looking for connections that are perhaps more obscure, exciting, challenging, provocative or amusing.

By allowing ideas to flow without restriction and recording them on paper as they occur you can begin to move away from simple ideas into new directions, exploring areas of interest that might not have occurred to you at the outset. If possible, discuss your ideas with other people, as they will often have a different perspective from yours, which may provide valuable insights.

ORGANISING THE PROCESS

Start by writing down the idea that you want to explore; this will be the focal point for your brainstorming session. One idea will readily act as a catalyst for further ones if you can free your mind and thoughts. Expand your concept one level at a time, writing down your initial responses as subdivisions of the original idea. These subdivisions should then prompt more ideas and hence further subdivisions.

How you record this process is important, as you will need to be able to access the information easily. One way to do this is with a spider graph, which starts with the initial subject or idea in the centre, and subsequent related ideas linked by a 'web' travelling outwards. Similarly, the family-tree graph places the focal idea at the 'root' with the different trains of thought branching up and out.

SIFTING THE INFORMATION

Ideas can flow fast in a brainstorming session, so you may quickly find that you have a great deal of information that requires sifting. You will need to be discerning to identify the ideas that have the most potential. Shortlist the best ideas by highlighting them, and then decide which have the most relevance for your design brief before you take them further through research and development. Try to identify whether any ideas overlap, and if so where, as this is valuable information that can be used to strengthen your concept.

Don't be afraid of extremes, as these can lead to new and invigorating ways of thinking, and, of course, they can always be tempered to make them appear less radical.

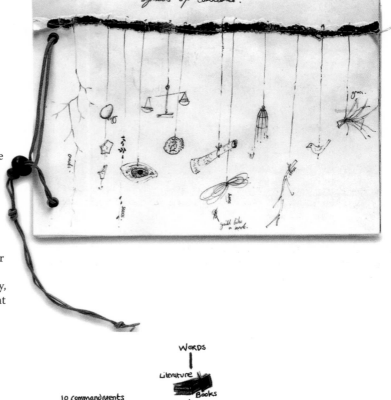

Above Sketches and notes record a brainstorming session in which appropriate symbols and wording were explored for a conceptual piece based on the burden of conscience.

Right A spider graph shows the train of thought and new ideas that arose during a brainstorming session on the subject of religion.

Research

RESEARCH IS THE PROCESS OF SYSTEMATIC INVESTIGATION WITH THE PURPOSE OF INCREASING KNOWLEDGE AND FINDING NEW OR BETTER SOLUTIONS. ONCE YOU HAVE YOUR INSPIRATION, YOU NEED TO GAIN AS MUCH KNOWLEDGE ABOUT IT AS YOU CAN, IN ORDER TO BROADEN YOUR OUTLOOK AND ENRICH YOUR DESIGNS.

BROADENING YOUR HORIZONS

Begin your research by accumulating a wide range of information. If, for example, your object of interest is a fish – you might find it beautiful, stimulating or even repugnant – and you want to form a design around the subject or the feelings it inspires, it might be beneficial to actually handle a fish, to feel its texture and weight, to know in detail how it looks, feels, smells and tastes. If, specifically, the look or feel of a fish interests you, more academic research would explain exactly how the scales of a fish protect, move and reflect light. Research of a more general nature might reveal important elements that could affect the interpretation of a design, such as surrounding symbolism. In this case, a fish is commonly recognised as a symbol of Christianity. It is this kind of information that can become the catalyst for many ideas and unexpected design directions.

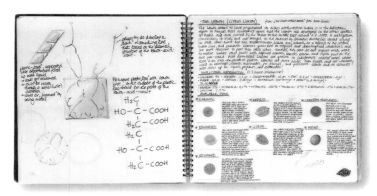

Above Lemons are researched in depth so that everything that can be gleaned about the lemon as a subject is explored – from type and chemical composition to tools for squeezing – in order to broaden the designer's knowledge of the subject.

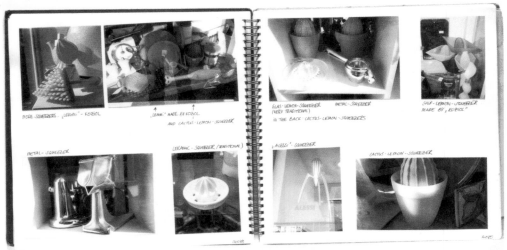

Left and below Magazine clippings that include an image of a stealth bomber are collated in a sketchbook to research striking forms seen in man-made objects and architecture.

RESEARCH MATERIAL

There are so many sources of research material that it would be quite impossible to identify them all. Consider where the information you need is most likely to be found. For example, if you wanted to research the Art Deco movement, a library would be the obvious place to start, but if you were looking for innovative methods of containment it might be more fruitful to examine containers and products in the shopping centre. The internet has become a useful resource, and search engines can reveal less obvious sources of information.

FILTERING THE RESEARCH

When your research is design-specific, it will be necessary at some point to filter the material, and you will need to return to the original concept and the design brief to check that you have not strayed too far from either one.

Research need not be exclusively led by a narrow design question. It may be an ongoing process of gathering information that informs a particular body of work. It is important to be open to new ideas and directions during the research process, and to retain and collate information so it can be referred to as part of your overall portfolio. Try to be discerning about how you use your research, but keep any good material that proves unsuitable for one project, as it could be the inspiration or information needed for future work.

Above Various images of different types of flower are researched with a view to using them as inspiration for the form of a ring.

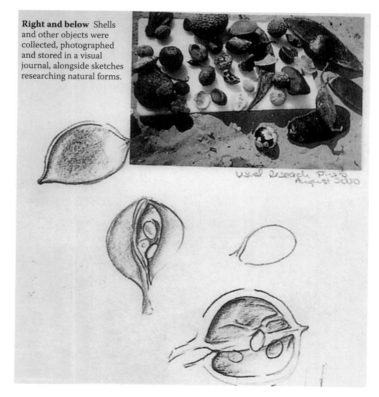

Right and below Shells and other objects were collected, photographed and stored in a visual journal, alongside sketches researching natural forms.

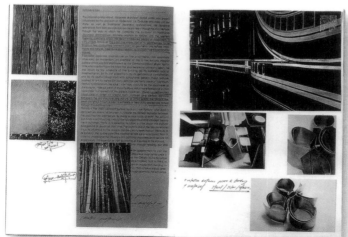

Above Notes and images based around Japanese architecture are researched and collated alongside images of jewellery samples and models of the final bangle designs.

Samples and test pieces

ONCE THE THEORETICAL ELEMENTS OF YOUR DESIGN ARE COMPLETE – SKETCHING, BRAINSTORMING, RESEARCH – YOU CAN TURN YOUR ATTENTION TO THE SAMPLES AND TEST PIECES THAT ARE GOING TO GIVE YOUR FINISHED DESIGN ITS PRIMARY VISUAL AND SENSUAL CHARACTERISTICS.

INFORMATION AND CLARIFICATION

If you have a material in mind for the fabrication of a piece, it is advisable to take time to locate the material and collect samples so you can check its quality and its suitability for the purpose. If you want to explore different ways of treating that material, perhaps to create a different look or texture, or even to alter its properties, you will need to conduct a series of tests.

Samples and test pieces are physical pieces used as part of an information-gathering and clarification process. They present another valuable opportunity to ensure that you are making appropriate decisions. Samples are usually concerned with detail and concentrate on small segments of a larger scheme. For example, you might make samples of a commercially manufactured material such as latex because you are concerned about the suitability of 0.533mm latex in comparison

Above Test pieces explore a variety of materials and textures that could be used to express the delicate texture and form of a spider's body.

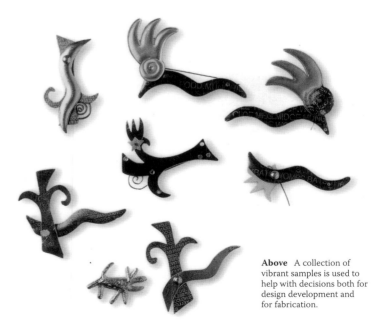

Above A collection of vibrant samples is used to help with decisions both for design development and for fabrication.

Above A deluge of paper samples is used to test different combinations of colour and shape, and to create inspirational textures and forms.

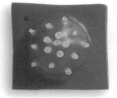

with 0.813mm. You would want to have samples of these materials for trials as well as for future reference.

Samples can be a limited example or a 'taster' of a technique, in much the same way as a knitting or fabric swatch shows a small segment of the whole. If you find you are interested in a particular process, samples are a way of exploring and progressing it.

Above Various test pieces and samples are kept as part of the process of understanding materials, forms, textures and processes to enlighten, broaden and inform design development.

Above Acrylic test pieces try combinations of colour, texture and process so that these outcomes can be assessed and brought to bear on the design process.

INSPIRATION AND POSTERITY

As well as a means of answering technical and aesthetic questions, samples are a useful source of inspiration because they are about choice; samples and test pieces are precious tangible illustrations, often the first windows into what can actually be, rather than ideas in your head or designs on paper. They can be lovely and desirable objects in themselves, as they are usually relatively simple and pure statements – uncluttered and informal.

Collectively, they also have the potential to form a catalogue of materials, processes, textures, colours and so on. So always keep the pieces and treat them with care. They should be collated with notes that record why, how, and when they were made and what they relate to. A technical journal is a logical place to record this material, but if samples are swatches of fabric or materials that relate directly to a design and are part of the decision-making process, it might be more appropriate to keep them in your sketchbook.

Left Silver and copper are used with traditional oriental lacquering techniques to explore a range of different combinations of colour and pattern.

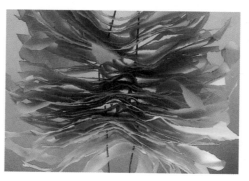

Left With a focus on a loose layered effect, paper has been treated, shaped and formed before being assembled as a sample that will inform the final design.

Shape

THE SHAPES YOU CHOOSE FOR YOUR DESIGNS ARE OF PRINCIPAL IMPORTANCE, FOR THEY WILL CONVEY MOST OF THE INITIAL VISUAL IMPACT OF A PIECE OF JEWELLERY. THE WAY SHAPES ARE HANDLED THROUGH THE DESIGN PROCESS CAN ALTER THE LANGUAGE OF A PIECE IN BOTH SUBTLE AND SIGNIFICANT WAYS.

SUITABLE CHARACTERISTICS

Think of shape as a building block that can be used to ensure good aesthetic and visual balance. It can be treated as a frame or as a vehicle for more complex aspects of design, but care needs to be taken when embellishing the basic shape, or the design may become unnecessarily cluttered or overstated.

It is essential to establish at the beginning what is required from your shape by referring to your concept – should the shape be bold, sleek, inviting, tactile, oriental, organic or something else? Draw a few basic shapes that might be suitable, and then consider how you might develop them to further express the concept and add character to your design.

To design effectively, you must try to understand the identity of a chosen shape. A square, for example, can be seen in simplistic terms as an orderly shape because it has equal sides, while a circle is less so because it has no beginning or end. A triangle is a strong, centred, directional shape because it comes to a point. A simple, basic shape is easy to

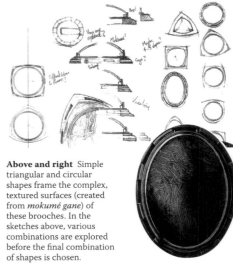

Above and right Simple triangular and circular shapes frame the complex, textured surfaces (created from *mokumé gane*) of these brooches. In the sketches above, various combinations are explored before the final combination of shapes is chosen.

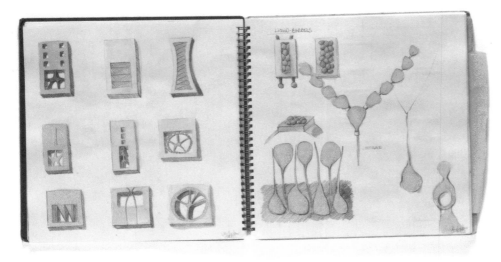

Left Through these abstract studies of a lemon, the suitability of different shapes is considered. The designer has made a series of subtle changes to a basic four-sided shape, as well as alterations to the interior pattern. The simplicity of the frame means that the busy patterns do not have to compete with each other for attention.

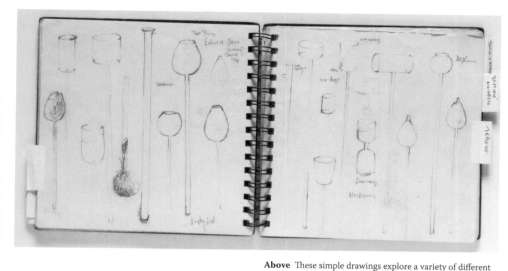

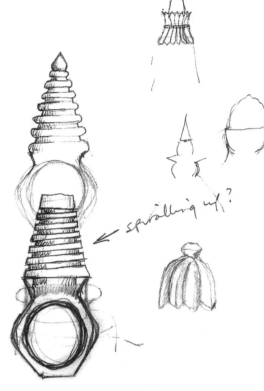

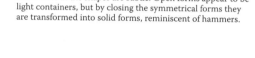

understand and work with because its impact and character can be easily modified by alterations to the edges or interiors so that its identity is changed.

With practice, you can tailor the properties of any shape to redefine its basic personality – try out a few simple alterations to see the effects that can be achieved. Don't be afraid to explore extremes; the most surprising and pleasing results frequently come through being daring and testing the boundaries.

Above These simple drawings explore a variety of different shapes. Each has its own character, even though the differences in the shapes are subtle. Open forms appear to be light containers, but by closing the symmetrical forms they are transformed into solid forms, reminiscent of hammers.

Right and below For this collection of silver jewellery, architectural sketches are developed and transformed into simple, elongated cone shapes. The surfaces of the cones are deeply scalloped to suggest the forms of the original architectural structures that inspired them.

TIPS

- Begin by exploring all possibilities, without fear of being too radical.
- Narrow your focus to shapes that are relevant to the design brief.
- Having selected the shapes that seem most appropriate, test them as models to aid the decision-making process.
- Consider how internal shapes can alter or emphasise the appearance of a piece.

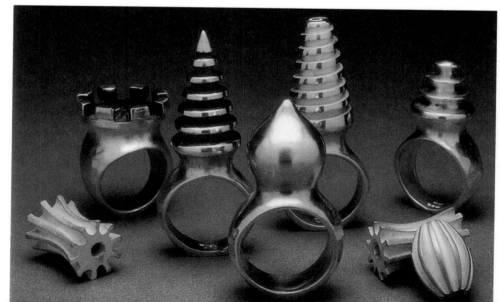

Form

JEWELLERY IS A THREE-DIMENSIONAL DISCIPLINE THAT RELATES DIRECTLY TO THE MOBILE, VARIABLE FORM OF THE BODY, WITH ITS CURVING, ROUNDED SHAPES. AS SUCH, THREE-DIMENSIONAL OBJECTS CAN OFFER A RICH, VISUAL AND TACTILE EXPERIENCE, AS THEY ARE EXPLORED THROUGH 360°.

INSIDE AND OUT

A good design is distinguished from an ordinary one by attention to detail, both large and small, so always check that you have considered all aspects of form and are conscious of the potential of the different faces of a piece throughout the design process. This helps to achieve a cohesive design in which all aspects of form have been addressed.

Form is not just about the parts of a piece that can be seen. In a good design the back of a piece should complement the front. To find that the back is a thing of beauty in itself is like discovering a secret – one that will make a piece infinitely more satisfying and memorable.

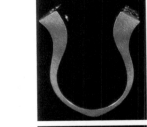

Left Shaped sheets of coloured paper are stacked to form a solid, cylindrical bangle. Looking from above, the form falls away from the rim to give the centre a gentle, conical look that makes it visually interesting and yet physically satisfying at the same time.

Right Three-dimensional form is used to manipulate the degree of translucency of this resin pendant. The resin is carved into a curvaceous form, thinning from a full body to a knife-edge at the base – the internal texture of the piece becomes visible as the form thins, and the translucency of the resin increases.

Left and above Drawings indicate different views of a two-part ring, and show it both fully assembled and separated. The measured drawings allow the forms to be visualised and checked before the design is finalised and the ring is fabricated.

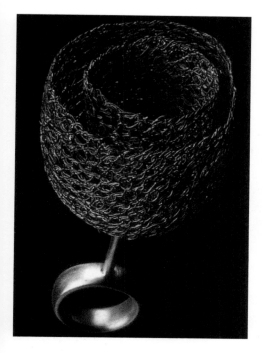

Left The outer voluminous form on top of this silver ring acts as a container for a smaller form that nestles inside it. The smaller form adds depth and further interest to the design.

Right These airy, three-dimensional forms are made from wire. Lines and intersections create different patterns according to the angle at which they are viewed. Tiny glimpses of solid forms that relate to the linear structure are suggested by sheet detail.

TWO DIMENSIONS INTO THREE

When you begin designing, your drawings may be rather two-dimensional, because you are likely to be drawing from a single viewpoint. Form is difficult to convey on paper, so it is important to learn how to draw in three dimensions, using contour and perspective. Measured drawing is an accurate and relatively simple way of exploring form: by projecting the shape into three dimensions, the different elevations of a piece can be connected to check that decisions about detailing and proportions are sympathetic and plausible.

TIPS

- Always consider designs three-dimensionally.
- Develop drawing skills so that you can explore 3-D forms on paper.
- Form can be fluid and changeable; consider how movement affects form, and vice versa.

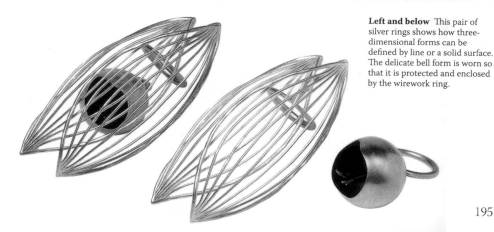

Left and below This pair of silver rings shows how three-dimensional forms can be defined by line or a solid surface. The delicate bell form is worn so that it is protected and enclosed by the wirework ring.

Texture

JEWELLERY IS A TACTILE MEDIUM, DESIGNED TO BE HANDLED AND WORN, SO THE WAY IT FEELS IS CLEARLY AN IMPORTANT ELEMENT OF ITS DESIGN. THE SURFACE FINISH OF A PIECE CAN LIFT IT FROM THE ORDINARY TO THE EXTRAORDINARY BECAUSE OF THE WAY IN WHICH IT STIMULATES AND ENTERTAINS OUR SENSES.

EVOCATIVE TEXTURES AND MATERIALS

People often think of jewellery as being highly polished, but although a mirror finish has its place, there are many other interesting textural surfaces, and texture should never be overlooked in the design process. Metal, the most commonly used material in jewellery design, has a hard surface, but through applying appropriate processes it can be made to appear soft, inviting and even velvety.

Most of the materials used in jewellery-making present opportunities for exploring and exploiting a wide range of exciting textures, however it is important when choosing a material and texture to consider whether they will wear well for the intended lifespan of the piece, whether that be a month, a year, a decade or a lifetime.

Left and below The inspiration for textures can come from anywhere, from the natural world to man- or machine-made objects. Visual and technical journals are useful tools for recording all manner of textures for future reference.

Left and right This key-shaped bangle uses patination to highlight lettering, and the carefully applied surface of green and oxide gives the feeling of antiquity. In the related ring, with a secret to unlock, patination is used in a different way to create a visual texture that emphasises the shape.

VISUAL LANGUAGE

Our perception of texture is ingrained as part of a common visual language – we expect an object to be old if it has a tarnished surface or is covered in the familiar green patina caused by weathering. This kind of knowledge is useful in creating pieces that evoke a particular response. Physical and visual texture can be readily employed to imitate commonly recognised surfaces, and therefore to reinforce the design intention. For example, a silver surface can be etched into stripes, gold-plated and oxidised to suggest a tiger's pelt – it may not feel like fur, but the visual connection is readily made.

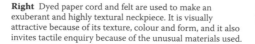

Above For this round brooch, a delicate visual texture reminiscent of dyed silk is cleverly made in metal using patination and wire to alter the *mokumé gane* technique.

> ## TIPS
>
> • Consider how the surface of a material can be improved by a textural finish.
> • Remember that texture can avoid the difficulty involved in achieving a highly polished surface, and can add frailty to a piece.
> • Consider how a finish or texture might wear, and what measures can be taken to protect it.

Right Dyed paper cord and felt are used to make an exuberant and highly textural neckpiece. It is visually attractive because of its texture, colour and form, and it also invites tactile enquiry because of the unusual materials used.

Colour

COLOUR IS ONE OF THE MOST IMMEDIATE AND EFFECTIVE WAYS OF ATTRACTING ATTENTION TO WORK – WE ARE A VISUALLY SENSITIVE SPECIES, AND COLOUR IS A VERY IMPORTANT STIMULUS. COLOUR IS A USEFUL DEVICE FOR ENRICHING JEWELLERY AND ENHANCING THE MUST-HAVE FACTOR.

TRADITION AND INNOVATION

In past centuries, jewellery was a mainly metal-based discipline. As jewellery was associated in many cultures with prosperity, precious metals such as silver and gold were the primary materials used. Colour was added by the inclusion of stones or coloured beads, or through enamelling. Seeds, feathers and other brightly coloured objects were no doubt used as well, but these were generally a poor-man's substitute for the valuable materials that were accessible only to the wealthy.

Scientific advances mean that contemporary jewellery has a much wider palette of materials. In the 1980s titanium came in and went out of fashion, while plastic has gone from strength to strength since its introduction – because it is constantly being developed, it has infinitely more possibilities than titanium, which quickly became ordinary.

Original ways of including colour in jewellery are continually being explored by designers who aim to establish their design style through explorations into unusual materials and techniques.

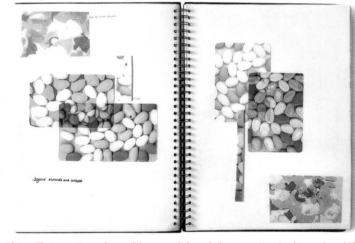

Above The springtime colours of the sugared almonds, here seen in a visual journal, could be used as the inspiration for a future collection of bridal or fashion jewellery designs.

Left The vibrant blue in this feather brooch, set with diamonds, is created using anodised titanium.

Right A pair of silver pendants is made even more attractive by lustrous, deep red seed-like beads.

THE LANGUAGE OF COLOUR

The way people feel and react to colour is to a large extent personal; however, certain colours are generally understood to have particular 'personalities' – blue, for example, is believed to be calming, and red aggressive, or suggestive of passion or lust. Culture also plays a part in people's attitudes towards different colours: a Western bride would be unlikely to wear red at the altar, whereas a Chinese bride may well do so, because in traditional Chinese culture red is an auspicious colour linked with religion.

In the West, colour can also be a metaphor for the seasons and the cycle of life: light and pale colours indicate spring and youth; intense or bright colours symbolise summer and maturity; dark and faded colours are associated with autumn and old age; and white or washed-out colours symbolise winter and death.

Knowing what a colour means in a particular context allows you to focus on how it can be used in combination with form, texture and other relevant factors, to make the design intention of a piece more readily realised and understood.

Right These wonderful, pod-like forms are richly coloured on the inside. The muted exteriors appear to be simple, organic shapes, while the interiors are little treasure-troves of colour that demand your attention.

TIPS

• Remember that the range of alternative materials used in contemporary jewellery design means that choice in colour is virtually limitless.

• Consider how the physical surface affects colour. For example, a shiny surface that reflects a sheen will have a different affect to the same colour in matt.

• Consider how changing the amount and intensity of a colour can influence the character of a piece.

Left Resin is cast into quirky, curvaceous forms to make a neckpiece of opaque, translucent and transparent green. The strands of dyed nylon filament embedded in the transparent forms add visual texture as well as colour to the piece.

Right Humble paper is transformed through cutting and assembly with silver to make a collection of vivid bangles. The layers of orange, red and pink are subtly varied in places to add additional interest and visual allure.

Emotion

JEWELLERY HAS BEEN USED TO APPEAL TO OUR EMOTIONS FOR CENTURIES, AND A LOOK AT THE HISTORY OF ITS DESIGN REVEALS PIECES THAT HAVE INSPIRED REVERENCE, FEAR, JOY, LAUGHTER AND SORROW – WHETHER VISUALLY OR SYMBOLICALLY – FROM ANCIENT EGYPT TO THE PRESENT DAY.

HORROR

Some emotions are personal, while others are shared by groups of people. For example, fear of spiders (arachnophobia) is relatively common, and even those who are not actually phobic may still feel uncomfortable when facing a large, hairy spider. The inclusion of elements that might cause people discomfort or uneasiness can be a good way of attracting attention to a design, as people tend to be drawn to that which is fearsome or disturbing.

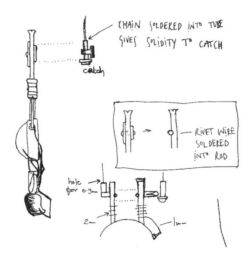

CHAIN SOLDERED INTO TUBE GIVES SOLIDITY TO CATCH

catch

RIVET WIRE SOLDERED INTO ROD

hole for o.g...

2mm   1mm

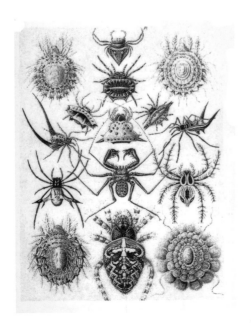

Left and right Spiders' bodies were researched and detailed technical drawings were made before the making of a frighteningly large and realistic spider pendant. Hung from a staring, dismembered eyeball, it cannot fail to attract attention.

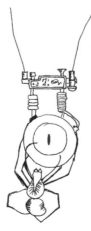

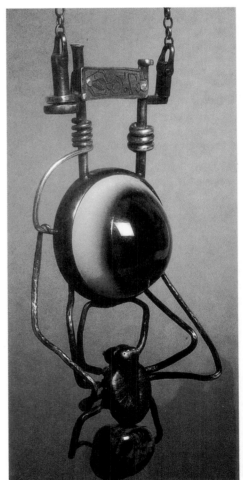

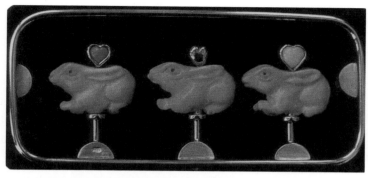

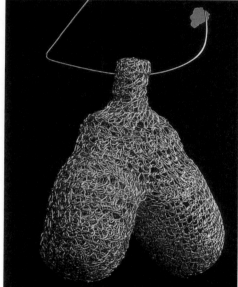

HUMOUR

Humour is another human quality that is often exploited in jewellery-making. A design that includes humour and has the ability to make people smile will generally be appealing. There are many ways of provoking mirth in jewellery design. Think of jewellery that makes you smile or laugh as a visual joke. You might consider using a title that helps explain the joke. Ideally, however, the visual image should convey sufficient information for the joke to be understood, with the title merely confirming the punchline – otherwise, as it is not always possible for the viewer to know the title, the joke might fall on deaf ears.

Jewellery is generally regarded as a serious subject, so a design that incorporates humour has the advantage of surprise. It should not be hard to find themes that will raise a smile, but because jewellery is a small canvas, you may need to keep the idea simple – children's humour, puns and familiar humorous and comic images are all useful sources of inspiration.

Far left A cat fishing on the edge of a bowl, and a predator fish with a human face, are a pair of simple, endearing images that were considered during the development of a ring design. The designer appears not to take life – or jewellery – too seriously.

Above The three adorable bunnies in this brooch are a sure-fire recipe for producing a smile, but the title 'Menagerie à Trois', twists the image of innocence by adding innuendo. As in many good jokes, it is the unexpected that provokes laughter.

Left The shape of this brooch speaks for itself, but the title 'The Jewels' confirms the unbelievable. The pendant is crafted from silver and steel to make a provocative, tongue-in-cheek piece.

TIPS

- Remember that the most effective designs rely on appealing to one emotion per piece.
- Explore a wide range of possibilities, but make sure your concept is in good taste.
- Seek inspiration in the emotions that tend to have the greatest impact.

Function

THE IDEA THAT ALL ASPECTS OF DESIGN ARE REPRESENTED IN A FINISHED PIECE IS FUNDAMENTAL TO JEWELLERY DESIGN. THE FUNCTION OF A PIECE SHOULD THEREFORE BE CONSIDERED NOT AS A SEPARATE, PRACTICAL CONCERN, BUT AS POTENTIALLY INTEGRAL TO THE OVERALL DESIGN.

INVENTIVE SOLUTIONS

The function of a piece may be a simple issue, such as the need for a catch to open and close a neck chain. But in some cases it can be more challenging – for example, a ring might be required to light up when a trigger is activated by a finger passed though the form.

If your design is biased towards function, it is important to explore various possibilities and learn more about that function. If, for example, your piece is to act as a fastening, then brainstorming (*see pages 186– 187*) and researching (*see pages 188–189*) different ways of fastening will turn up a number of options – buttons, safety pins, locks and latches are just a few possibilities – and will feed the design process.

One way to broaden your knowledge is to explore other fields; looking to jewellery alone for solutions is very limiting and restrictive. Instead, think of all the different methods of fastening there are – in the kitchen, on clothing, in industry and so on – and then consider how you might translate these solutions into a jewellery format.

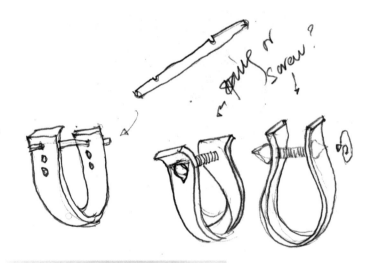

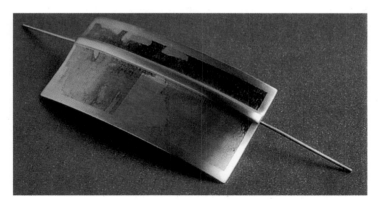

Above The pin on this simple silver brooch contributes significantly to the balance of the composition and visual aesthetic, rather than just being a functional addition.

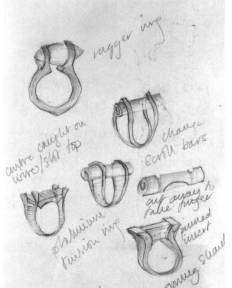

Left and above Changing the size of a ring has always been a problem for jewellery designers. This series of drawings explores various ways of changing the size of a ring so that the function of the piece is an essential element, absolutely integral to the design.

Right The function of this swirling piece is initially a conundrum – the flexible form allows it to be moulded by the wearer before it is secured to clothing or hair using hook-and-loop fastening.

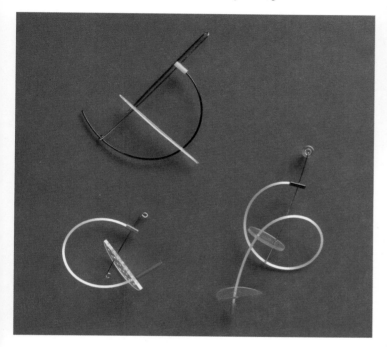

Above The steel pins in this set of brooches are an important element of the design – the wires used for the pins help to describe the shape and also serve a functional purpose.

Below The clean lines of this silver and acrylic brooch are enhanced by the simplicity of the steel pins. These double as a stand so that the form can be displayed as a miniature sculpture when not worn.

FUNCTION AND AESTHETICS

In many cases functional elements must be included in a design to enable satisfactory fabrication. One example is hollow work, which often requires air holes to be included to avoid explosions during soldering. These need only be small holes drilled into the form, but rather than having them only fulfil a utilitarian purpose, a better solution might be to incorporate them into the design so that they become a feature, rather than a potential eyesore.

Often the only way you can make a piece function properly is by adding an element that you would rather keep hidden from view. Hiding a purely functional element is not always easy, so consider making it a prominent, well-designed feature of the piece, something beautiful that will add to the design, rather than being simply a practical necessity.

TIPS

- Decide early on whether the function of a piece is to play a large role in its design.
- Always consider whether or not the fastening on a piece of jewellery could also have an aesthetic role to play.
- Think about the way in which a piece will be worn and how this might affect its function.

Materials

THERE ARE NO TABOOS REGARDING MATERIALS IN JEWELLERY DESIGN. IT IS THE APPROPRIATENESS OF A MATERIAL AND HOW IT IS TREATED THAT ADDS QUALITY AND VALUE TO A DESIGN, AS CAN BE SEEN IN THE TRANSFORMATION OF HUMBLE MATERIALS SUCH AS PLASTIC AND PAPER, OR RIBBON AND TIN, FOR EXAMPLE.

TRADITIONAL MATERIALS

If asked which materials they most associate with jewellery-making, most people would name the 'noble' metals – gold and platinum. There are historic reasons for this, as traditionally jewellery was a means both of investing wealth and displaying worth so that others could appreciate the financial status of the wearer.

There are also practical reasons for using gold and platinum: in their pure, unalloyed state they are inert metals – that is, they are chemically inactive and so they do not oxidise or react to the body. This factor, combined with the value added because of their relative scarcity, makes them highly desirable for jewellery.

For those who could not afford gold, there was silver, which was sufficiently scarce to be prestigious, but less so than gold. Although silver does oxidise, it does not react with the body excessively, and can be worn by most people.

Pure gold and silver are in general too soft for jewellery-making; they are ductile, malleable metals and lose their form too readily, so both are usually alloyed – mixed with other metals – to make them workable.

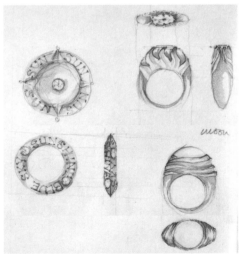

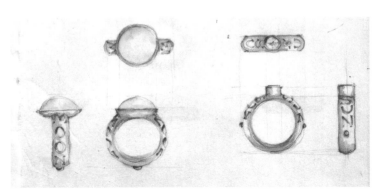

Left The white bloom, achieved through pickling silver, contrasts with the gold that has been used as detailing on the dense cluster of stems of this ring.

Below These two rings have been deftly crafted to look like ribbon. One is made of palladium – a metal that is rarely seen in jewellery – and the other is gold, a more traditional and obvious choice.

Above Pearls and diamonds, and gold and diamonds are used to depict the moon and the sun respectively. In one set of designs lettering (SUN, SUNSHINE, BLUE-SKY and MOON) is used as a means of explaining the concept, while in the other the materials are used as a subtler indicator.

NATURAL AND SYMBOLIC MATERIALS

Natural materials have been used throughout the centuries, for decoration or to introduce colour to metal pieces. In ancient cultures, some materials were also valued for their symbolic connotations – for example, in traditional Chinese culture pearls, said to be the tears of dragons, are associated with sorrow, and jade is considered lucky because it warms to the human body and is thought to be capable of projecting the luck of the wearer.

Often the symbolic meaning of a material is related to the strength or vulnerability of that material. Opals, for example, are considered unlucky, which is due to the fact that they have a high water content and so can be tricky to set – if set in a loose collet, they might shrink in warm weather and fall out in cool weather.

Other natural materials, such as crystals, are believed to have qualities that may aid healing and promote spirituality. Knowing what a material symbolises can help to make your design intentions clearer.

> ### TIPS
>
> • Remember that any material used in a way that is appropriate and sensitive is fitting for jewellery design.
> • Try to challenge the perceived value of a material through good design and craftsmanship.
> • Consider including precious materials; they can increase the acceptance and value of a piece made predominantly from alternative materials.

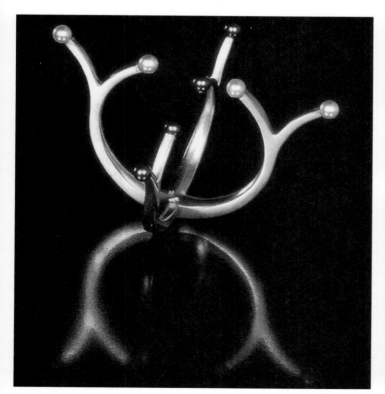

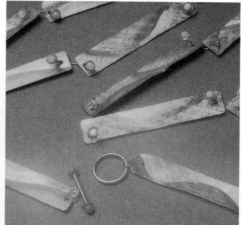

Far left Although the gold and pearls used in this marvellous ring are traditional materials, the form is clearly contemporary. The design's modernity helps to rejuvenate the conventional materials, while also ensuring that the piece retains desirability.

Left Tin plate, a material not normally associated with jewellery, is used to make chain links that have been coupled with precious platinum and gold leaf in various shades.

Below The sun, moon and stars are represented in gold and diamonds in this brooch, but the traditional silver is replaced with white gold and niobium.

Processes

THE PROCESSES AVAILABLE TO JEWELLERS TODAY ARE AS VARIED AS THE MATERIALS USED, AND THE POSSIBILITIES OPEN TO A DESIGNER ARE LIMITED ONLY BY THE DESIGNER'S OWN IMAGINATION AND KNOW-HOW. HOWEVER, SUCH CHOICE CAN MAKE IT DIFFICULT TO DECIDE WHICH PROCESS TO SPECIALISE IN.

KNOWING THE FACTS

The complexity of some jewellery-making techniques and processes can make them unsuitable unless you have an in-depth knowledge of the particular procedure, so designing to include them may not be straightforward. You may need to spend some time researching processes either by reading up about them in good technical manuals, or learning about them in a workshop environment. Some processes, such as *mokumé gane* (also known as burl metal, which involves producing a laminate from mixing two or more metals), may be more difficult to access for example, as they require specialist machinery or materials that are not commonly found. You will need to try and gain access to them through the relevant expert, or a suitably equipped specialist educational establishment.

Left and below The ancient art of lacquerwork is coupled with simple, modern jewellery forms, and the happy outcome is refreshing-looking jewellery and a new lease on life for the technique.

Above Brass wire is used to make sample patterns and forms. The resulting models allow a designer to assess the design potential of the sample, as well as provide an opportunity to push the boundaries of the process.

SIGNATURE TECHNIQUES

To refine basic jewellery-making skills so that a well-crafted piece of jewellery can be realised is challenge enough, so as a designer-maker the most productive course may be to concentrate on a technique that really inspires you and motivates you to keep on making and designing. Focusing on perfecting and exploring a specific sphere of activity can help you to establish a distinctive design style, and also a reputation for skilful handling of a particular process.

Some designers become master craftspeople of a particular process by developing a technique in a pioneering and unique way. Whether you choose to design and master techniques whose sheer complexity prohibits others from following suit, or alternatively, take an easier path and use simple, existing techniques in an original way, the overriding concern must be to make the process part of the whole concept (*see pages 184–185*). With good design and an open and enquiring attitude, you can be innovative with any technique. Exploring new avenues in whichever process you choose can be a means of establishing your style and name as a designer-maker who specialises and excels in the application of that process, thereby making it a signature technique.

TIPS

- **Consider how to use and combine processes to determine an individual style of your own.**
- **Make exploratory samples and models; this can help achieve unexpected and exciting results.**
- **Collate material and test results in a technical journal; this will enable you to repeat and develop processes easily.**

Above Knitting is used as a means of defining three-dimensional form. The combination of knitted silver and rubber cord gives the design a quirky feel, while the ambiguity of the form invites the imagination to suggest what it might represent.

Left Modern explorations in bonding techniques have revolutionised the metals that can be used to make technical advances in the ancient Japanese art of *mokumé gane*. Some of the combinations of metals in these three brooches are unique, and have never been achieved before.

Gallery

With numerous gems on which to feast your eyes, this chapter of the book offers tremendous scope for developing your jewellery-making skills further. Wirework, beadwork, silver jewellery, texturing and gold jewellery employ many of the techniques discussed and practised in earlier chapters of the book. No matter what stage of development you are at, there will be something here that you can emulate. For those looking to follow a particular style, there is also a collection of pieces that fall under the umbrella: design inspiration. Almost all pieces in this chapter could qualify under more than one heading, however, so do not confine yourself to one section if you are looking for inspiration.

Wirework

THERE ARE MANY SIMPLE PIECES OF JEWELLERY TO BE MADE USING WIRE. A WIDE RANGE OF PLEASING DESIGNS CAN BE ACHIEVED BY TWISTING, BENDING, PLAITING AND KNITTING WIRE. YOU CAN INCORPORATE BEADS, JEWELS, PEBBLES AND OTHER FOUND MATERIALS INTO THE FINISHED PIECE.

Fantasy Bird
This elegant silver pin was inspired by the exotic birds of South America. The bird's shape is made from a single length of silver wire. A narrower gauge wire is used to create the feather embellishments. Tiny silver beads are incorporated into the tail feathers, while a bright blue beady eye completes the design.

Precious Wire and Beads
This intricate-looking bracelet uses French knitting techniques to create its chunky, yet airy design. It is made from a coil of very fine metal wire that has been threaded with tiny metal beads.

Wire and Marbles
Before being assembled, each component of this design involves wrapping an iridescent marble in silver wire. A little loop is incorporated at each end of the marble during the wrapping process. The links for the components are coils of loosely spiralled wire.

Dog and Bone Bracelet
This quirky design uses a thick brass wire to create a series of fun dog and bone shapes. These are decorated simply using coils of very fine metal wire, wrapped around each shape a number of times. Each component is then joined to the next using jump rings. The piece is finished with two fasteners.

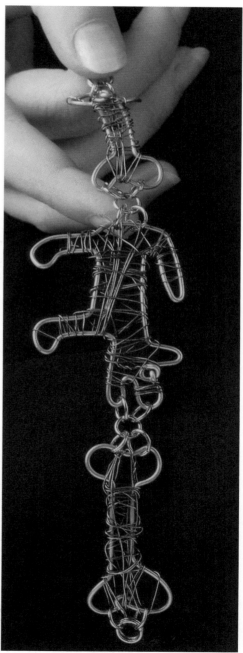

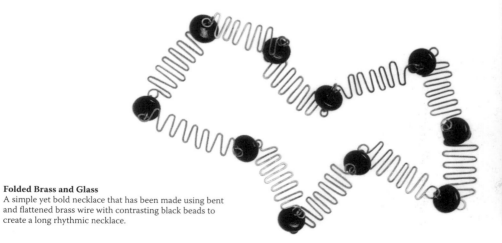

Folded Brass and Glass
A simple yet bold necklace that has been made using bent and flattened brass wire with contrasting black beads to create a long rhythmic necklace.

Statement Ring
Different gauges of wire have been manipulated to make this ring. The shank is made from several strands of the thickest wire, bound together with narrower strands. The green, transparent stone is incorporated into the design, with the thicker-gauge wire holding it in place. The piece is reminiscent of the tendril-like designs that emerged during the Art Nouveau period.

Wires and Washers
This is a design that could be made using a wide range of found materials, including watch and clock pieces. Washers of different sizes are grouped together to make interesting, three-dimensional components for the earrings. Each group is held together using brass wire, bound through the centre. The discs are held together using jump rings and each one finished with an earring hook.

Copper Bangle
Nine strands of narrow-gauge copper wire have been plaited and hammered flat to make this rustic bracelet. The design is not unlike those made by African tribespeople.

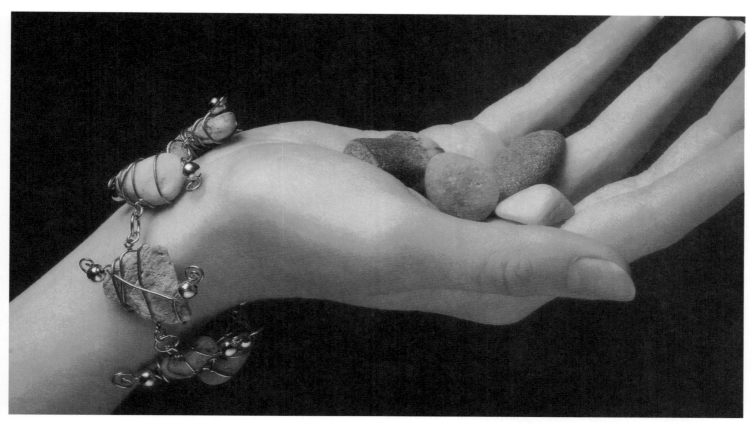

Pebble Bracelet
Each of the pebbles in this design is wrapped tightly in copper wire before being incorporated into the final piece. A small hoop is made at either side of each pebble during the wrapping process, and a small metal bead attached at each end. The pebbles are then joined together simply, by connecting a small jump ring to each small hoop and using larger jump rings to link all the components together.

Spiralling Earrings
A pair of simple spiral earrings, made using green aluminium wire. An initial loop is formed by wrapping the end of the wire around the tip of round-nosed pliers. The wire is then manipulated by hand to form a spiral, round and round, until the desired size is achieved. A final, closed, loop is made through which the ear hooks are attached.

Beadwork

BEADS FOR MAKING NECKLACES, BRACELETS AND EARRINGS EXIST IN ALL SHAPES AND SIZES, AND CAN BE INCORPORATED INTO A DESIGN IN MANY DIFFERENT WAYS. THE EXAMPLES HERE RANGE FROM KNOTTING BEADS ONTO LINEN THREAD TO ATTACHING THEM TO ONE ANOTHER USING ANTIQUE GOLD FINDINGS.

Natural Ceramic Beads

For this simple design, earthy-coloured ceramic beads are widely spaced on a linen thread to create a natural-looking piece. Necklaces like this can be made quickly using a wide range of beads – glass, wood, ceramic, papier mâché. The beads are held in place by tying knots in a double length of thread at intervals. It is up to you to decide how frequently you want the beads spaced. This particular piece is long enough to fit over the head, so needs no fastening.

Bright Sparks

Clusters of tiny bright beads dangle at the end of these drop earrings. They are threaded on narrow-gauge gold wire. The same wire is used for making the ear hooks.

Polished Stones

A number of highly polished and rounded stones have been made into beads and threaded together to make a bracelet. A length of silver wire is passed through each bead and each end manipulated to form a coiled wire hook. Once the first bead is complete, the wire from the next bead is threaded through any one of its hooks before its own hook is then finished. Each bead is attached to the next in the same way.

Sea-green Necklace

Multiple strands of tiny, angular beads have been strung close together to make this tight-fitting necklace, fastened at the rear with an elegant silver clasp. This example uses a single colour to dramatic effect, but similar pieces could be made using a different colour per strand, or alternating strands of two colours.

Pretty Pearls
This necklace has an elegant Victorian look to it. Smooth round and oval beads in pastel pinks, lilacs and creams – some of them with floral decoration – are connected together using delicate, antique gold filigree findings.

Hoops and Beads
Chunky blue beads alternate with large silver hoops in this contemporary-looking piece. Each is joined to the next using jump rings. Some of the hoops are made from smooth, round wire, while others have a textured surface.

Necklace by Jenny Turtill
This curious piece alternates cuttlefish castings with haematite beads. It is reminiscent of tribal pieces, many of which incorporate bone and ivory. The cuttlefish castings have been made individually, rather than using a number of identically cast components. This gives the piece a more authentic, rustic, handcrafted feel.

Ethnic Necklace
The combination of brass and beads gives this piece a Middle Eastern feel to it. The colour scheme is predominantly orange and brown, with tiny specks of brilliant blue.

Texture

ADDING TEXTURE TO A JEWELLERY DESIGN CAN BE A VERY SATISFYING WAY TO GIVE IT MORE CHARACTER. THERE ARE MANY TECHNIQUES TO CHOOSE FROM – EMBOSSING, ETCHING, PLANISHING, CHASING – AND A NUMBER OF THEM HAVE BEEN DEMONSTRATED IN THIS BOOK.

Textured Necklace by Alan Vallis
Central to this textured silver necklace is a dark-red, oval carnelian stone suspended in a rub-over setting at the base. The lace-like silver components are hung from a string of carnelian beads.

Gold Medallion
This gold medallion has been strung onto a length of ethnic beads with a range of earthy colours and soft smooth shapes. An intricate symmetrical design has been worked into the surface of the gold to complete the look.

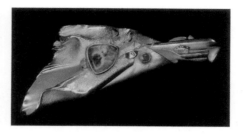

Silver Brooch by Ruta Brown
For this brooch, a sheet of silver has been reticulated and folded while warm to create its interesting, organic shape. The textured silver has been further decorated with gold and set with quartz and ruby.

Symbol Necklace and Earrings by Alan Vallis
This necklace has two rows of roundel-type beads alternating with large-scale silver components. Taking inspiration from African tribal examples, the pieces are near identical in shape and form, but vary in size. The flat surfaces have been planished to give them shape and texture. The matching drop earrings are made from the same components.

Reticulated Necklace by Ruta Brown
This free-form piece has been made using several sheets of reticulated silver. To give the necklace an even more textured surface, a number of stones have been added, attached to the silver sheet using tiny wire hooks.

Gold Buttons by Gerald Benny
A matching set of 12 identical gold buttons. Each has been textured to give it this crinkled effect, and has a bright blue enamelled centre.

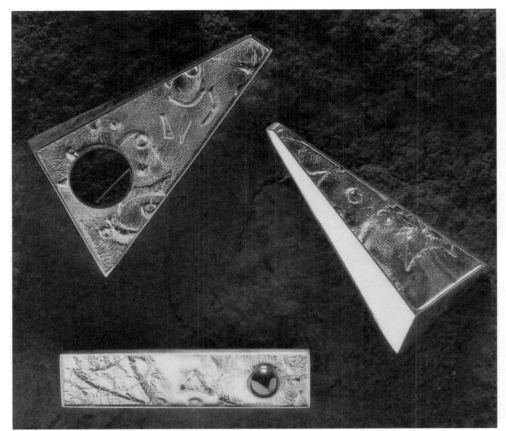

Three Brooches by John Hill
Reticulation means having veins, fibres or lines, which exactly describes the appearance of silver after this type of treatment. Sheet silver is heated and pickled several times in order to remove most of the copper oxides present. The resulting pure silver is heated again, to just below melting point, and a second flame is passed along the metal and back again. The centre of the silver melts and solidifies during this process, forcing the fine silver surface, which has not melted, to move and twist as the silver below cools.

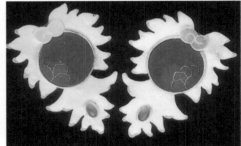

Silver Earrings by Jinks McGrath
This pair of textured silver earrings has been set with enamelled domes and moonstones. The very tips of the outline of each piece have been tipped with gold.

Embossed Copper Brooch
The design for this brooch involves hand-drawing a motif onto copper foil and heat-treating the metal to give it colour. The techniques used are very simple and can be achieved in no time at all. You can use a ballpoint pen to create the texture on the copper foil and a single flame to heat the metal, moving it to and fro until it changes colour. The copper is mounted on a piece of thick card, and its edges folded towards the rear to secure it. The piece is completed with a piece of felt glued to the back of the brooch, to conceal the folded copper edges, and a brooch back is attached, also using glue.

Punched Metal Brooch
Very rudimentary stone-setting techniques are used to secure the stone at the centre of this piece – it is simply placed in the middle of a brass six-pointed star, the points of which are raised to secure it. This focal component is then placed at the centre of two different-sized circles cut from brass and aluminium, which have been punched with a decorative design.

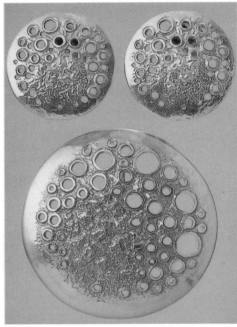

Brooch and Earrings by Alan Vallis
Each of these slightly domed discs has been pierced with holes of varying sizes. The surface has been reticulated to give it the molten silver texture, and the edges have been burnished smooth.

Silver Earrings by Jenny Turtill
The surface texture of these earrings has been achieved by using etching techniques. This is a process in which some areas of the surface are protected while others are treated with an acid solution. The acid removes the top layer of silver to leave the desired pattern.

Silver Earstuds by Jenny Turtill
Each of these earrings has been etched and gold plated. The effect is to give the appearance of gold that has worn away to reveal a highly polished silver layer below.

Striking Neckpiece by Chris Morphy
This piece is composed of a number of lightly textured brass plates that have been pierced in the corners and joined together using jump rings. Increasing in size as they near the centre, the three largest plates are set with oval tigerion stones. A stem and leaf design has been chased into the plates using a punch and a chasing hammer, and is created in such a way that it moves continuously from one metal plate to the next, as if the components were a single piece.

Medieval-style Bangle by Chris Morphy
An elegant brass bangle with medieval undertones. The surface design has been created using both chasing and repoussé techniques. While chasing involves marking or modelling the metal on the top surface, repoussé is a relief pattern that is made from the underside of the silver.

Silver jewellery

WORKING WITH SILVER TAKES YOU INTO THE REALM OF PRECIOUS JEWELLERY-MAKING. THESE STUNNING PIECES HAVE BEEN MADE USING SOME OF THE MORE ADVANCED TECHNIQUES DESCRIBED IN THIS BOOK – CASTING, FORGING AND STONE-SETTING.

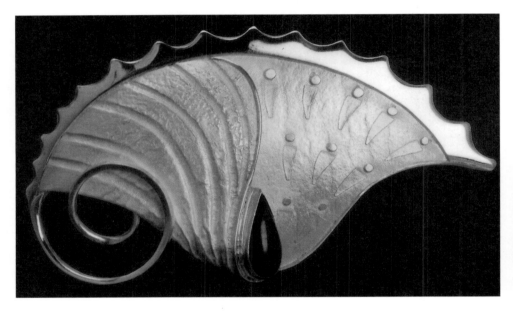

Silver Brooches by Pat McAnally
A pair of elegant silver brooches with organic, fossil-like and shell-like forms. In the first (*above*) the silver is set with a teardrop-shaped lapis lazuli stone in a gold bezel setting. The second (*right*) is set with pink and green tourmaline and has additional interest in the gold decoration. The slightly veined surface texture of each brooch is achieved by heating the metal in a process known as reticulation. It contrasts with the highly polished elements of each piece.

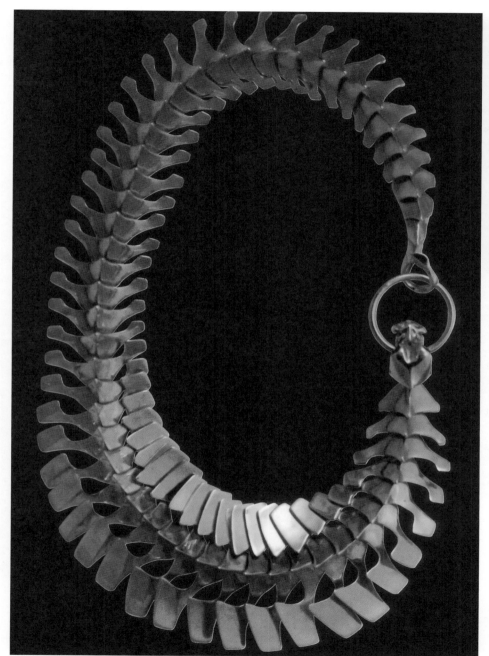

Silver bracelet by Rebecca Smith
A delicate silver bracelet made from over 50 tiny silver balls. Each ball has been handmade, which accounts for the irregularity that gives this piece its original appearance. The balls are made simply by placing short lengths of wire onto a charcoal block and heating them until they roll up into balls.

Cast Silver Necklace by Alan Vallis
For this piece, 50 separate components have been cast. Each is similar in shape and size and, together, they interlock to create a very striking piece that resembles the stylised spine of a fish or reptile.

Silver Necklaces by Jinks McGrath

These two necklaces have been made from pre-cast components. Casting offers plenty of scope for creating pieces with a more uniform appearance. In the first necklace (*left*) a rectangular component is repeated many times to achieve the length of the piece. Each part has tiny hooks at each end and is joined to the next using jump rings. The second piece (*below*) has identical circular components that are secured one to the next using a simple pin. Each of the necklaces is constructed in such a way that there is considerable movement in them when worn. In both of these examples, the components for each one are identical to one another, but this does not have to be so. You could alternate two or three different components, depending on the look you are trying to create.

Indian Bracelet

A silver bangle with intricate surface decoration. The open form has been shaped using a mandrel. It makes the piece easy to slip onto the wrist without the need for an additional fastening mechanism.

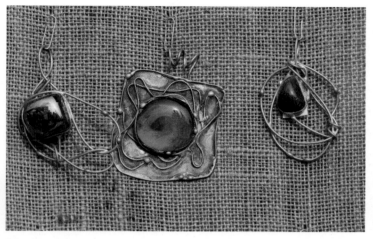

Stone-set Pendants
A set of three pendants made using a combination of sheet silver and silver wire. Each has an organic feel to it: the wirework is random, there is no symmetry and the stone is not always central to the piece.

Silver Earrings by Daphne Krinos
The blackened colour of these earrings was achieved by oxidising the silver. It gives the metal a soft look, which is offset beautifully by the bright gold of the decorative details.

Silver Mask by Alan Vallis
This elegant necklace has an Art Deco feel to it. A detailed mask motif is suspended between two oval stones set in silver and offset by three rows of Chinese carnelian beads. The same beads are used for the necklace itself, which has an elegant fastening to the front: two simple hooks thread through jump rings attached to either side of the mask.

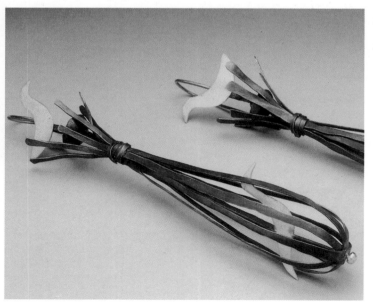

Gold jewellery

THIS HANDFUL OF INSPIRATIONAL PIECES HAS BEEN MADE USING GOLD. THEY RANGE FROM A SIMPLE, MEDIEVAL-LOOKING RING TO PIECES THAT COMBINE GOLD WITH SILVER IN A NUMBER OF WAYS. BETWEEN THEM THEY USE A WIDE RANGE OF TECHNIQUES INCLUDING DOMING, OXIDISING AND STONE-SETTING.

Necklace by Alexandra Coppen
An unusual fastening makes the back of this gold necklace more interesting. One end of the chain is soldered to the textured disc. At the other end of a chain a length of narrow-gauge gold bar is attached, and it is this that slips through the hole at the centre of the disc to secure the piece when worn.

Silver and Gold Necklace by Jinks McGrath
This necklace has been made using a simple technique for overlapping joints. Holes are drilled into each unit where the join is to be. A length of wire is soldered in a hole in one unit and a second unit is slotted over the wire. A jump ring is then dropped onto the wire and soldered in place before the excess wire is cut and filed.

Pendant by Jinks McGrath
The smooth, gently domed surface of this pendant has been fashioned from white, yellow and red 18-carat gold. An ornate decorative top, set with a round sapphire, is also functional and provides the means by which a chain is attached to the piece.

Gold Necklace by Gerald Benny
A gold necklace with matching earrings, set with diamonds and opal. The strong geometric shapes echo those that featured in much Art Deco jewellery of the early 20th century, which in turn took inspiration from ancient Egyptian and Mesoamerican forms.

Rub-over Settings by Daphne Krinos
A bright, clear stone is set at the centre of each of these pieces, each one housed in a simple rub-over setting. The stones contrast beautifully with the alternating discs of oxidised silver and gold.

Gold Ring
This striking design sees a large cabochon amethyst set in gold. The round-wire shank is simply shaped and the stone is mounted in a bezel within a round-wire ring.

231

Historic inspiration

JEWELLERY DESIGN IS A GREAT MEASURE OF CHANGING FASHION. PIECES FROM DIFFERENT ERAS, LIKE THOSE PRESENTED HERE, DEMONSTRATE MANY TRENDS IN THE USE OF TECHNIQUES AND MATERIALS. WHEN CONSIDERING THE DESIGN OF A PIECE, IT CAN ALWAYS BE HELPFUL TO LOOK TO THE PAST FOR INSPIRATION.

Cluster Brooches
These white and coloured paste cluster brooches date from around 1785. They started out as buttons, but have since been adapted to give them greater longevity. Pieces like this can still be found for similar adaptations or for incorporation into a larger contemporary design. Harvey & Gore, London

Oval Cluster Ring
A wonderful inspiration for a large statement ring, this piece is set with many tiny clear glass stones. Rings like this, c.1790, were often given as gifts. The underside of this sentimental jewel is inscribed '*amitié*' meaning friendship. Harvey & Gore, London

Pendant Earrings
A handsome pair of girandole pendant earrings set with rock crystal. They date from around 1760 and are typical of the period in that they incorporate many bright faceted stones for catching the light. They are the perfect inspiration for a light-looking elegant design. Harvey & Gore, London

Delicate Necklace
This necklace with oval pink pastes mounted on pinchbeck dates from 1820. Pinchbeck is a form of brass – an alloy of copper and zinc which is mixed in such proportions that it resembles gold. It is no longer used for making jewellery. Harvey & Gore, London

Regard Ring
In 'regard' rings such as this, the choice of stones would spell out a message – an idea that could be equally effective for today's jewellery designers. In this ring from 1810, stones resembling rubies, emeralds, garnets, amethysts and diamonds have been used. Harvey & Gore, London

Pendant Cross
Religious pieces can be a valuable source of inspiration for jewellery designers. There are countless examples of cross-shaped pendants for necklaces going back centuries. This particular piece – a somewhat stylised version of the form – is dated around 1820. Harvey & Gore, London

Micromosaic Necklace
Micromosaic jewellery, such as this necklace, made c.1860, began to appear in Western Europe after the discovery of classical ruins in Greece and Italy. The technique involves using many tiny pieces of glass to create images and decorative patterns. Late 19th-century jewellers sought to imitate this ancient art in jewellery-making, and some continue to do so today. Beauty & the Beasts, London

Cuff Bracelet
A large, late 19th-century, paste and gilt cuff bracelet. It was made for the French actress Sarah Bernhardt. Designs like this are easily adapted for a contemporary interpretation – perhaps for a cuff that is textured before shaping around a mandrel and set with stones. Steinberg & Tolkein, London

Crescent Brooch
Ancient symbols and motifs often make the most striking centrepieces in jewellery-making. This is because they are often very simple in outline. They can be useful in pieces in which the emotional impact is integral to the design. This paste brooch, c.1875, uses one of the oldest motifs in the history of jewellery design. In fact, the crescent is one of the oldest symbols in humanity, seen in use by many cultures across the centuries. Harvey & Gore, London

Gilt Metal Brooch
This early piece dates back to the mid-19th century. It was made by Roman art jeweller Fortunato Pio Castellani, and reflects his great love of ancient Greek and Etruscan styles. Pieces like this offer inspiration for those seeking striking geometric designs. Beauty & the Beasts, London

Teardrop Brooch
When selecting stones for a piece, always consider how they will catch the light. Faceted stones reflect more brilliantly than non-faceted ones, and iridescent ones reflect all sorts of colours. The opaline stones in this piece, c.1725, reflect all manner of bright yellows, pinks and purples. Harvey & Gore, London

Floral Brooch
Plants and flowers have long been imitated in jewellery design. A wealth of inspiration can be sought in late 18th-century pieces, like this brooch, c.1790. Harvey & Gore, London

Harp Brooch
A paste lyre brooch c.1800. It was fashionable at the turn of the 19th century to look to the cultures of ancient Rome and Greece for inspiration. Lyres and harps were popular motifs for at least a quarter of a century. Harvey & Gore, London

Striking Hairpin
Designers through the ages have paid particular interest to colour in their works, and this yellow and amethyst paste flower from around 1770 demonstrates this perfectly. It was as much a part of the function of pieces like this to draw attention to the extravagant hairstyles popularised by the French queen Marie Antoinette as it was to be a striking ornament in its own right. Harvey & Gore, London

Shoe Buckles
Although shoe buckles like this, dating from the 1790s, are no longer worn, they provide ample inspiration when it comes to designing brooches and belt buckles. It is even possible to find pieces like this, which could be adapted. Harvey & Gore, London

Hair Ornament
This is an example of how the function of a piece can be integral to the design. Although most of this hairpin is obscured when worn, it is nevertheless beautifully crafted from tortoiseshell. Designed during the second half of the 19th century, it also has a feature seen in many pieces of the period – the insect sitting at the top of the hairpin is attached in such a way that it quivers with any movement of the head.

Face Brooches
This fabulous collection of face brooches includes examples from c.1890 to 1970. Not only do they span a wide period of time, but they also cover many different styles and materials. As such, they offer great inspiration for an exciting range of creative designs.

Jet Necklace
Using a strong, single-colour stone can result in striking effects, as demonstrated by this French piece, dated around 1910. A fashion for wearing jet jewellery emerged in France during the late 19th century and persisted well into the first years of the 20th century. Beauty & the Beasts, London

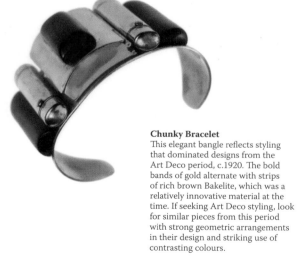

Chunky Bracelet
This elegant bangle reflects styling that dominated designs from the Art Deco period, c.1920. The bold bands of gold alternate with strips of rich brown Bakelite, which was a relatively innovative material at the time. If seeking Art Deco styling, look for similar pieces from this period with strong geometric arrangements in their design and striking use of contrasting colours.

Art Nouveau Sautoir
Princess Alexandra, Queen Victoria's granddaughter, did much to popularise this form of necklace. Inspired by the designs of French master craftsman René Lalique, it would have been worn over a high-necked dress. Steinberg & Tolkein, London

Romantic Brooch
This intricate design from the former Czechoslovakia, dated around the 1930s, takes inspiration from pieces designed over 100 years earlier. Floral designs like this epitomise those emerging during the Romantic period that flourished in Europe in the late 18th century. Steinberg & Tolkein, London

Crystal Tassel Sautoir
Modernist designs from the 1920s and 1930s offer inspiration for the contemporary jeweller. They are often minimalist in their use of colour and material, which is in tune with many design considerations today. This piece is typical of a style first popularised by couturier Paul Poiret in the 1920s. It became an essential accessory for the Jazz Age flapper. Steinberg & Tolkein, London

Floral Brooch

An early 1930s diamanté floral brooch made by Coro, a leading jewellery manufacturer, established in New York in the early 19th century. The piece gently imitates nature, with its cluster of flowers atop the delicate spray of leaves.

Harlequin Pin

An enamelled image of a dancing harlequin. Figures of all kinds were popular for enamelled pieces, allowing wider scope with the range of bright colours available. Steinberg & Tolkein, London.

Cocktail Jewellery

These pretty American bird pins are fine examples of the countless enamel cocktail pieces that were worn during the 1930s. Creatures of all kinds make wonderful motifs for enamelled jewellery, where there is greater scope for working with colour. Each of these birds is studded with sparkling diamanté. Steinberg & Tolkein, London

1940s Brooch
This mid-1940s vermeil silver brooch typifies the most popular style of decorating a wartime suit. Compared to the Coro piece on the previous page, it offers a more fluid, stylised interpretation of a spray of flowers.

Snakechain Necklace
Part of a set, this late 1940s to early 1950s snakechain necklace is signed by New York firm Trifari. 'Trifarium', a new metal alloy developed by the company, served the 1950s craze for ultra-shiny, non-tarnishing costume jewellery.
Steinberg & Tolkein, London

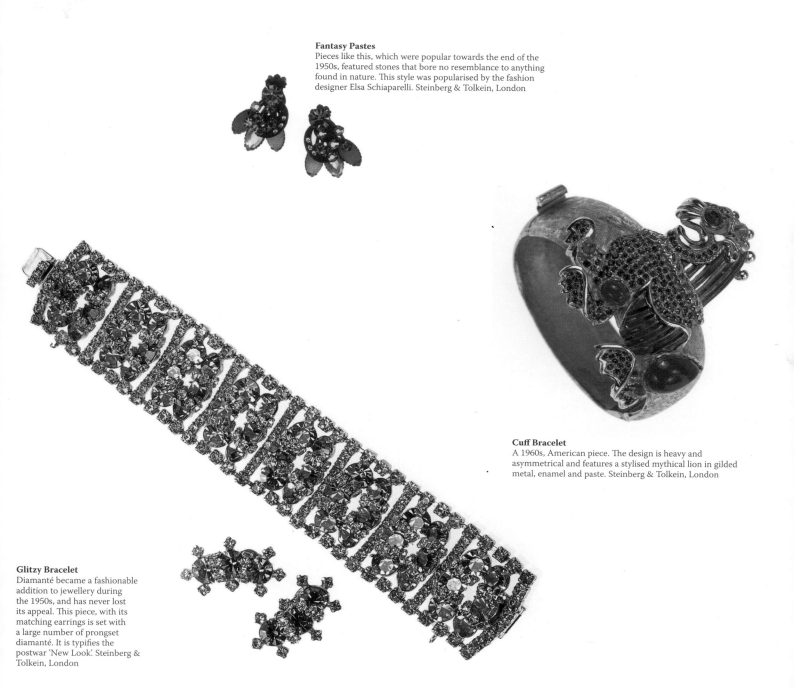

Fantasy Pastes
Pieces like this, which were popular towards the end of the 1950s, featured stones that bore no resemblance to anything found in nature. This style was popularised by the fashion designer Elsa Schiaparelli. Steinberg & Tolkein, London

Cuff Bracelet
A 1960s, American piece. The design is heavy and asymmetrical and features a stylised mythical lion in gilded metal, enamel and paste. Steinberg & Tolkein, London

Glitzy Bracelet
Diamanté became a fashionable addition to jewellery during the 1950s, and has never lost its appeal. This piece, with its matching earrings is set with a large number of prongset diamanté. It is typifies the postwar 'New Look'. Steinberg & Tolkein, London

243

Technical information

ALTHOUGH PRECISE MEASUREMENTS ARE NOT ALWAYS CRITICAL, THERE WILL BE TIMES WHEN YOU NEED TO KNOW SPECIFIC MEASUREMENTS. DEPENDING ON SUPPLIERS, THESE MAY BE IN METRIC OR IMPERIAL, AND IT IS IMPORTANT THAT YOU ARE ABLE TO MAKE ACCURATE CONVERSIONS.

BASE METALS AND THEIR PROPERTIES

This list is not comprehensive, but describes the most commonly used metals and the most readily available.

Copper: A warm reddish-pink in colour, tarnished and oxidises very quickly. Very soft and malleable. Not suitable for unsoldered chains or in very thin sheet since it bends too easily.

Gilding metal: A warm golden yellow in colour, similar to gold. Malleable and less prone to oxidisation than copper.

Brass: Pale straw yellow colour when polished. Harder to bend and shape than copper. Casts well.

Aluminium: Dull greyish-white in colour. This metal is extremely malleable and lightweight, and is therefore excellent for stamping and forming. It cannot be soldered with hard solders, but is suitable for cold fixing methods, such as riveting. It is possible to colour it with bright dyes in a process known as anodising.

To calculate the approximate weight of a finished jewellery piece when made in another metal, find the metal in which the piece is currently made in the left-hand column, then read across the chart to find the metal in which you would like to make the piece. Multiply the current weight of the piece by the number in that column.

	18K gold	14K gold	9K gold	Silver	Copper
18K gold	1.00	0.89	0.72	0.66	0.58
14K gold	1.12	1.0	0.81	0.75	0.65
9K gold	1.38	1.23	1.0	0.92	0.80
Silver	1.50	1.33	1.09	1.00	0.87
Copper	1.73	1.53	1.24	1.14	1.00

WAX TO METAL CONVERSION CHART

Use the following calculations to figure out the weight of a wax model when it has been cast in metal.

Wax to silver
Weight of wax x 10.5 = weight when cast in silver

Wax to 9k gold
Weight of wax x 11.2 = weight when cast in 9K gold

Wax to 18K gold
Weight of wax x 15.4 = weight when cast in 18K gold

To convert ounces to grams: multiply by 28.35

To convert grams to ounces: multiply by 0.0352

PRECIOUS METALS

24K gold: Pure gold is so soft and malleable that it is unsuitable for the construction of jewellery. It is therefore alloyed with varying quantities of other metals, usually copper, silver, zinc, palladium and platinum, to improve its strength, alter its working qualities, and even to change its colour.

22K gold: Rich yellow in colour, this is also very soft.

18K gold: Most commonly a rich warm yellow in colour, but also available in white, red and green. Extremely malleable and ductile. Useful for all jewellery-making purposes.

14K gold: Like 18K, available in a range of colours. Good working qualities.

9K gold: A pale yellow in colour. This hard gold is widely used in commercial jewellery manufacture. (Some countries use 10K gold.)

Silver: A lustrous white colour. Pure silver is too soft for most jewellery making, so it is alloyed with varying quantities of copper to improve its working qualities.

Britannia silver: White in colour. This is not known as true silver, although it contains a high proportion of silver. It is most useful for bezel or run-over settings, since it is extremely malleable. It is often used by silversmiths, because it oxidises less than sterling silver.

Sterling silver: White in colour. This has a slightly lower ratio of silver and is excellent for all jewellery-making purposes.

METAL GAUGES

The thicknesses of wire and sheet metal have been specified in both millimetres and inches throughout this book. Most metal suppliers sell their products using either or both of these measurement systems. However, some suppliers specify metal thicknesses primarily in gauges, so below is a conversion table for two of the most commonly used gauge systems.

Inches	Millimeters	B & S gauge	Birmingham gauge
0.008	0.203	36	1
0.009	0.229	34	2
0.011	0.274	32	3
0.112	0.305	30	4
0.114	0.356	28	5
0.016	0.406	27	6
0.019	0.483	26	7
0.021	0.533	25	8
0.023	0.584	24	9
0.027	0.686	22	10
0.032	0.813	21	11
0.035	0.889	20	12
0.039	0.991	19	13
0.042	1.067	19	14
0.048	1.219	18	15
0.051	1.295	18	16
0.056	1.422	17	17
0.060	1.524	17	18
0.063	1.603	16	19
0.065	1.651	16	20
0.072	1.829	15	22
0.077	1.956	14	23
0.086	2.184	14	24

Inches	Millimeters	B & S gauge	Birmingham gauge
0.092	2.337	13	25
0.104	2.642	12	26
0.110	2.794	12	27
0.124	3.150	11	28
0.136	3.454	10	29
0.150	3.810	9	30
0.167	4.242	8	31
0.183	4.648	7	32
0.200	5.080	6	33
0.216	5.486	5	34
0.240	6.096	4	35
0.252	6.410	3	36
0.270	6.858	3	37
0.276	7.010	2	38
0.284	7.214	2	39
0.300	7.620	1	40

To convert inches to millimetres: multiply by 25.4

To convert millimetres to inches: multiply by 0.0394

To convert fractions of an inch to decimal inches: divide the top figure by the bottom figure.

SOLDER MELTING TEMPERATURES

	Hard °C	°F	Medium °C	°F	Soft °C	°F
9-carat gold	755–795	1390–1465	735–755	1355–1390	720–650	1330–1200
14-carat gold	750–785	1380–1445	-	-	710–730	1310–1350
18-carat gold	790–830	1455–1525	730–765	1350–1410	700–715	1290–1320
silver	745–778	1375–1430	720–765	1330–1410	705–725	1300–1340

ANNEALING TEMPERATURES

	°C	°F
Copper	370–650	700–1200
Brass	430–750	800–1380
Gold (not 24 carat)	650–750	1200–1380
Silver	600–700	1120–1300

MELTING TEMPERATURES

	°C	°F
Copper	1080	1980
Brass	900	1660
Gold (not 24 carat)	880–1000	1600–1830
Silver	890	1640

RING GAUGES

The table below shows the most common ring gauge systems, together with their equivalent measurements in millimetres and inches. These measurements are the inside circumference of the ring. Always add the depth of the metal you are using to this measurement, to allow the two ends to meet in a neat seam. When you have finished your calculations, round up the figure to the first decimal place.

US	UK	Europe	Millimetres	Inches
½	A		37.825	1.490
¾	A ½		38.424	1.514
1	B		39.022	1.537
1 ¼	B ½		39.621	1.561
1 ½	C		40.219	1.585
1 ¾	C ½		40.818	1.608
2	D	1	41.416	1.632
2 ¼	D ½	2	42.015	1.655
2 ½	E		42.613	1.679
2 ¼	E ½	3	43.212	1.703
3	F	4	43.810	1.726
	F ½		44.409	1.750
3 ¼	G	5	45.007	1.773
3 ½	G½		45.606	1.797
3¾	H	6	46.204	1.820
4	H ½		46.803	1.844
4 ¼	I	7	47.401	1.868
4 ½	I ½	8	48.000	1.891
4 ¾	J		48.598	1.915
5	J ½	9	49.197	1.938
5 ¼	K	10	49.795	1.962
5 ½	K ½		50.394	1.986
5 ¾	L	11	50.992	2.009
6	L ½		51.591	2.033
6 ¼	M	12	52.189	2.056
6 ½	M ½	13	52.788	2.080

US	UK	Europe	Millimetres	Inches
6 ¾	N		53.466	2.107
	N ½	14	54.104	2.132
7	O	15	54.743	2.157
7 ¼	O ½		55.381	2.182
7 ½	P	16	56.020	2.207
7 ¾	P ½		56.658	2.232
8	Q	17	57.296	2.257
8 ½	Q ½	18	57.935	2.283
8 ½	R		58.573	2.308
8 ¾	R ½	19	59.212	2.333
9	S	20	59.850	2.358
9 ¼	S ½		60.488	2.383
9 ½	T	21	61.127	2.408
9 ¾	T ½	22	61.765	2.434
10	U		62.403	2.459
10 ¼	U ½	23	63.042	2.484
10 ½	V	24	63.680	2.509
10 ¾	V ½		64.319	2.534
11	W	25	64.877	2.556
11 ¼	W ½		65.476	2.580
11 ½	X	26	66.074	2.603
11 ¾	X ½		66.673	2.627
12	Y		67.271	2.650
12 ¼	Y ½		67.870	2.674
12 ½	Z		68.468	2.680

Glossary

Abrasives: The natural or man-made sand-like particles used to smooth or clean away marks on a surface, as can be found adhered to abrasive papers.

Acetone: A flammable liquid used to remove setter's wax/cement.

Adhesive: Sticky substance, such as glue, used for sticking things together.

Alloy: A mixture of metals.

Aluminium: A lightweight, light grey, malleable, ductile metal.

Anneal: To soften metal by heating and cooling at the correct temperature. Soft metal is easier to work.

Anvil: Heavy metal stand with flat top and bottom with a round protruding nose. Used for shaping, flattening, hardening, etc.

Argotec: A white powder mixed to a paste either with methylated spirits or water and then painted onto silver prior to heating to avoid firestain.

Base metal: Non-precious metal such as aluminium, brass, copper, gilding metal, nickel, pewter, steel and titanium.

Bearer wire: The metal ring inside the bezel that forms the 'shelf' on which the stone sits.

Bevel: The slope on the edge of a metal surface.

Bezel: The rim of metal that is used to secure a stone in a rub-over setting.

Binding wire: Steel wire that ties and holds parts together for soldering.

Bobs: Another term for polishing mops used with a pendant motor or flexible shaft machine.

Borax: A flux used for soldering. It is mixed to a paste with water and painted onto the areas to be soldered.

Bronze: A pale yellow metal used for casting that is generally an alloy of copper and tin.

Buffs: Also polishing mops – fabric polishing ends.

Bullion: Gold and silver.

Bur: Metal tools for grinding, for use with a pendant motor or a flexible shaft motor.

Burnish: To polish by rubbing.

Cabochon: A smooth-shaped, polished stone.

Carat: a measure used to express the purity of gold, with 24 being the purest.

Catch: A means of securing a bracelet, neckpiece or the like.

Chenier: Silver/gold tubing. Can have walls of different thickness for different uses, e.g. hinges, choker and joints.

Claw setting: A setting for a faceted stone that uses wires to hold the stone. It has an open back, which allows light to reflect off the stone.

Compound: Also polishing compound – generic name for a greasy media containing abrasives used in the polishing process.

Coping saw: A hand saw used like a piercing saw for cutting wood and plastics.

Copper: A reddish-coloured, malleable, ductile metal.

Creasing hammer: A steel hammer with a fine cylindrical face.

Die: Steel tools used for shaping by stamping or a cutting tool such as used for cutting screw threads.

Die wrench: Also die stock – a tool for holding dies to facilitate the cutting of screws.

Dividers: Metal implement with two fine points. A screw action spaces the distance at which the two points are kept apart.

Doming block: A steel form with hemispherical depressions used to form domes.

Doming punches: Steel punches with rounded heads used with a doming block to make domes.

Draw: A term for pulling in, as in 'drawing wire'.

Drawplate: A steel plate with graded holes that can be round, triangular, D-shaped, square, oval or rectangular. Annealed wire is drawn through the plate until the desired shape and size are achieved.

Ductile: A term used to describe a material that is yielding or pliable.

Engraving: The removal of metal using steel tools called gravers.

Faceted: A term used to describe gemstones that have been cut so that their form is covered in small, polished, flat surfaces.

Ferrous: Containing iron.

Fibre grips: Protective covering used to protect material from being damaged by the steel jaws of a vice.

Fibula: A brooch where the pin is integral to the form, similar to a safety pin.

Findings: A term used to describe the commercially made fittings for jewellery purposes.

Finish: A term used to describe the cleaning up of a piece by sanding and polishing.

Firestain: A layer of subcutaneous discoloration on sterling/standard silver that is the result of annealing or soldering.

Fittings: Functional components such as catches, clips and joints as used in jewellery.

Flux: The generic term used to describe a chemical used as an antioxidant as part of the soldering process.

Fretwork: A term used to describe a sheet that has been pierced with a number of holes to make an ornamental pattern.

Gauge: A standard of measurement such as the thickness of sheet or the diameter of wire.

Girdle: The fine line around a faceted stone where the top and bottom facets meet.

Gold: The metal most commonly associated with jewellery, it is naturally found as a rich yellow colour although it can be alloyed to be white, red or green in colour.

Grain: A term used to describe a rounded bead of metal that has been formed to hold a stone in place.

Gravers: Steel tools used to cut away metal in engraving and setting.

Hammer: A tool for beating or striking metal.

Hyfin: A white polish used after Tripoli during the polishing process.

Imperial: Non-metric standard of measure or weight.

Join: A term used to describe the meeting of two or more pieces for soldering.

Joint: Another term used to describe a join.

Jump ring: The generic word for ring forms used in jewellery for joining, linking, articulation and chain making.

Lathe: A tool used for cutting rotary objects.

Malleable: A term used to describe a material that can be readily formed, rolled etc.

Mallet: Non-metal-faced hammer.

Mandrel: A form, generally made of steel, used to support metal while it is being formed.

Metric: Relating to measurement based on the decimal system.

Mica: Heat-resistant transparent sheet on which pieces to be enamelled are placed.

Mineral oil: Oil used for lubrication in sharpening gravers.

Mould: A hollow form into which molten wax or metal can be poured for casting.

Nickel: A pale silvery metal also known as nickel silver.

Nitric acid: Colourless acid that goes slightly blue when added to water and is used for 'bright dipping' silver for etching.

Non-ferrous: Metals not containing iron.

Oxides: Black or shadowy areas that appear when some metals are heated in air. Can be removed by pickling.

Paillons: Term for pieces of solder, taken from the French word 'flake'.

Patina: A surface finish that develops on metal or other material as a result of exposure to chemicals or handling.

Pendant motor: A motor with a hand-held flexible drive shaft with a variety of different tools used for drilling, polishing, texturing, etc.

Perspex: A proprietary thermoplastic resin.

Pewter: A dark grey-coloured, tin-based metal that is extremely ductile.

Pickle: A chemical used to remove the oxides that are a result of heating.

Pin: A piece of wire with a sharpened end used to fasten an object.

Planishing: Polishing or flattening by hammering with a mirror-finished hammer face.

Platinum: Whitish-grey precious metal.

Precious: A term used to describe diamonds, sapphires, rubies and emeralds when referring to stones or gold, silver and platinum when referring to metals.

Prong: The term used to describe a tine or spur made in a claw stone setting, for example.

Pumice: Abrasive powder mixed with water and used after pickling to clean the metal.

Punches: Hardened steel tools used in forming or texturing metal.

Pyrex: A type of glassware resistant to heat.

Rasp: A coarse file.

Rivet: Method of joining - usually a small pin passing through two or more planes and spread over on both ends.

Rod: Straight solid wire.

Setter's cement: Also setter's wax – A hard substance that can be softened by warming used to support jewellery pieces for stone-setting.

Shank: Straight or plain section of a ring or twist drill bit.

Sheet: A piece of metal that is normally uniform thickness.

Shot: Also burnishing media – Polished steel media used to burnish metal in barrel polishing. Solid metal shape such as pellets or spheres.

Silver: A light grey metal that is malleable and ductile.

Solder: A fusible alloy for joining metals.

Sprue: A passage through which molten wax or metal can be poured into a mould, the wire on a casting or casting master that corresponds to the sprue passage.

Sprung tweezers: Also crosslock tweezers, self-locking tweezers or fibre grip tweezers – tweezers that close when you release them that are used as a soldering aid.

Steel: A grey ferrous metal often used for tool making.

Table: The top face of a faceted stone.

Tallow: Rendered fat or grease.

Tang: End of file, graver, tool.

Taps: Tools used for cutting thread in a hole.

Temper: To alter the hardness of steel.

Template: A shaped, thin plate used as a guide to define a form.

Triblet: Another term for a mandrel.

Vernier: A sliding scale used for accurate fractional measurement.

White spirit: Also mineral spirits – a flammable liquid used for thinning stop out varnish for etching and for removing pitch in repoussé.

Work hardening: The hardening of a material by manipulation.

Wrench: Also stock – an instrument for holding taps and dies or other such equipment.

Resources

UNITED STATES

Tools

Allcraft Tool & Supply Co
135 West 29th Street #402
New York, NY 10001
Tel: +1 (800) 645 7124

Anchor Tool & Supply Inc
PO Box 265
Chatham, NJ 07928
Tel: +1 (201) 887 8888

Armstrong Tool & Supply Co
31747 West Eight Mile Road
Livonia, MI 48152
Tel: +1 (800) 446 9694
www.armstrongtool.com

Frei & Borel
PO Box 796
126 Second Street
Oakland, CA 94604
Tel: +1 (510) 832 0355
www.ofrei.com

Indian Jeweller's Supply
601 East Coal Avenue
Gallup, NM, 87305
Tel: +1 (505) 772 4451
www.ijsinc.com

Metalliferous
34 West 46th Street
New York, NY 10036
Tel: +1 (212) 944 0909
www.metalliferous.com

Myron Toback
25 West 47th Street
New York, NY 10036
Tel: +1 (212) 398 8300
www.myrontoback.com

Paul Gesswein and Company, Inc
255 Hancock Avenue
PO Box 3998
Bridgeport, CT 06605
Tel: +1 (203) 366 5400
www.gesswein.com

Rio Grande
7500 Bluewater Road NW
Albuquerque, NM 87121
Tel: +1 (800) 545 6566
www.riogrande.com

Precious Metals

David H Fell & Company
6009 Bandini Blvd
City of Commerce, CA 90040
Tel: +1 (323) 722 6567
www.dhfco.com

T B Hagstoz and son
709 Sansom Street
Philadelphia, PA 19106
Tel: +1 (215) 922 1627
www.hagstoz.com

Handy & Harman
Camden Metals
12244 Willow Grove Road
Camden, DE 19934
Tel: +1 (302) 697 9521
www.handytube.com

Hauser & Miller Co
10950 Lin-Valle Drive
St Louis, MO 63123
Tel: +1 (800) 462 7447
www.hauserandmiller.com

CR Hill Company
2734 West 11 Mile Road
Berkely, MI 48072
Tel: +1 (248) 543 1555
www.crhill.com

Hoover & Strong
10700 Trade Road
Richmond, VA 23236
Tel: +1 (800) 759 9997
www.hooverandstrong.com

Belden Wire and Cable Company
PO Box 1327
350 NW N Street
Richmond, IN 47374
Tel: +1 (765) 962 7561
www.belden.com

Copper and Brass
NASCO
PO Box 1
Salida, CA 95368
Tel: +1 (800) 372 1236
www.enasco.com

Revere Copper Products, Inc
One Revere Park
Rome, NY 13440
Tel: +1 (800) 448 1776
www.reverecopper.com

CANADA

Tools
1400 Ages Drive
Ottawa, ON
K1B 4K9
Tel: +1 (613) 526 4695
www.busybeetools.com

Lacy and Co Ltd
69 Queen Street East
Toronto, ON
MSC 1R6
Tel: +1 (416) 365 1375
www.lacytools.com

Precious Metals
Imperial Smelting & Refining Co Ltd
451 Denison
Markham, ON
L3R 1B7
Tel: +1 (905) 475 9566
www.imperialproducts.com

Johnson Matthey Ltd
130 Gliddon Road
Brampton, ON
L6W 3M8
Tel: +1 (905) 453 6120
www.matthey.com

UNITED KINGDOM

Tools
J Blundell & Sons
25 St Cross Street
London EC1N 8UH
Tel: +44 (0207) 437 4746
www.jblundells.uk.com

Buck & Ryan
Shop 4, Southampton Row
London WC1B 4DA
Tel: +44 (0207) 636 7475
www.buckandryan.co.uk

EMC Services
Unit 1
Tollemache Business Park
Offton, Ipswich
Suffolk 1P8 4RT
www.emcservices.net

Frank Pike
14 Hatton Wall
London EC1N 8JH
Tel: +44 (0207) 405 2688

Rashbel UK Ltd
24-28 Hatton Wall
London EC1N 8JH
Tel: +44 (0207) 831 5646
www.rashbel.com

Le Ronka
Unit 3 Sandy Lane
Stourport-on-Severn
Worcestershire
DY13 9PT
Tel: +44 (01299) 873 600

H S Walsh
44 Hatton Garden
London EC1
Tel: +44 (0207) 242 3711
www.hswalsh.com

Etch Resist Film and Enamels
Diatherm
Gresham Works
Mornington Road
North Chingford
London E4
Tel: +44 (0208) 524 9546

Precious Metals
Cookson Precious Metals Ltd
59-83 Vittoria Street
Birmingham
B1 3NZ
Tel: +44 (0121) 200 2120
www.cooksongold.com

Copper And Brass
J F Ratcliff (Metals) Ltd
New Summer Street
Birmingham
B19 3QN
Tel: +44 (0121) 359 5901
www.jfratcliff.co.uk

Smiths Metal Centres
42–56 Tottenham Road
London N1 4BZ
Tel: +44 (0207) 241 2430
www.smithmetal.com

Findings
Exchange Findings
49 Hatton Gardens
London EC1N 8YS
Tel: +44 (0207) 831 7574

Samuel Findings & Jewellers Ltd.
14 St. Cross Street
London EC1N 8UN
Tel. +44 (0207) 831 0657

H A Light Findings Ltd
The Rical Group
Tramway
Oldbury Road
Smethwick
West Midlands
B66 1NY
Tel: +44 (0121) 555 8395
www.lightfindings.co.uk

T H Findings
42 Hylton Street
Birmingham
B18 6HN
Tel: +44 (0121) 554 9889
www.thfindings.com

Gemstones

Capital Gems
30B Great Sutton Street
London EC1V 0DU
Tel: +44 (0207) 253 3575
www.capitalgems.com

R Holt & Co
98 Hatton Garden
London EC1N 8NX
Tel: +44 (0207) 430 5284
www.holtsgems.com

Levy Gems Ltd
26–27 Minerva House
Hatton Garden
London EC1N 8BR
Tel: +44 (0207) 242 4547
www.levygems.com

Manchester Minerals
Georges Road
Stockport
Cheshire
SK4 1DP
Tel: +44 (0161) 477 0435
www.manchesterminerals.co.uk

Casting

Casting House (Gold, Silver)
1 Augusta Street
Birmingham
B18 6JA
Tel: +44 (0121) 236 6858

West One Castings
(Gold, Silver)
24 Hatton Garden
London EC1
Tel: +44 (0207) 831 0542

Weston Beamor
(Platinum, Fine Casting)
3–8 Vyse Street
Birmingham
B18 6LT
Tel: +44 (0121) 678 4131
www.westonbeamor.co.uk

AUSTRALIA

Precious Metals

A & E Metal Merchants
68 Smith Street
Marrickville
NSW 2204
Tel: +61 (2) 8568 4200
www.aemetal.com.au

Johnson Matthey
64 Lillie Crescent
Tullamarine
Melbourne
Victoria 3043
Tel: +61 (3) 9344 770064
www.matthey.com

Index